MYSTICISM AND
RELIGIOUS TRADITIONS

MYSTICISM AND
RELIGIOUS TRADITIONS

EDITED BY

STEVEN T. KATZ

OXFORD UNIVERSITY PRESS
Oxford   New York   Toronto   Melbourne
1983

OXFORD UNIVERSITY PRESS
Oxford   London   Glasgow
New York   Toronto   Melbourne   Auckland
Delhi   Bombay   Calcutta   Madras   Karachi
Kuala Lumpur   Singapore   Hong Kong   Tokyo
Nairobi   Dar es Salaam   Cape Town

and associate companies in
Beirut   Berlin   Ibadan   Mexico City   Nicosia

First published by Oxford University Press, New York, 1983
First issued as an Oxford University Press paperback, 1983

Library of Congress Cataloging in Publication Data
Main entry under title:

Mysticism and religious traditions.

1. Mysticism—Comparative studies—Addresses,
essays, lectures. I. Katz, Steven T., 1944–
BL625.M894   1983   291.4'2   82-22508
ISBN 0-19-503313-2
ISBN 0-19-503314-0 (pbk.)

Printing (last digit):   9 8 7 6 5 4

Printed in the United States of America

Contents

Contents

Editor's Introduction

I

The relationship between mysticism and religious traditions is a much discussed issue. The predominant scholarly view has favoured seeing this dialogue as fraught with strain and tension. Thus, mysticism is usually depicted as, in essence, an autonomous realm of experience which only uneasily fits in with more traditional and widespread religious beliefs, practices, and communities. The mystic is that rare soul whose life soars above dogma and community, leaving the sober majority behind to its mechanical, if irrelevant, religious teachings and practices. Moreover, so the regnant scholarly orthodoxy has it, at the exalted level of *the* mystic experience the specificity of given religious systems is transcended in a sense of oneness which is common to all true mystics. Here in the presence of the Absolute, the self is no longer 'Jew nor Greek, male nor female' and all true seekers come to know—to feel—the sameness which is the Ultimately Real. Tragically, the mystic must descend from his height and then, caught up again in the fetters of tradition and history, space and time, he must express what is truly inexpressible in the inadequate symbols and syntax of his particular faith community. Thus, the One becomes the many and the absolute becomes Krishna and Allah, God and Tao, and is alluded to through such inadequate symbols as Torah and Koran, Mantra and Gospel, Koans and Chants.

This common image, however, is as suspect as it is widespread, for it may well be a fundamental error to juxtapose the mystic and his tradition, the mystic individual and his socio-religious environment. The oppositional model may, after all, not be the correct one for describing and analysing this interaction. It is this possibility that has brought the present symposium into being. The essays in this volume have been written in order to reconsider this relational issue afresh with the hope that a more adequate schematisation of this dialectical encounter can be arrived at. That is to say, the present essays are attempts to reconsider, in various ways, the question: 'What relation(s) does obtain between mystics and the religious communities out of which they emerge and of which they are a part?' Or to frame the query in another form, can we, as is so commonly assumed, come to understand mysticism aright if we pluck it out of its socio-historical parameters and separate it from its philosophical-theological environment, thus treating it as a pure, non-relational, unmediated sort of human experience? Or, in contradistinction to this currently dominant interpretation, is it necessary in order to understand mysticism to ground the mystic in his polyform context so that one comes to realize what may well be the *necessary* connection between the mystic's way and his goal; the mystic's problematic and the mystic's solution to this problematic; the mystic's intentions and the mystic's actual experiences? To put this in another idiom, what we are concerned to inquire into is: just how Muslim is a Sufi and can one be a Sufi without being a Muslim? How Jewish is Jewish mysticism? Can one who is not an observant, learned Jew, be a Kabbalist? Or do the 'four ells of the *halachah* (Jewish law)' set definite, if not complete, parameters for the kabbalistic universe as they do for the rabbinic? Does Christian mysticism represent a universal religious experience or is it necessarily related to Christian dogma, especially in its christological character? In other words, can one be a Christian mystic if one denies classical christological claims? Is *nirvāṇa* attainable without subscribing to the Buddhist teaching of 'no-self'? Can Enlightenment be won without holding to the Buddhist doctrine of impermanence? This more localized, more historically and theologically concrete, way of raising the central difficulty(s) helps bring to the surface the essential concern involved in discussing the relationship of mystic to established religious communities, to wit: do Muslims have essentially pre-formed Muslim experiences, Jews specifically Jewish experiences, Christians christological experiences, Buddhists Buddhist enlightenments and so on. And if so what does it mean? There are no easy answers to these hard questions, but this difficulty is not a justification for lack of effort, or acceptance of all too easy, if more comfortable, answers. Certainly, if we want better to appreciate the world's mystical heritage we cannot ignore the critical thrust of these interrogations. Only a satisfactory descriptive schema which does justice to these matters, which is not too reductive on the one hand nor too intuitionistic on the other, will serve our purposes.

In the essays prepared for this collection these issues have been taken up anew and taken up with a sustained interest in the details of the matter before us, as well as with particularly acute methodological acumen. All the contributors have recognized and help us to recognize that to begin to approach these substantive and theoretical matters properly one must know a good deal about specific religious traditions and communities as well as about particular mystical authors and groups. Without such knowledge one might generate theories which, while ingenious, bear little relation to the evidence and which do not stand up to serious technical analysis. Many of the best known accounts of mysticism are indeed the product of *a priori* metaphysical and theological requirements, and not the result of any close encounter with the mystical sources of the world's religions. Such presentations, whatever their appearance, are quite independent of the data and allow of no contradiction. They are proclaimed to be 'true' no matter what the details of scholarly research reveal. Rejecting this dogmatic approach as out of place in the serious academic study of mysticism, the contributors to this volume have attempted, on the contrary, to engage the texts and traditions of the world's religious and mystical communities. They have done so in order to offer accounts of this many-sided, multi-layered material which will not only titillate the imagination but also reveal themselves to be the result of intimate study of the requisite sources coupled with methodological sophistication. Moreover, and especially, our contributors offer their theses as, at least in theory, possibly discomfirmable, i.e. they are open to scrutiny and scholarly discussion—they argue from the texts and traditions and allow others to consider these same materials and to respond. There is no wish to offer new dogmas in place of the old.

II

Though no separate bibliography of mystical works and secondary studies is appended to this volume it should be noted that the original sources and secondary literature referred to in the substantial notes which conclude each of the essays collectively constitute quite a complete 'bibliography for further study.'

Before concluding, it is my pleasant task to thank a number of individuals who helped in various ways in the preparation of this volume. First, to Ms. Patsy Carter of Baker Library, Dartmouth College, who helped to locate and procure a wide range of volumes needed in my research. Indeed, the entire staff of Baker Library deserves a 'Thank you' for their help in so many ways. Second, to Mrs. Peggy Sanders and Mrs. Fran Dupuis who helped in the secretarial duties connected with this project. Third, to Mr. Allen Kelley, Mr. Charles Scott, and Ms. Cynthia Read of Oxford University Press, New York, whose wise counsel was, as always, much appreciated. I want also publicly to thank the contributors for their participation in the project. All were a joy to be associated with. Last, my greatest debt is to my wife, Rebecca, who aided in this, as in all my work, in innumerable ways, and most importantly by just being there.

Steven T. Katz

The 'Conservative' Character of Mystical Experience

STEVEN T. KATZ

I

It is a commonplace of the study of mysticism[1] to see it as the paradigm of religious individualism and radicalism.[2] The mystic, it is said, is the great religious rebel who undermines the orthodox establishment, placing his own experience above the doctrines of the accepted authorities, and who not infrequently engenders serious opposition even to the point of being put to death for heresy. The martyrdom of Al Ḥallāj[3] and similar episodes are highlighted in almost all descriptions of mysticism. Now it is of course true that Al Ḥallāj was martyred, as were Ortlieb and Priscillian of Avila, among others. And again, Eckhart and Teresa of Avila, like many before and after them, were briefly excommunicated for heresy, as were the Sufis during the reign of Al-Mu Hamid (870–893), and the Franciscan Spirituals of the thirteenth century, while the Kabbalists were always suspect and the Hasidim were actually put 'under the Ban' by the Gaon of Vilna and his followers.[4] These incidents must *not* be taken as presenting the entire account, however, nor even as representing the typical relation between mysticism and established religion, for the relationship(s) of the two are far more varied and dialectical than is usually appreciated. This paper will examine this dialectic, showing in the process that, while it is true that mysticism, in its many different guises, contains elements of radical challenge to established religious authority and tradition, at the same time it also embodies characteristics which are anything but radical. And it is on these normally neglected features, which I have chosen to label 'conservative', that this study will focus. Let me assert my position clearly lest misunderstanding arise: it is not my intention to argue that mysticism, or more accurately mysticism*s*, is *only* a conservative phenomenon; rather, the aim of this paper is to reveal the two-sided nature of mysticism, that it is a dialectic that oscillates between the innovative

3

and traditional poles of the religious life. To recognize only one of these poles – it does not matter which – is to misrepresent the phenomenon.

II

Concern with the conservative element(s) of the mystical experience(s) has grown out of my earlier research on mysticism.[5] These earlier studies can be summarized as follows. I began with a question and an epistemological generalization based on the study of the data and reflection thereon. The question I tried to answer was: 'Why are mystical experiences the experiences they are?' And in order to begin to answer this query, I adopted as a working hypothesis the epistemic thesis that there are *no* pure (i.e. unmediated) experiences. Neither mystical experience nor more ordinary forms of experience gives any indication, or any grounds for believing, that they are unmediated. That is to say, all experience is processed through, organized by, and makes itself available to us in extremely complex epistemological ways. The notion of unmediated experience seems, if not self-contradictory, empty at best. This seems to me to be true even with regard to the experiences of those ultimate objects of concern with which mystics have intercourse, e.g., God, Being, nirvāṇa, etc., and this 'mediated' aspect of all our experience seems an inescapable feature of any epistemological inquiry, including the inquiry into mysticism. Yet this constitutive epistemic element has been overlooked or underplayed by every major investigator of our subject. Thus, contrary to the prevailing scholarly view – that of James, Stace, Underhill, Otto, and even Zaehner and Smart – we must recognize that a right understanding of mysticism is not just a question of studying the reports of the mystic after the experiential event but also of acknowledging that the experience itself, as well as the form in which it is reported, is shaped by concepts which the mystic brings to, and which shape, his experience. Straightforwardly, what is argued is that, for example, the Hindu mystic does not have an experience of x which he describes in the, to him, familiar language and symbols of Hinduism, but rather he has a Hindu experience; his experience is not an unmediated experience of x but is itself the at least partially preformed anticipated Hindu experience of Brahman. Again, the Christian mystic does not experience some unidentified reality which he then conveniently labels 'God', but rather has the at least partially, prefigured Christian experiences of God, or Jesus, and so forth. Moreover, as one might anticipate, it is my contention, *based on what evidence there is*, that the Hindu experience of Brahman and the Christian experience of God are not the same. (I have defended this thesis in my earlier work and will offer further support of this important claim in section III of the present paper.)

The significance of these theoretical and methodological considerations is that they entail that the forms of consciousness which the mystic brings to an experience set structured and limiting parameters on what the experience will be, i.e. on what will be experienced, and rule out in advance what is 'inexperienceable' in the particular, given, concrete context. Thus, for example, the nature of the Christian mystic's pre-mystical consciousness informs the mystical consciousness in such a way that he encounters Jesus, the Trinity, or a personal God rather than the non-personal, 'not this, not that', Buddhist doctrine of nirvāṇa.

This hermeneutical understanding and its accompanying epistemological perspective require, in turn, a fresh study of the entire corpus of mystical literature, across cultures and traditions. Above all, the interpenetration of the mystical event and the religious tradition out of which the mystic grows has emerged as a central concern requiring new and innovative study. The remainder of this paper will explore the implications of these considerations, particularly as they manifest themselves in the attempt to understand the relationship that obtains between mystical experiences and their historic socio-religious contexts.

One further preliminary observation is yet required. It must constantly be borne in mind that however we might view the nature of mysticism and mystical experience, the only evidence we have, if we are not mystics ourselves, and even mystics really do not have a privileged position here[6], is the account given by mystics of their experience. These are the data for study and analysis. No scholar can get behind the autobiographical fragment to the putative 'pure-experience' – whatever one holds that to be. Whatever the truth of the nature of the commingling of theory, experience and interpretation that goes into the mystics' 'report', the *only* evidence one has to call upon to support one's analysis of this material, and hence one's description of this relationship, is the given recording of the mystic – the already 'experienced' and 'interpreted' first person recording.

This fact recognized, the first discrete subject that must be analysed is the relatively little-studied character of mystical literature. This literature is complex and involves 'creative', 'formative', and 'interpretive' elements of different sorts and at several different levels: (*a*) first person reports; (*b*) the mystic's own later 'interpretation' of his own experience; (*c*) the 'interpretation' of third persons from within the same tradition about other peoples' first person reports; (*d*) the 'interpretation' of third persons from other traditions (Buddhists on Christianity, etc.). And all of these cases can be more or less highly ramified. Then again, this literature takes many shapes which are not merely incidental or tangential to their content. These forms include: biography, biblical exegesis, aphorisms, theoretical and theosophical treatises, poems, polemics, dogmatics, and didactic compositions. And all of these genres enrich and complicate the decoding of mystical reports.[7] Moreover, recognition of the myriad elements within this preliminary taxonomy only begins the discussion. The analysis of each of these perspectival stances and literary types now must be extended and enriched, especially with regard to the pre-experiental structures and modalities which influence the having and the being of the mystical experience, as well as the form(s) in which the experience(s) are reported.

Mystical experience(s) are the *result* of traversing the mystical way(s), whatever specific *way* one happens to follow, e.g. the Jewish, Sufi, or Buddhist. What one reads, learns, knows, intends, and experiences along the path creates to some degree (let us leave this somewhat vaguely stated as yet) the *anticipated* experience made manifest. That is to say, there is an intimate even necessary connection between the mystical and religious texts studied and assimilated, the mystical experience had, and the mystical experience reported. In each mystical tradition, as in each of the larger religious communities in which the mystical traditions inhere, there is an inherited theological-mystical education which is built upon certain agreed sources. The layperson, like the mystical tyro, begins to move upwards along the spiritual spiral in part, even in large part, by studying these established texts and traditions, working all the while at appropriating them for him or herself.

To understand the significance of this educational process by which the individual's religious sensitivities mature, and the role played in this maturation pattern by inherited religious-mystical documents, let us take as a paradigm the role of the Song of Songs in

Western mystical traditions. Jewish mystics have continually favoured the study of the Song of Songs, reading it as the ultimate biblical expression of God's love for Israel and then again for the individual Jew. While all biblical books were sources for Kabbalistic speculation, none was so preferred as the Song of Songs. Beginning with the mysticism of the rabbinic period, e.g. the *Shiur Koma* and then later the *Targum on the Song of Songs*, through the writings of the medieval Kabbalists and Hasidic masters (eighteenth century on), the Song was a profound inspiration. It pre-formed the imagination of the Kabbalistic mind even as the Kabbalistic mind interpreted it according to its own radical theosophical hermeneutic.

Consider as an example of this influencing activity the 'descriptions' of God provided in that strangest of all Jewish mystical compositions, the *Shiur Koma*,[8] which have their root in the description of the Lover (interpreted as God) in the Song of Songs 5.10–16.

> My beloved is all radiant and ruddy, distinguished among ten thousand.
> His head is the finest gold; his locks are wavy, black as a raven.
> His eyes are like doves beside springs of water, bathed in milk, fitly set.
> His cheeks are like beds of spices, yielding fragrance.
> His lips are lilies, distilling liquid myrrh.
> His arms are rounded gold, set with jewels.
> His body is ivory work, encrusted with sapphires.
> His legs are alabaster columns, set upon bases of gold.
> His appearance is like Lebanon, choice as the cedars.
> His speech is most sweet, and he is altogether desirable.
> This is my beloved and this is my friend, O daughters of Jerusalem.

Having absorbed, in the most profound sense, this biblical vision of the Song, the Jewish mystic 'saw' and reported:

> 1. Rabbi Yishmael said: Metatron the Great Lord said to me: I bear this testimony on behalf of YHVH, ELOHIM of Israel, the living and enduring EL, our Lord and Master,
> . . . that His height, from His Seat of Glory and up (is) 118 ten thousands (rebaboth) parasangs,
> . . . from His Seat of Glory down (is) 118 ten thousands (rebaboth) parasangs,
> . . . His total height (is) 236 ten thousand thousands parasangs.
> . . . From His Right Arm to His Left Arm (is) 77 ten thousand (parasangs),

. . . from His Right Eye to (His) Left Eye (is) 30 ten thousands
    (parasangs),

. . . the Skull on His Head (is) three and one-third ten thousand
    (parasangs);

. . . the Crowns on His head (amount to) 60 ten thousands (parasangs)
    equaling the 60 ten thousands of the tribes of Israel.

Therefore is He called the Great, the Mighty and the Awesome EL.

---

7. Rabbi Nathan, the pupil of R. Yishmael said: He also gave me the
measure of the nose right and left, as well as that of the lips and cheeks.
Also he gave me the measure of the forehead, he also set down rules for
every cubit.

. . . Holy, Holy, Holy is the YHVH of Hosts, the whole earth is full of His
    glory.

. . . [The measure of] His eyelids, [is] like the measure of His eyes.

. . . The right [eye] is named HDR, VVLD

. . . the left [eye is named] APDH [in Lemberg APRH] ZZYHV.

. . . The height of His ears [is] like the height of His forehead.

. . . The right [ear] is called AZTHYYA.

. . . The left [ear is called] MNVGHV.

. . . Hence, the total measure [of the Divine Stature] is ten thousands of ten
    thousands ten thousand thousands parasangs in height, and one
    thousand thousand ten thousands of parasangs in width.[9]

. . . The width of the forehead is equal to the height of the neck and so is
    the shoulder.

. . . The length of the nose [is] like the length of the small finger.

. . . The height of the cheek is equal to half the roundness of the head.

. . . These measures are also found in human beings.

. . . [The size of] His lips: seventy seven parasangs.

. . . His upper lip is called GBRH, TYA

. . . the lower one HZRGYA.

. . . His mouth is fire consuming fire. . . .

. . . My friend is white and ruddy, distinguished among ten thousand.
    His head is bright as the finest gold,
    His locks are like waving foliage and black as a raven.
    His eyes are doves by streamlets of water.
    His cheeks are as a bed of roses . . .
    Two thousand, ten thousand parasangs.
    And whoever does not conclude with this verse (Song of Songs 5: 10–
      16) is in error.

[ch. 5, vv. 10–16 of The Song are now quoted to conclude the description][9]

That is to say, what the rabbinic mystic 'saw' was not independent of what he had studied in order to 'see'. The author of the *Shiur Koma* did not make the heavenly ascent unaided, did not seek out transcendance unguided, did not perceive the divine without a prior, biblical, education which prepared him for his moment of supreme encounter, did not order and assimilate his experience without the help of the canonical description. He sought what Solomon had described, he found what Solomon had said there was to find.

When rabbinic mysticism evolved into the very different system of medieval Kabbalah, the formative power of the Song remained central even though it was read for novel reasons and in novel ways. At the heart of Zoharic Kabbalah and then Lurianic Kabbalah is the doctrine of the *Sefiroth* – their primordial fragmentation in the 'upper world' and the eventual re-integration of the now fragmented Sefirothic realm through human action, i.e. through the keeping of the *mitzvot* (a remarkably 'conservative' feature, indeed the most conservative feature possible in a Jewish context). In simpler terms, the essence of medieval and later Kabbalistic speculation is an explanation of how the imperfect world we inhabit came to be and how its imperfection, understood as 'separation' and 'disunity', can be overcome. The primary mystical symbol of this separation was the 'separation' of the upper nine *Sefiroth*, taken as 'male', from the tenth *Sefirah*, the *Shechinah*, which is taken as 'female'. The most explicit sexual language is used to describe the desire of the 'male' and 'female' principles and their hoped-for 'coupling' (the Hebrew term used is *zivvug*, already used this way in rabbinic literature, e.g. *Midrash to Ps*, LIX). Moreover, in the Zoharic world-view the 'exile of the Shechinah' is inseparable from the 'exile of Israel', its earthly reflection. Thus, the reunification of the 'male' *Sefiroth* with the *Shechinah* is also the symbol of Israel's redemption by a loving God.[10] Study of the *Zohar* and related texts is at first surprising and disturbing (and therefore forbidden to those not rabbinically learned as well as to those below the age of mystical maturity, namely, forty[11]) precisely because of its extreme sexual imagery and its use of sexual allegory as the most appropriate representation of the interaction of the 'upper' and 'lower' worlds, of the interaction of God and Israel.

> . . . R. Isaac said: 'There is still a higher sphere in which is contained and consummated the love-union of the Divine aspects which are never

thereafter separated.' R. Judah asked: 'Who is worthy to know of it?'
R. Isaac replied: 'He who has a portion in the world to come.'[12]

The religious imagination of the Jewish mystic was saturated with
this structural architectonic and the sexual-anthropomorphic imagery that was interwoven with it. Our interest in this complex
pattern of Kabbalistic sexual imagery, however, stems from the fact
that it returns us to, and reinforces, the point of the present argument:
that the Song was seen as the pre-eminent source of the 'revelation' of
this 'secret doctrine' which lay at the heart of Zoharic Kabbalah. It
was the sexual explicitness of the Song that was one of the main
sources that suggested this line of exegesis to the Kabbalist in the first
place and then legitimized the full working out of an entire Jewish
theosophy in such terms thereafter. A close study of the biblical loci
cited by the *Zohar* as the revelatory justification of its more
systematic mystical exposition will reveal how often it cites the Song
as the root of its teaching on the essential matter of the final *Tikkun*
('repair', i.e. re-unification of the *Sefiroth*, the Messianic age), as well
as all partial *Tikkunim* achieved in the realm of the *Sefiroth* – these
Tikkunim being described, of course, in sexual metaphor. The
absorption of the Song by the medieval Kabbalists resulted in the
adoption of unification (not Unity) – conceptualized after the pre-
eminent, this-wordly model of the sexual union of husband and
wife – as the pattern for all further conjecture on this elemental
theme.

To summarize, then, it can be seen that the Song was first studied in
a variety of ways in Jewish tradition, was subsequently experienced as
learned, and finally was reported first as in the *Shiur Koma*, then as in
the *Zohar*, etc. Let there be no confusion: later Kabbalists from
Nachmanides and Moses de Leon to Isaac Luria and Shneur Zalman
of Liady, did *not* experience a neutral something or 'nothingness'
which they then reported in the symbols of transcendental sexuality
and the accompanying language of the *Sefiroth*, nor again did they
even experience that 'Person' revealed to the Talmudic sages in the
Shiur Koma, reporting this experience in the technical vocabulary of
medieval Kabbalah. Rather, they experienced what they had learned
to experience, what their piety, training and education had prepared
them to experience, what they would claim their preparation had
made it possible for them (and only them, i.e. those with such
knowledge) to experience, namely a Jewish gnostic, theosophical

reality, shaped by the imagery of the Song (and the whole Torah[13] more generally, though likewise mystically deconstructed and engaged.)

To extend this analysis, consider now, as an alternative but parallel example, the continual use of the Song by Christian mystics. Over and over again, since at least the time of Origen's commentary on the Song,[14] Christian mystics of both sexes have used its imagery as a key to understanding their Christian experience of God's love, and especially of their encounter with Christ in mystical ecstasy. Though the most basic Christian exegesis of the Song sees it as an allegory of Christ's love for the Church (cf. Eph. 5.23), mystics, while accepting this interpretation, also favour a more personal exegesis emphasizing the individualistic interpretation whereby Jesus is the male Lover of the Song and the individual, especially the individual soul, is the female beloved. It was in particular this emphasis on the soul's love for Christ which passed into the medieval Christian mystical tradition through such works as Bernard of Clairvaux's famous commentary containing eighty-six Homilies on the Song. As a consequence, medieval Christian mystics, having been raised to seek Christ as 'Lover', indeed so experience him, and this is so in the case of both male and female mystics. Schooled on the christological rendering of the Song, Christian mystics quite naturally anticipated such a christological love encounter, had such an encounter, and subsequently described such an encounter. Theirs was no 'pure' happening only retroactively explained or interpreted in terms of Christ the Lover of the Song of Songs, rather Christ the Lover is the living content of their experience. No one who has read, for example, Teresa of Avila's *Autobiography* with an open mind can doubt the correctness of this analysis.

> He [Jesus] bade me not to suppose that He had forgotten me; He would never abandon me, but it was necessary I should do all that I could myself.
>
> (29) Our Lord said all this with great tenderness and sweetness; He also spoke other most gracious words, which I need not repeat. His majesty, further showing His great love for me, said to me very often: 'Thou art Mine, and I am thine.' I am in the habit of saying myself, and I believe in all sincerity: 'What do I care for myself? I only care for thee, O my Lord.'[15]

Or again, note the language used by Teresa in *The Interior Castle* to describe true ecstatic moments: 'in genuine raptures, for then I believe God ravishes the soul wholly to himself, as being his very own and his bride, and shows her some small part of the kingdom she has thus won.'[16] Likewise, Ruysbroeck remarks: 'Christ our Lover teacheth us four things . . . He shows us the use and purpose of our labour and of all our life, that is to say, the loving meeting with our Bridegroom,'[17] while Julian of Norwich says of Jesus: 'He is our Very, True, Spouse, and we His loved wife, His fair maiden, with which Wife He is never displeased.'[18] In addition, Catherine of Siena tells how in April 1542 Jesus revealed to her his intention of 'espousing her soul to him in faith',[19] after which Jesus placed a ring of marriage on Catherine's hand held out to her beloved by Mary.[20] The classic account of this remarkable episode deserves to be quoted in full.

> Then Jesus took from His left hand and from the finger next to the little finger a ring as described above [viz. a gold ring adorned with a magnificent diamond and enamelled in red], and while the Queen of Heaven continued to hold Catherine's hand Jesus Christ placed this most beautiful ring upon the finger which is called the index, next to the long finger of her left hand, saying, 'I give thee this in token that thou shalt always remain my spouse and in token that thou shalt never be led astray by the tempter in anything', and He added, 'Now thou are my bride indeed.' Then Jesus kissed her on the mouth, and Our Lady in the same spot and moment did likewise, and Catherine, excusing herself to Jesus that she had no words to thank Him as her heart desired, only said, 'My Lord I thank Thee that Thou hast deigned to take this wretched creature for Thy Bride.'

Teresa of Avila reports a similar event, as did the fourteenth-century mystic Colette, and Bernardene Florigni, Marina de Escobar, and Columba Schoneth, among others. Comparable phenomena continue to be reported by Christian mystics into the contemporary era, e.g. Celestine Fenouil, who also received Christ's stigmata at the age of 17 (in 1866), and Marie Julie Jahenny who manifested the stigmata in March 1873 as well as the signs of a mystical betrothal through the appearance of a mystical ring in February 1874.[21]

This use of the Song of Songs is full of intrinsic fascination but for our purposes its interest lies in the fact that it is tied to a broader consideration of prime significance: the conception of God as lover. That is, the image and idea of God as lover derived from the Song is part and parcel of a larger theological and metaphysical schema revealed in the Bible which conceives of God in personal terms and which lends itself to the language of the Song of Songs specifically and the language of love generally. The biblical text as a whole, with due allowance for differing exegetical emphases, thus contributes significantly to shaping the ontological-spiritual frame of reference in which the mystic moves and 'experiences'.

Of course, the biblical ontological schema is often enlarged upon in other sources, e.g. the Plotinian neo-Platonic tradition, but when this happens the argument, though more complex, remains basically intact; these non-canonical texts become 'canonical' through a process of domestication, rationalization and synthesis. The christianization of Plotinus at the hands of pseudo-Dionysius is a typical example of this process at work in mystical circles, in the same way that Aquinas's 'Aristotle' was for medieval Catholic scholasticism, and as Maimonides's and Avicenna's 'Aristotle' had been earlier for medieval Judaism and Islam respectively. Not that this process of integration and synthesis of alternative traditions is an easy matter, or even a terribly satisfactory conceptual enterprise, but the tensions between the amalgamated traditions usually go unrecognized. When it *is* recognized for any of many reasons, then one sees discord and charges of heresy. But this is the exception rather than the rule – especially once these syntheses are fully conceived and in place. Thus, medieval mystics of all three monotheistic faiths had little difficulty seeing neo-Platonism as compatible with the Torah or Koran, while rationalist philosophers, after the initial success of Arabic theologians in reconciling Aristotle and the Koran, came to view this reconciliation not only as useful but also as true. In other words, the sources of the 'canonical' tradition became broader, but no less stable. As a consequence, and despite claims to the contrary, for example, as advanced by W. T. Stace,[22] Western mystics do not experience 'God' in 'neutral' or monistic ways and then *interpret* this experience for expediency's sake in theistic language, but rather, based on their prior study of canonical sources such as the Song and other texts and source traditions, they have theistic and even more specifically personal, intimate, theistic experiences, e.g. God as lover, Christ as lover, etc.

Notice too that even within the theistic camp, and in the course of reading the same text, e.g. the Song of Songs, the doctrinal hermeneutic determines in advance how the meaning-content of the Song is experienced. I stress: how it is *experienced* – not merely how it is interpreted retroactively. Thus, Jews experience God as lover, though due to other pre-conditions (and pre-conditioning) of Jewish experience, they do not experience him in those most intimate and absorptive terms used by many, especially female, Christian mystics. Then again, Jewish mystics know only of, and thus only experience what Christians call 'God the Father'. On the other hand, Christians do not generally experience 'God the Father' as their lover but rather Jesus. Thus Bonaventure can write: 'There is no other path [to God] but through the burning love of the crucified.'[23]

The concrete meetings of mystic and beloved in Christian tradition, moreover, are almost always with the Christ whose physical body and wounds, etc., are seen and *felt* by the Christian initiate. Indeed, this feeling of sharing in Christ's wounds is a striking feature of many Christian mystical occasions. Citing Bonaventure again:

> There is no other path but through the burning love of the crucified, a love which so transformed Paul into Christ when he *was carried up to the third heaven* (2 Cor. 12.2) that he could say: *with Christ I am nailed to the Cross. I live yet not I, but Christ lives in me* (Gal. 2.20). This love also so absorbed the soul of Francis that his spirit shone through his flesh when for two years before his death he carried in his body the sacred stigma of the passion.[24]

It is not at all surprising, thus, to find that Francis of Assisi's manifestation of the stigmata has many parallels in later, as well as earlier, strata of the Christian mystical tradition, in the experiences of Catherine of Siena, Lukardis of Oberweimar, Gemma Galgani, Domenica Lazzari, and Louise Lateau, among others. While this tradition seems to have its origin in a literal interpretation of Paul's remark in Galatians: 'I bear the *stigmata* of the Lord Jesus in my body' (6.17), it is primarily associated with Francis. The powerful impression Francis's stigmata made on his contemporaries can be judged from this report published soon after his death:

> And this said [so Elias wrote] I announce to you great joy, even a new miracle. From the beginning of ages there has not been heard so great a wonder, save only in the Son of God, who is Christ our God. For, a long while before his death, our Father and Brother appeared crucified, bearing in his body the five wounds which are verily the Stigmata of the Christ; for his hands and feet had as it were piercings made by nails fixed in from above and below, which laid open the scars and had the black appearance of nails; while his side appeared to have been lanced, and blood often trickled therefrom.[25]

Similar recordings of sharing in Christ's suffering as part of the intense love-relation which the Christian mystic feels can easily be multiplied manyfold. Julian of Norwich, Suso, Tauler, Teresa of Avila, John of the Cross, provide numerous examples of this phenomenon. Suso gives this description:

> [Jesus addresses him thus] 'I will put on these my coat of mail, for my entire passion must thou [Suso] suffer over again according to thy strength . . . my torments must thou then diligently carry in thy heart with a motherly heartfelt love.'[26]

To which Suso, upon reflection, replies:

> 'I desire that thou wouldst unlock for me the entire treasure of thy Passion.'[27]

The 'intentionality' involved in this lived moment is exemplified in Lukardis of Oberweimar's striking experience. Yearning to share in her Lord's Passion she prayed that his experience of pain might always be present to her own experience. In response to her fervent prayers her wish was answered.

> For she saw in the spirit that she ought to pass through a certain door in which she found Jesus Christ as it were recently fastened to the cross, scored with the weals of the scourges and most pitifully dripping with blood. As she looked intently upon Him the servant of God fell at His feet swooning and almost lifeless. Then our Lord said to her: 'Rise up, My child, and help me'; by which she understood that she ought not to be content with merely calling His sufferings to mind but that she was meant to help Him by voluntarily sharing in His Passion. At Christ's word, accordingly, recovering at last something of her strength, she answered tremblingly: 'How can I help thee, my Lord?' And thereupon raising her eyes she saw His right arm loosened from the cross and hanging feebly down, by which it seemed to her that the pain of the suffering Christ was greatly intensified. So the beloved handmaiden, drawing near in tender compassion, strove to tie up the arm again to the cross with a thread of silk, but she could not succeed. Accordingly she began to lift His arm with her hands and with deep groanings to hold it in its place. Then our Lord said to her: 'Place thy hands against My hands, and thy feet against My feet, and thy breast against My breast, and in such wise shall be so much helped by thee that My pain will be less.' And when the servant of God had done this she felt interiorly the most bitter pain of the wounds both in her hands and in her feet and in her breast, although the wounds were not yet manifest to the outward eye. It was after this that she formed the habit of knocking her

> hands together with great force so that the noise was heard far and wide as
> from the collision of two planks.[28]

Here the shaping power of the traditional symbolism of a religious
community is felt with great intensity and immediacy.

With respect to other aspects of the conditioning of consciousness
produced by the Christian theological context, consider this quite
standard advice regarding the art of contemplation offered by
Bonaventure to would-be mystics:

> Let us come now to our Lord's return from exile. Lend a diligent attention
> thereto, for this meditation is extremely devout. Return then into Egypt,
> and there visit the child Jesus. Perhaps you will find him out-of-doors, with
> other children; on perceiving you he will come to meet you, for he is good
> and full of affability. You will kneel and kiss his feet, then take him into
> your arms and enjoy some rest in his company. Perhaps after this he will
> say to you: 'We have been permitted to return to our native land; we start
> tomorrow morning. You have come at an excellent moment; you can
> return with us.' Reply to him gladly that you are greatly rejoiced thereat
> and that you wish to follow him wheresoever he goes. Continue to take
> your delight in his conversation after this fashion. Then he will take you to
> his mother, with tokens of great respect for her. Kneel before her and do
> her reverence, and the like to the old man Joseph, and stay with them.[29]

Of course one must understand such advice 'mystically'; yet, with all
due allowance, is it surprising that after following such a recommendation and meditating on the child Jesus and his celestial family the
Christian mystic experiences these entities as realities, or put the other
way round, experiences reality in the form of such entities?
Alternatively, Muslims, given the dynamics of Islamic tradition,
experience Muhammad in a variety of transcendental guises. Nor is
this to be wondered at given Islam's veneration of Muhammad as:
'God's lights, mystery of mysteries, Spirit of Spirits'.[30] Kabbalists, in
their turn, certainly *never* encounter Jesus as the Lover of the Song,
nor Muhammad in any form or on any basis! Christians almost
always see, feel, touch, love, in short, experience Jesus as the Christ,
rather than 'God the Father', and never experience Muhammad in
any transcendental modality. Muslims never see Jesus as the Christ,
though they respect him as a prophet, but they often see Muhammad
in his primordiality as Logos, pre-existent perfect man, Prophet, and
the like. All this and more is not only the effect of doctrinal orthodoxy

post hoc, but also of the shaping influences of doctrinal orthodoxy *propter hoc*.

This discussion of the intimate interconnection of the religious and canonical literature studied and subsequent mystical experience can, and should, be considerably broadened at this juncture, the role played by the Song of Songs being typical, rather than exclusive. Hence the role of the Torah in its entirety, as understood by Kabbalists, i.e. as the eternal and perfect 'Word of God', must be appreciated. The affirmation of the eternal validity of the Torah[31] is a foundation of *all* conservative approaches to Judaism, whether mystical or not, and something insisted upon by all Kabbalists.[32] The elaborate exegetical tradition of the Kabbalists is based on precisely this conservative principle, i.e. God's word as revealed in the Torah is inexhaustible in its meaning and meaningfulness. The ramifications of this methodological and theological assumption can be seen in the saturation of Kabbalistic language by the biblical idiom; this saturation is little short of extra-ordinary. Nor must it be forgotten that most Kabbalistic treatises, including the *Zohar*, the most famous of all Jewish mystical compendia, take the form of biblical commentaries. The very novelty of the Kabbalistic interpretation of Scripture is grounded in the first instance in the highly traditional, conservative belief in the authority of the Torah as God's own will. One would not concern oneself with the Torah if it were not what the Jewish tradition claimed it to be. The further Kabbalistic speculations which promulgated such esoteric beliefs as that the Torah was God's 'name', and also that the Torah was a living organism, odd as these doctrinal notions might be, are not only developments growing out of biblical and talmudic traditions, but even more importantly for our present discussion, are predicated on the traditional view of the Torah as *Torat Emet*, God's own truth.

Similarly, the imagination of the Muslim mystic is, as Louis Massignon and Paul Nwyia[34] among others have shown, thoroughly saturated with the language of the Koran. Muslim mystics saw the Koran exactly as Jewish mystics saw the Torah, i.e. as the perfect 'Word' of Allah. The Muslim faithful even went so far as to argue for the uncreated, co-eternal nature of the Koran, which echoes certain midrashic writings on the nature of the Torah. As Massignon has rightly said: '[the Koran] is the essential textbook of his [the Sufi] sciences, the key for his Weltanschauung.'[35] In his classic study, *Essai sur les origines du lexique technique de la mystique musulmane*, Massignon gives the following description, so fundamental to our inquiry that I quote it at some length.

> 1. La source principale, à consulter d'abord, c'est le Qor'ân; puisqu'il s'agit de musulmans qui en connaissaient le texte par coeur, et le récitaient assidûment, pour composer le cadre de leurs méditations quotidiennes. Leur but était, en s'astreignant à réciter sans relâche ce texte d'un bout à l'autre (*khatm*), d'acquérir la science de l'*istinbât*: c'est-à-dire l'*élucidation* immédiate du sens de chaque verset, considéré en composition, à sa place parmi les autres. C'est la règle hanbalite: 'Ne t'en va pas (comme les commentateurs critiques) chercher deux passages séparés du Qor'ân pour les confronter; lis le Qor'ân du commencement à la fin.' Celui qui médite un texte pour en vivre tend à substituer à la consultation analytique et morcelée de ses éléments isolés (procédé d'indexage juridique, cher aux gens de loi) la considération synthétique et simultanée de l'ensemble.[36]

Massignon's summary remarks should be thoroughly assimilated, for they contain the essence of the matter, namely, that the whole consciousness of the Muslim mystic has been, to coin a term, 'Koranized'. When the Sufi, such as Ibn ᶜArabī, goes on to speak of the perfect Muslim as a Koran in his person[37] he is extending the meaning of Koran as the Hasidim do when they speak of their Zaddik as a 'Torah' in a parallel sense.[38] In these cases, the basic meaning of the Koran (as of Torah) is not lost or diminished; rather it is heightened. The use of such analogies is a mark of respect, a respect that is rooted in a specific tradition, i.e. of the Koran or Torah respectively. Even more fundamental in this context is the near universal Sufi concern with *taᶜwil*, the spiritual exegesis of the Koran which also functions as profound, mystical self-interrogation. *Taᶜwil* is the dialectical complement of *tanzil*: one brings the Koran from above, the other returns the Koran to its transcendental source. According to a classic text: 'He who practises the *taᶜwil* is the one who turns his speech from the external (exoteric) form towards the inner reality (*ḥaqīqat*).'[39] This mystical exegetical process must not be assimilated to the distinction between form and spirit or sign and reality.

> The symbol [the exoteric aspect of the Koran] is not an artificially constructed *sign*; it flowers in the soul spontaneously to announce something that cannot be expressed otherwise; it is the *unique* expression of

the thing symbolized as of a reality that thus becomes transparent to the soul . . . To penetrate the meaning of a symbol is in no sense equivalent to making it superfluous or abolishing it, for it always remains the sole expression of the signified thing with which it symbolizes.[40]

That is, the Sufi does not reduce the Koran to a set of arbitrary signs, and even less does he eliminate the Koran altogether; rather, he is engaged in the task of raising the Koran through mystical means back to its Source: Allah. In other words, it is only the Sufi who knows the true depth of the Koran; he alone is aware of the full reality it reveals. At the deepest level, the mystic becomes conscious, as must we, that there is no secret *above* or *behind* the sacred text: the text *is* the secret! – if only one knows how to 'read' it. Of course, this means that the text can no longer be viewed as primarily a historical or literary narrative, though it is always this too. Rather, it is the stuff of creation, containing the building blocks of the universe arranged according to a transcendental wisdom. Here is the basis of the Muslim tradition of Koranic letter mysticism which parallels, if it is not derived from, Jewish Torah letter mysticism as it is found throughout Jewish mystical writings,[41] and most clearly exemplified in the *Sefer Yezirah*, the outstanding witness to this cosmological conceptual orientation.[42] Early Christian mystics are known also to have speculated on the letters of the Greek alphabet, the language of their canonical scripture. Likewise, in the Middle Ages the astounding speculations of Joachim of Fiore, for example, reflect a profound study of the Hebrew Bible and the New Testament, interpreted in such a way as to justify a radical understanding of history. But for all its radicalness the interpretation is constantly 'drawn out' of the text, through a special Joachimite exegetical approach to scripture. One example is his constant play on the number 12 as it appears in the Bible, or his mystical trinitarian speculations on the letters of the Tetragrammaton as they appear in translation, IEVE. The letters are not arbitrary signs even in translation(!), but communicate the deepest mystery of the three-in-one Godhead. One is reminded here of Philo's exegetical writings as well, but with Christian materials one important methodological distinction, is necessary. Despite the attempts of some like Joachim to derive mystical meanings from the New Testament text it must be recognized that the Church does not make the same claim for the New Testament even though, it is traditionally said to be inspired by the Holy Spirit, as Jews, Muslims, and Hindus, for example, make for the Torah, Koran, and Vedas respectively. And this is due to the fact that, whereas one might describe the other traditions as centring their understanding of 'revelation' in a text, i.e. the text is God's 'Word', Christianity centres it in the person of Jesus; Jesus is *the* revelation, the 'Word become flesh', rather than the text of the New Testament per se.

The scripturally educated experience of mystics of the monotheistic traditions provides a paradigm which now must be the basis for further research. Even when mystics have provided a radical hermeneutic for searching out the meaning of their particular canonical scripture, their recognition of a given scripture as canonical and not another is, *ipso-facto*, at least in part, a 'conservative' phenomenon. The Jewish mystic may do wonders with the Torah but it is still the Torah and not another source with which he does those wonders. The same is true of Sufis who chant the traditional *tahlil* formula: 'Lā ilāha illā' llāh' (There is no god but Allah) as opposed to 'Om', and the same obtains in reverse for Gurus who intone the sacred syllable 'Om' rather than 'La ilāha illā' llāh'.

Then again, in those more usual instances in which mystics give a radical exegesis *not* of scripture, but rather of experience – arguing that they have *directly experienced* what scripture describes or prescribes (whichever text they hold to be scripture) – their experiential assertions and reports are both meant by them and understood by the larger faith community to which they belong and in the midst of which these proclamations are made, as *confirmations* of the inherited, authoritative tradition of scriptural interpretation(s), and not as heretical assertions that threaten the pillars of the regnant orthodoxy. Examples of this phenomenon abound. The *Merkavah* (Chariot) and *Heichalot* (Palaces) texts of the rabbinic period, as well as segments of the later Kabbalistic interpretation of scripture, are examples from the Jewish tradition. The teachings of Rābiᶜa; the *Kitāb al Riᶜāya lihuqūq Allah wa'l Qiyām biha* ('The Observance of the Law of God and the Abiding Therein') of Al Muhāsibī; the Koranic commentary of Jaᶜfar as Sādiq (d. 765); the mystic prayers of Dhūᶜn Nūn, and perhaps above all, the works of Al-Ghazzāli and IbnᶜArabī, are a very small sample of relevant Islamic writings. Christian materials ranging from Gregory's *Morals on Job* and Bernard's *Sermons on the Canticles*, to John of the Cross's *Canticles*, show similar intent and structure. The classical Buddhist commentaries on the *Āgamas* and *Nikāyas* show a strong conservative pattern, especially the best known of all commentaries, those composed by Buddhaghosa.[43] Zen texts exemplify conformity to this pattern. Their concern is to enable experience of the teachings of the Buddhist community, heavily emphasizing each individual's emulation of the Buddha's achievement. The Hindu exegetical tradition throws up many relevant examples, the best of which is Shankara's commentaries on the Upanishads, which, for all their novelty, are intended to be, were understood to be, and in many respect in fact are, highly conservative, traditional expositions of basic Hindu doctrine.

All these mystical personalities intended and experienced, they had *knowledge by acquaintance*, what their communities taught as *knowledge by description*. They had existential knowlege of what their co-religionists knew only through propositions. This existential knowledge moreover is quite specific, even to confirming minutiae of theological doctrine. For example, Teresa of Avila not only encounters Jesus but also receives existential verification of the doctrine of the Trinity,[44] while Jewish mystics always experience reality as conforming to the *halachah* (Jewish Law). That is to say, such experiences are highly specific, more often than not reinforcing the structures of established religion even down to its most technical doctrinal detail.

Even when mystics teach radical doctrines of one sort or another (those cases incorrectly fastened on as the 'essence' of mysticism by many students of religion) note should be taken of the attempt made by these very individuals to 'domesticate' their radical teachings by locating them within the larger orthodox and communal frame of reference. Thus, even radical Kabbalists referred to their wisdom as 'revelation(s) of the Prophet Elijah', the traditional keeper of the messianic secret and hence a pillar of Jewish orthodoxy. As Gershom Scholem has noted:

> since he [Elijah] was conceived as the vigilant custodian of the Jewish religious ideal, the Messianic guardian and guarantor of the tradition, it was impossible to suppose that he would ever reveal or communicate anything that was in fundamental contradiction with the tradition. Thus by its very nature, the interpretation of mystical experience as a revelation of the Prophet Elijah tended far more to confirm than to question the traditional authority.[45]

As a consequence, mystics saw their own teaching, and others saw it likewise, as either (*a*) the older teachings in a new guise; (*b*) a personal confirmation of existing doctrine; (*c*) a legitimate extension of traditional teaching; or (*d*) a new, but authoritative, stage of tradition. This is evidenced in the classical pseudepigraphic attribution of the thirteenth-century work, *Zohar*, to the great Talmudic sage of the second century Rabbi Simeon bar Yochai, and again in the claims by such Kabbalistic luminaries as R. Abraham ben David of Posquieres (12th c.) and R. Isaac Luria of Safed (16th c.) to have received their doctrines from Elijah. Still more radical, yet at the same time more conservative, is the claim of R. Joseph Karo, the author of the famous code of Jewish Law, the *Shulchan Aruch*, to be the student of no lesser a guide than 'The Spirit of the *Mishnah*',[46] the earliest classical corpus of rabbinic law.

In Sufi tradition we encounter the same phenomenon. All mystical wisdom is said to derive from Muhammed, who is depicted as the first and greatest Sufi. Thus, the Sufis saw their own path as both inspired by the example of Muhammed and expressly taught by him, while the *ḥadīth* was constantly invoked as the source and authority of Sufi practice and ideology. Even in those cases where the Sufis have recourse to *ḥadīth* which are not generally accepted by the legal schools the very fact that the Sufi seeks to ground and justify his experience by reference to the *ḥadīth* is itself important. It reveals the desire of the Sufi to stand within the Koranic and Muhammedan tradition rather than to deviate from it. Thus, Al Ḥallāj, supposedly the arch-heretic of Islam who was gruesomely martyred in 922 A.D., writes:

> All the lights of the Prophets proceeded from his [Mohammed's] light; he was before all, his name the first in the book of Fate; he was known before all things, all being, and will endure after the end of all. By his guidance have all eyes attained to sight . . . All knowledge is merely a drop, all wisdom merely a handful from his stream, all time merely an hour from his life . . .[47]

Again the divine revelation to Muhammed through the intermediary of the angel Gabriel is also a legacy of the Prophet to later Sufi thought, many Sufis receiving guidance from a variety of angels and heavenly spirits in achieving their mystical wisdom and salvation. Additional, relevant, examples abound in the Sufi material but must wait for another occasion for further elaboration of investigation.

Hindu tradition is also instructive on this point. Although not regarding the Vedas as the revelation of a Divine Revealer–as the Torah and Koran are regarded in their respective traditions–Hindus do hold the Vedas to be *śruti* (revelation i.e. that which is 'heard') of a 'transcendental' (for lack of a better term) origin, and to contain cosmic wisdom. Indeed, they see the uncreated origin of the scripture as the source of its authority, for all created things are inferior by definition. The lifelong engagement of the Hindu with the Vedas is predicated on this belief, as are the many rites and liturgical practices involving the Vedas which the Hindu employs in the search for Brahman, or one's 'true self'.

The same structural dynamic is evident in Christian mysticism. The 'revelation' vouchsafed in the mystical encounter with Jesus, Mary, or the like, is usually 'orthodox' in point of doctrine, e.g. touching the Trinity, the Incarnation, or original sin. Even when the Christian mystic believes him or herself to be the recipient of a novel experience or revelation, the 'novelty' is legitimized, as well as domesticated, by the fact of its transmission through the ultimate authority of the Church: Jesus, or one of his heavenly circle. Thus one can see without further examples or exegesis that, even when mystics seem to proclaim innovations of doctrine or practice, the relationship of mystics of the various traditions to the sources of authority and legitimacy in those traditions is, in character and function, less anarchic or revolutionary than conservative.

To conclude this part of our discussion of texts, a word about the unsatisfactoriness of reading mystical sources in translation is in order. To some extent this is, of course, a problem that mystical literature shares with all other literature: every translation is necessarily an interpretation. But we should not stop at this generalization. It is important to recognize that the study of mystical documents in translation is fraught with difficulties. There are, first of all, instances of blatant over-interpretation in translations. Martin Buber's *Tales of the Hasidim*, for example, are radically different from the originals. Whereas the authentic Hasidic tales are mystical, gnostic, Kabbalistic, ritualistic, saturated with folk-magic and superstition, other-worldly, and deeply concerned with Torah and *mitzvot*, Buber's are anti-mystical, anti-gnostic, anti-Kabbalistic, anti-ritualistic, this-worldly, pansacramental, anti-magical, and anti-halachic (i.e. opposed to Torah and *mitzvot* as traditionally understood).[48] Those who, like Stace, rely on Buber for Jewish mystical materials to compare with other mystical traditions will be badly misled.[49] But Buber's eisegesis and similar cases, like D. Suzuki on Zen, need not detain us, for serious scholars will, one hopes, be able to spot such theological revisionism.

More troublesome, however, is the challenge posed by texts which are translated more subtly and with genuine concern for accuracy. In such instances there is, lying below the surface of the text, difficulty on at least three important counts: First, the connotative senses of words are lost. Let us, for the sake of simplicity, return to our example of the Song of Songs. When a learned Jew hears certain Hebrew words which appear in the text of the Song of Songs, he connects them to a whole world of rabbinic discourse and hence the words gain a depth, a richness that is lacking in their merely denotative, dictionary sense. This kind of connotative force is, in fact, one of the most striking features of midrashic exegesis, and a prominent element in Kabbalistic thought and reasoning. Take as an example this interpretation from R. Abraham b. Isaac Ha Levi Tamakh's *Commentary on the Song of Songs*: In interpreting v. 7 of ch. 2, 'I adjure you, Oh maidens of Jerusalem by the gazelles and by the does of the field', he comments on the Hebrew words *zeba'ot* (gazelles) and *ayalot* (does) as follows:

> The mystical interpretation is that the people are adjuring the two forces that make up the universe: the upper and the lower world. The first is alluded to by a play on the word *zeba'ot*, which is equated with *zeba' ha-Shamayim*, the heavenly host; the lower world is derived from a play on *'ayala = 'eyley ha-'arez*, the mighty of the land, or the mighty in strength that fulfil His word, and in whose merit the world was created. The Midrash refers to this verse when it states that God warned heaven and earth that their sins might cause the departure of His presence, while in His divine wisdom he really desires to remain with them.[50]

And this interpretation, in fact, draws on allusions and textual references to be found in: *Midrash Leviticus Rabbah*; the biblical books of Nehemiah, Hezekiah, and Psalms; *Midrash Song of Songs Rabbah;* and *The Commentary of Nachmanides*. In comparison, the Christian exegete Gilbert of Hoyland comments on Song 3.3, 'Have you seen Him whom my soul loves', as follows:

> Have you seen him whom my soul loves? The sight of the Bridegroom is not one, or simple, or uniform. Abraham danced to see his day: 'he saw it

and rejoiced'. Jacob saw the Lord face to face and his life was spared. Moses saw him, but only his back. Isaiah saw the Lord seated on a lofty throne. Ezekiel saw him. Daniel saw him in the likeness of man although He had not yet assumed human nature. But every vision of this kind before the Incarnation was revealed in bodily appearance but not in the reality of a human body. The apostles saw him in the very reality of the flesh and they touched and handled him.

Yet both the former and the latter saw God inwardly by faith. He said to Philip: 'he who sees me, sees also my Father'. That this sight is a matter of faith is made clear by what follows: 'Do you not believe that I am in the Father and the Father is in me? . . . If not my words, accept the evidence of my deeds'. To prove that Philip sees the Father, the Lord argues that Philip sees the Son; what conclusion follows except that the Lord meant Philip's vision of both Father and Son to be understood as the vision of God through faith. So the Lord adds to the argument for belief: 'Do you not believe that I am in the Father and the Father is in me? . . . If not my words, accept the evidence of my deeds'. For if Christ dwells 'in our hearts by faith', and if those hearts of ours are cleansed by faith, why is He not also seen in our hearts by faith? As for the visions mentioned previously, some given in a likeness, others in the flesh, both sets are full of delight or of profit, but completeness is reserved for the third set of visions, those given through faith.[51]

In offering this christological interpretation, Gilbert draws on the connotations of *visio* in the Latin Vulgate, i.e. he refers to allusions and references in John 14.9, John 14.10-11, Ephesians 3.17, and Acts 15.9. Further examples are as unnecessary as they are plentiful.

Let us turn to a second difficulty created in the process of translation. Even when scrupulous care is taken, translators inevitably must use words in 'translation' which lead to fundamental problems of understanding.[52] This danger is particularly strong when, in the course of translating religious treatises, the translator has to find a 'translation' for the ultimate objects or realities of one tradition, in the language of a different tradition. *Brahman* becomes 'God', while *Mu* becomes 'Nothingness', as do the German *Nicht* and the Hebrew *Ayin*. But the Chinese Buddhist *Mu*, the *Nicht* of Eckhart, and the *Ayin* of Lurianic Kabbalah are *not* equivalent to the English terms 'Nothing' and 'Nothingness'. 'Nothing' and 'Nothingness' become intelligible – 'mean' – only within the syntactical and semantic structures of English which, in turn, receive their English meaning only in relation to a given ontology (or ontologies). *Ayin*, however, is tied to the rules of Hebrew grammar and receives its meaning only in connection with the metaphysical schema of the Kabbalists – their unique understanding of God as *Eyn Sof* (literally 'without end'), the Godhead to which no attributes can be assigned, and yet which is related necessarily and dialectically to certain manifestations (i.e. *Sefiroth*) of the Godhead and not to others. Indeed, the word 'God' is itself only a 'translation' for the various Hebrew terms of the Bible, and presents numerous problems. Thus, for example, while in English we have one term 'God', the Kabbalists would make a great deal of the different 'Names of God' in the Bible, believing each to refer to a different *Sefirah*, i.e. to a different Divine attribute.[53]

Third, the translation of texts implies the adoption of a *principle of translation*: that languages are composed of 'arbitrary' signs which stand for given realities though no necessary connection exists between sign and reality, and thus any one of many signs can 'stand for' a given referent. However, religious texts are often, if not always, believed by the faithful, and especially by mystics, to be more than arbitrary signs. In several traditions, at least, religious texts are taken to be the *literal* revelation of God and hence, in principle, untranslatable in a very special way. For example, Jewish mystics took the Torah as a unique reality whose every jot and tittle had cosmic significance. Here the 'power of speech' is given its maximum sense: the Hebrew letters, words, and names possess the power of creation and more.[54] It is through them – 'God spoke' – that worlds are created, ordered and destroyed; there is a casual nexus between revelation – Divine speech – and creation.[55] Special potency is found in the names of God,[56] most of all in the Tetragrammaton, whose proper employment can achieve cosmic elevation, spiritual salvation, and all forms of practical magic. The Muslim interpretation of the Koran is virtually the same.[57] Unaffected by any human consciousness – hence the importance of the traditional insistence on Muhammed's illiteracy,[58] – the Koran is Allah's co-eternal wisdom. Thus, even one who knows scant Arabic and intones its words by rote achieves higher spiritual states in as much as he is held to be sharing in Allah's own wisdom. As the speech of Allah, the words have the power to bring God and man together by virtue of their point of origination, comprehension aside. Then again, among the most important Sufi spiritual exercises is the practice of *dhikr Allah*, the remembrance and repetition of Allah's sacred names, especially the traditional formula: *La ilāha illā'llāh'* – 'There is no god but Allah.'[59]

It is not surprising, therefore, to find in Islam a long tradition of 'letter mysticism', comparable to that found in the Kabbalistic tradition. The most pronounced interest in this type of mysticism is among the Hurufi but it has been taught throughout Islam. According to such theories the shape and position of the letters of the Arabic alphabet are not arbitrary but reveal the deepest secrets of creation of which they are building blocks: 'The meaning of the Four Sacred Books is contained in a Single Alif.'[60] Al-Alawi, reworking the thought of 'Abd al Karīm al Jīlī, has written: 'All that is in the revealed books of the Koran is in the Fātihāh[61] and all that is in the Fātihāh is in Bismi'Llāh 'r-Raḥmāni 'r'Raḥīm.[62] And all that is in Bismi'Llāhi 'r-Raḥmāni r-Raḥīm is in the letter Bā,[63] which itself is contained in the point[64] that is beneath it.' He then goes on to explain the meaning of this cryptic remark thus:

> Whenever I speak of the Point I mean the Secret of the Essence which is named the Oneness of Perception (*Waḥdat ash-Shuhūd*), and whenever I speak of the *Alif* I mean the One Who Alone *is* (*Wāḥid al-Wujūd*), the Essence Dominical, and whenever I speak of the *Bā* I mean the ultimate Manifestation which is termed the Supreme Spirit, after which come the rest of the letters, then single words, then speech in general, all in hierarchy. But the pivot of this book turneth upon the first letters of the alphabet on account of their precedence over the others. *The Foremost are the Foremost, it is they who are brought nigh.* These are Alif and Bā, and they hold in the Alphabet the place that is held by the Basmalah in the Qoran, for together they make up Ab which is one of the Divine Names. By it would Jesus speak unto His Lord, and he used it when he said: 'Verily I go unto my Father and your Father', that is, unto my Lord and your Lord. And now, if thou understandest that these two letters have a meaning that thou knewest not, be not amazed at what we shall say of the Point, and the rest of the letters.
>
> The Point was in its hidden-treasurehood before its manifestation of itself as Alif, and the letters were obliterate in its secret essence until it manifested the inward outwardly, revealing what had been veiled from sight by donning the various forms of the visible letters; but if thou graspest the truth, thou wilt find naught there but the ink itself, which is what is meant by the Point.[65]

Given this understanding of language and its relation to reality, that is as a consequence of this contention, we may be able to describe this matter to some degree, even a high degree, in languages other than Arabic, but none of these other languages can 'mean' the same thing for the 'meaning' is ontic not semantic.

This same problem also emerges in regard to Eastern texts. The Hindu tradition has always held the Vedas to be *śruti*, revelation, though whose revelation, i.e. whether of one Supreme Deity such as the God of Judaism or Islam, or of a secondary deity, or of no deity at all, is a subject of considerable debate. Some sources attribute their authorship to Prajāpati while others favour Brahman or the Supreme Spirit.[66] In any case, whoever their revealer or none, the Vedic text was traditionally considered eternal and of transcendental origin. As such it has been used over the centuries as a source of meditation and devotion by Hindu mystics. It has always been held to contain 'gnosis', i.e. 'knowledge', which is the primary meaning of the name *Veda*, whose possession allowed one to understand and hence control, or at least influence, the elemental cosmic forces. The ritual formulae of the Vedas, in the form of *mantras*, when properly chanted and pronounced become the magical means of gaining transcendental wisdom and power.[67] The adept who knows how to use a *mantra* 'achieves its union with that Consciousness which manifests itself in that "text" or formula, and being so a vedic *mantra*, can, according to the context, be corroborative or minatory, exert beneficent influence in the cosmos, and, of course, bring about communication with the unseen.'[68] The most concentrated magical power resides in the name *Brahman* which 'assumed in definite contexts, more specific connotations such as the fundamental power inherent in the holy word and ritual and in the vocabulary of the poets their products considered in one of their characteristic aspects. The gods are strengthened by *brahman*; it can gain the victory in battles, protect the people, give offspring, dispel darkness.'[69] That the study of the *mantra* has spawned various esoteric practices, perhaps the best known of which is *mantra-yoga*, is thus not surprising. The *mantra* possesses a mystical energy which inheres in the power of speech as manifest in the Sanskrit alphabet similar to the Kabbalistic and Sufi understandings of Hebrew and Arabic respectively. This parallelism of the power of the Sanskrit alphabet is also seen in the *bījākshara mantras* (the mystical 'seed syllable' *mantras*), which, along with the *gayatri mantras*, are the most religiously significant of all *mantras*. These *mantras* are said to represent the *anusvāra*, i.e. the overtone of the nasal sound of the Sanskrit alphabet. The best known *bījākshara*, the sound *oṁ*, made up of three sounds, *a u m*, is the mystic sound *par excellence*. Its three sounds are said to contain within themselves all the wisdom of the three *Vedas*, the worlds and the three chief deities, all concentrated into one mystically potent sound point. In the *Upanishads* this mystical utterance is given prime importance. The whole of the *Māndūkya Upanishad* is devoted to unfolding its meaning, explaining in its first verse that: 'Oṁ! – this syllable is this whole world. The past, present, the future – everything is just *Oṁ*.' Meditation on this syllable brings spiritual elevation, recitation of it as the name of *Brāhman* brings communion with the ultimate, which is known by this name. In the *Katha Upanishad* we are instructed:

> The word which all the Vedas repeat, and what they say is [equivalent to] all austerities, seeking which men lead the religious life, that word I [Yama] declare to you summarily. It is *Oṁ*. For this syllable alone is *brāhman*; for this syllable alone is supreme; for knowing this syllable alone, whatever one wishes, that is his. This is the best foundation, that is the supreme foundation. Knowing this foundation one enjoys bliss in the *brāhman* world.[70]

In Buddhism too this *mantra* tradition continued to be a source of meditation, though, of course, employed towards the different end of reaching *nirvāṇa* or *śūnya*. Both Hinduism and Buddhism insist, moreover, that the sacred syllable *Oṁ* and many other *mantras* are 'unintelligible'[71] in any descriptive sense.[72]

Enough has been said – though hardly enough to treat the subject exhaustively – to indicate that sacred texts, written in sacred languages and comprised of sacred alphabets, play important roles in the major mystical traditions of the world. This militates against 'translation' of these languages and the sacred texts composed in them, and returning to our thesis about the 'conservatism' of mysticism helps re-inforce the argument that mystical experience(s) are rooted in established religious communities, and grow out of, and are compatible with, the basic elements of those positive traditions. And sacred alphabets grown into sacred languages and sacred texts play an essential role in this context-laden phenomenon.[73]

One final series of closely interrelated remarks dealing with the radical hermeneutical dimension of mystical thought is now necessary to round off this analysis. It is usual in discussion of mysticism to focus, and not without some grounds, on the radical rather than the 'conservative' side of mystical exegesis, i.e. on the strange things mystics do with and to the inherited canonical texts of their traditions. For instance, the *Zohar*, although structured as a commentary on the Torah, is a very unusual commentary indeed. Zoharic exegesis often arrives at 'truths' unimaginable, as well as unsupportable, by more regularly accepted hermeneutical principles. And the same is of course true of the many hundreds of other Kabbalistic and later Hasidic commentaries on scripture. Muslim, Hindu, and Buddhist mystics likewise are prone to 'unorthodox' exegeses of canonical texts and teachings. And on the basis of these facts one can arrive at the usual conclusion: mystics are radical underminers of the established religious order. I have no wish to deny the radicalness of salient features of the exegetical hermeneutic of the mystical exegetes listed above, and of a great many other mystical exegetes as well. Yet I do want to turn the understanding of their exegesis around and from that point of view illumine an alternate side of the matter. Consider this seeming paradox: the very radicalness of the mystical hermeneutic is itself a conservative factor. By proposing this seeming paradox I want to suggest this: mystics *do* stretch texts in all directions through their employment of allegorical and symbolic readings; yet this very use of allegory and symbolism, as well as other varied hermeneutical devices, functions to *maintain* the authority of the canonical sources under interpretation rather than to destroy or transcend them, as is usually assumed. That is to say, the presupposition on which the mystical use of allegory and symbolic modes of exegesis depends is that the canonical books of one's tradition do in fact possess the *truth* and *authority* claimed for them. In the absence of this presupposition one need not bother with allegory or other hermeneutical aids; the texts could be dispensed with altogether in favour of the new 'higher', mystical truths vouchsafed to the mystics through their experience. But, in fact, there is no displacement of scripture; there is only 're-interpretation'. Through this 're-interpretation' the extant spiritual classics are shown to teach the very doctrines revealed anew to the mystic. Thus, the community is seen to have been all the time in possession of the 'truth' revealed a second time to the contemporary initiate. In this way the mystical hermeneutic reinforces, even exaggerates, the significance of canonical texts to a degree unheard of in the non-mystical hermeneutical tradition.

One or two brief examples will, I trust, make this argument clear. The writings of Philo of Alexandria present perhaps the best known, most direct, example of this truth. In radically re-interpreting the Torah through an extreme allegorical method, his intention was highly conservative: to affirm the ultimacy of the Torah as the supreme source of wisdom which included – here arose the need for allegory – all of Platonic philosophy and surpassed it. Similarly, the exegesis of the *Zohar*, of Isaac Luria and his circle, and of the *Baal Shem Tov* and the masters of Hasidism, while clearly 'changing' the *peshat*, the literal meaning of the Torah, in various theosophical ways, never denied the binding nature of the Torah and its commandments. Rather they raised it to a new cosmic centrality making it the regulative principle of their entire theosophical vision. The exegesis of Tauler, Suso, John of the Cross, and even Eckhart, who is almost always incorrectly made over into a non-medieval Christian pantheist of some sort, was meant to extend the existential as well as metaphysical significance of the New Testament 'kerygma' of Jesus and his 'Gospel'. Christian mystics never denied what the New Testament revealed, rather they reinforced it in the existential dimension, i.e. Jesus died for 'me'; they experienced Jesus' passion, even to Francis's *stigmata*, and the like. When the Sufi Yūnus Emre taught: 'When you seek God, seek Him in your heart – He is not in Jerusalem, not in Mecca nor in the Hajj', [74] he was not denying the value of pilgrimage to Mecca, and the *Hajj* was always an essential of the Sufi *tarīqa*. Rather he was going beyond the 'letter' of the Koran and *extending* – not *rejecting* – its meaning towards an interiorization of the Koranic teaching. That is to say, the literal pilgrimage, like all other Koranic precepts, was a *sine qua non* of Sufi practice and teaching. Having done what is required, however, the Sufi then went further. This tendency to go 'further' is common to all mystical traditions. At the same time, however, this interiorization, this going 'further', was justified by the conservative presupposition of the ultimacy of the Koran as Allah's eternal word. That is, the interiorization of the Koran is not something extrinsic to the original nature of the Koran, as many a Western interpreter of Sufism would incorrectly have it, but is of its very essence; as the Word of Allah it is 'endless', 'bottomless', 'infinite', containing *all* wisdom. The gnosis gained by the Sufi is thus hermeneutically deposited in the structure of the ontology of the orthodox theology of the Koran which the

Sufis share. The same can be said for the Kabbalistic treatment of the Torah. It is infinitely more than the literal composition with each word containing seventy faces, i.e. allowing of endless depths of interpretation and re-interpretation.[75] Such re-interpretation then was intended to extend one's praise of the Torah (or Koran, etc.), and thus of its Revealer, by discovering ever deeper, more profound levels of the Divine wisdom.

Within the context of historic Judaism, the dialectic of Torah as revealed word, both conservatively and radically interpreted, remained for the most part in balance, though not without tension. The same may be said for the history of the respective canonical texts in the mystical traditions of Christianity, Islam, and Hinduism. It is only when scholars or enthusiasts wrench the mystical traditions from their contexts that this sensitive dialectic is broken, with the resulting caricature of the whole. This is not to make any pretence that the present argument resolves all the difficult epistemological, hermeneutical, and theological problems raised by the varieties of mystical exegesis. Rather it is only to claim that there is more to the issue than is usually appreciated.

III

Having begun with the structure of mystical texts and the manner of their interpretation, let us now consider the still more essential question: what do the texts tell us? To answer this question aright, one philosophical category must be explored as a pre-condition of all further comment: ontology. Whereas mystical texts take many forms, e.g. biographies, aphorisms, biblical exegesis, manuals, and so forth, they all reflect and are dependent upon, more often than not in an unspoken fashion, pluriform *Weltanschauungen*.

Let us begin with the example of Christian mystics. Whether schooled on Plotinus and the Neo-Platonic tradition as it was known through pseudo-Dionysius, as most Christian mystics were, or on a more Aristotelian model or rather 'pseudo'-Aristotelian model as conveyed first through the spurious *Theology of Aristotle* and then by Aquinas, Christian mystics all presume an ontological skeleton which broadly approximates to this: there is a personal God who created (or emanated) the world. Men and women are his creation. The world and all else that is in it are his creation. The world and mankind are alienated from God as a result of original sin. A means of overcoming this alienation, however, has been provided by God through the mediation of Christ who is God Incarnate, the second person of the Trinity. The human soul is capable of responding to this mediation because it is created by the Divine Being, incorporates the Divine, or is (depending on the technicalities of the different thinkers) Divine in itself. However, even the soul's divine origin is no guarantee of salvation unless God in his grace awakens the soul from its sensual, this-worldly, imprisonment and turns it towards its maker and master. One could go on to flesh out this ontological description in technical ways but I have chosen to keep it as simple as is possible without distortion, so that its essential contours are clear. This ontological schema tells us: (*a*) how and what the world and man are, i.e. creations of a loving creator; (*b*) what the world is not, i.e. an accident, a meaningless surd, an illusion, a this-worldly immanent naturalism or the like. Thus, Christian mystics are taught to 'experience' God, and more especially Christ, in the form of a personal redeemer. They are not prepared to experience the one-ness of a natural pantheism in the manner of Richard Jefferies, nor the illusoriness of reality as are the Advaitans. No Christian mystic is an Advaitan, not even Eckhart, on whom we shall comment further below. Moreover (though as with Eckhart there are complex metaphysical and theological difficulties to face), the christocentric experience of Christian mystics manifests a striking dialectic: their Christian ontological commitment leads them to seek and to find a mystical-transcendent Jesus, while the finding of this Jesus for whom they were seeking reinforces their Christian ontology. This ontological-epistemological interpretation explains why Christian mystics are *Christian* mystics and why, contrary to popular *mis*-conception, most Christian mystics do not become 'heretics', are not hounded from pillar to post by the Church, and do not die the romantic, if painful, death of the martyr. Augustine, Francis of Assisi, Bernard, Suso, Tauler, Thomas à Kempis, Teresa, John of the Cross, all, though not free of tension, were in holy orders, lived out their lives in regularized Christian ways, continued all their life to participate in Christian ritual and sacramental activity, were not permanently excommunicated, did not die outside the Church. Even Eckhart, the most radical of the medieval monk-mystics, was excommunicated only after his death and then soon reclaimed by the

Church. In each case, the conservative factor provided by their Christian ontology is evident in their lives as well as in their visions and mystic experiences.

Henry Suso, a disciple of Eckhart's who was instructed in the mystical way by the master himself, records the following very Christian sort of experience, i.e. grounded in a thoroughly christocentric ontology. He tells us, in the third person in which his autobiography is written, the detail of one of his penances:

> As a physical proof that he was touched to the heart with compassion for his crucified Lord, the Servitor fashioned a wooden cross the length and width of his own body, studded it with thirty sharp iron nails, and carried it day and night on his naked back for eight years in honour of Christ's wounds. Shouldering this cross the first time and finding the pain more than flesh and blood could bear, he took it off and blunted the nails. But he soon repented of this unmanly act and filed them again to a sharp point. It moved back and forth on his bony back, cutting deep, bloody wounds which bit with a thousand teeth whenever someone touched him or even brushed his clothing. To help himself bear the pain he chiselled on the back of the cross the sweet name of Jesus.
>
> He secretly took a discipline with this cross twice a day, striking himself so vigorously that the nails stuck in his flesh and he had to jerk the cross to remove them. The first of these disciplines he took at the entrance to the chapter room in his nightly Way of the Cross, begging his beloved Redeemer to heal his Servitor's wounds by the merits of his own atrocious scourging. The second he took upon reaching the crucifix above the pulpit, this time with the intention of nailing himself to the cross, never to be separated from the divine derelict. He also took the discipline whenever his conscience pricked him for having taken inordinate satisfaction in eating, drinking, or some other bodily need.[76]

Given this biographical report it is not at all surprising to find that Suso is also the author of the *Little Book of Eternal Wisdom* (*Horologium Sapientiae*), the heart of which is a 'Hundred Meditations' on Christ's Passion (see its 'Prologue'). Nor is it to be wondered at that Suso received the following mystical experience:

> One day when, according to his custom, the Servitor was in his cell praying for the grace to suffer meritoriously, Jesus Christ appeared to him in the form of a seraph on a cross. This seraph had six wings; with two he covered his head, with two he covered his feet, and with two he flew. On the two covering his feet was written: 'Receive sufferings willingly.' On the two with which he flew: 'Bear sufferings patiently.' On the two which covered his head: 'Learn to suffer in a Christlike spirit'.[77]

Is there room for reasonable doubt that Suso's original Christian ontology, with the Easter Event at its centre, prefigures and 'intends' the mystical happening of which Suso's *Autobiography* tells?

Consider then again a major nor-Eckhartian Christian mystic, Teresa of Avila. Teresa of Avila has a quite definite conception of reality which is not of her own making but rather learned from her sixteenth-century Spanish Christian environment. It is within this inherited 'picture' of the world that she matures to womanhood and 'experiences' reality. She has a very specific understanding of how reality is constituted, namely, as a creature created by a loving omnipotent God, as well as of what the proper goal of life is, i.e. relation with Christ.[78] This ontological schema creates and shapes her expectations from the outset, while at the same time delimiting the parameters of her experience. In short, the medieval Catholic ontology is fundamental to the way Teresa knows the world. It dictates how the world is to be experienced and also what there is to experience, i.e. Christ. I state this ontological presupposition of Teresa's entire mystical adventure without complicating detail, so as to focus on the central issue: Teresa's experience, however extreme it may be considered in certain Christian circles,[79] is always a Christian, or, even more precisely, a Catholic experience. The fact that she finds Christ as her Bridegroom is not a retroactive post-experiential 'gloss' on an essentially amorphous, neutral event. She had read the Song of Songs and knew its Catholic mystical symbolism before as well as after her ecstacy. She had sought that which she would come to find, the encounter with Christ as lover. Hers was no search after *ātman* within the self or of the cessation of all feeling in the no-thingness of *nirvāna*. The union of the mystic with Christ, as lover and beloved, was of the essence of her Christian study. She was the heir of a long Catholic line of mystical piety which described itself in the terms and images of love, culminating especially in St. Bernard's description of the 'mystical marriage' as it appears in his no fewer than eighty-six sermons on the Song of Songs.[80] This particular late medieval emphasis allied itself with the scholastic ontology of the schools, to produce a *Weltanschauung* which pre-conditioned all of Teresa's spirituality. One reads her autobiography and is amazed that this should require comment, yet the secondary literature reveals that it does. Her life, far from embodying heretical apprehensions, though it certainly did include unusual ones, is a model of traditional piety. Her experiences are all most 'orthodox', her life a commitment to the

Reform, i.e. a stringent form of Catholic monasticism. Though opposition from the calced communities and certain other churchmen was a constant presence in her biography, the overwhelming impression is of 'orthodoxy' and conservatism. Everything Teresa did was Catholic, every ambition Catholic, every intuition Catholic, every reform Catholic – all for 'Christ's sake'.

Her life's work was to renew the Church through her reform. Though the term 'reform' may conjure images of rebellion, associated most closely with Luther and the Protestant Reformation, it must be emphasized that reform is, at least in large measure, a fundamentally conservative factor which looks back to a real or imagined 'Golden Age' in some earlier, pristine period of a religious community's history. Even if this nostalgia is for a mythical ideal, it must be counted more a conservative than a radical phenomenon. That it has its radical side as well there is no doubt, but no religious reformer sees his or her self or work as essentially radical (i.e. novel or 'new'), whatever the judgement of history may be.

This ontological rootedness may be perceived not only in Teresa but in her great disciple, John of the Cross.[81] He too shares Teresa's understanding of reality, i.e. that of late medieval Catholicism, and as a consequence his writings show a strongly conservative dimension, even in the midst of the most intimate revelations of the 'Dark Night of the Soul'. Thus, for example, in expounding Stanza II of the *Living Flame of Love* which reads:

> O sweet burn!
> O delicious wound!
> O tender hand! O gentle touch!
> Savouring of everlasting life,
> And paying the whole debt
> In destroying death Thou hast changed it into life.

John comments as follows:

We learn here that it is the Three Persons of the Most Holy Trinity, Father, Son, and Holy Ghost, Who accomplish the divine work of union in the soul. The 'hand', the 'touch', and the 'burn' are in substance one and the same; and the three terms are employed because they express effects peculiar to each. The 'burn' is the Holy Ghost; the 'hand' is the Father; and the 'touch' is the Son. Thus the soul magnifies the Father, the Son, and the Holy Ghost, extolling those three grand gifts and graces which They perfect within it, in that They have changed death into life, transforming it into Themselves.

2. The first of these gifts is the delicious wound, attributed to the Holy Ghost, and so the soul calls it the 'burn'. The second is the 'taste of everlasting life', attributed to the Son, and the soul calls it the 'gentle touch'. The third is that 'gift' which is the perfect recompense of the soul, attributed to the Father, and is therefore called the 'tender hand'. Though the Three Persons of the Most Holy Trinity are referred to severally, because of the operations peculiar to Each, the soul is addressing itself to but One Essence, saying, 'Thou hast changed it into life', for the Three Divine Persons work together, and the whole is attributed to Each, and to All. 'O sweet burn.'[82]

John, it should also be remembered, served as the spiritual guide to a group of nuns. How may one imagine they would encounter the mystical reality when they were instructed by him as follows:

> Jesus be in your souls: My daughters are thinking that I have lost sight of them because I do not write, and that I have ceased to consider how easily they can become saints and rejoice in the Bridegroom Whom they love with great gladness and in strong security. I will come to Veas, and you will see that I have not forgotten you. We shall then see the treasures obtained by pure love and on the pathways of everlasting life; the blessed progress you have made in Christ, Whose joy and crown are His brides. This crown ought not to be rotting on the ground, but rather borne by the hands of the seraphim, and placed with respect and reverence on the head of our Lord.
>
> When the heart is grovelling meanly on the ground the crown rolls in the dust, and is trampled on in every act of meanness. But when man shall 'come to a heart that is high', according to the words of David, then shall God be exalted with the crown of the heart of His bride; wherewith they crown Him in the day of the joy of His coronation, for His delight is to be with the children of men.[83]

It might be (incorrectly!) argued in response that Teresa and John of the Cross are atypical, that even Suso is unrepresentative of Catholic mysticism. Such a response would surely tell us more about the views of the scholar so responding than about medieval Catholic mysticism, yet let us entertain the hypothesis for the purpose of clarification. The desired clarification will be achieved if we conclude our present discussion with a brief look at Meister Eckhart, the most often cited supposedly 'unorthodox' Catholic mystic.[84] Eckhart's mystical writings do reveal a different image from those of the sixteenth-century Spanish mystics, and he is certainly as radical as any other Christian mystic in his formulations, yet his mystical ontological schema is still defined by the creative and legitimating parameters of medieval Catholic theology. Eckhart described his own project thus: 'It is the intention of the writer [Eckhart] – as it has been in all his works – to expound by means of the natural demonstrations of the philosophers, the doctrines taught by the Holy Christian Faith and the Scriptures Old and New Testaments.'[85] Moreover, as one might expect, and reinforcing our opening comments on mystical texts, most of Eckhart's mystical writings, in whatever form, are essentially mystical-metaphysical commentaries on canonical texts. In this way, he was carrying out the purpose of the Church, i.e. to preserve and teach the doctrine of Christ, the incarnate Word, revealed authoritatively in Scripture. Eckhart's mystical hermeneutic is imbued with traditional Catholic dogma: the Incarnation; the presence of the Word in the New Testament and in and through the Catholic Church; the debilitating effects on all men of 'original sin' and hence the need for grace which is revealed only through Christ. Then again, Eckhart had drunk deeply of the metaphysics of Aristotle and Aquinas, receiving his doctorate in theology in Paris in 1302, and continually and faithfully taught that the Catholic Church was the only true way to God: 'Let us know only Jesus Christ who alone is our light, our support and the way to the Father.'[86] Secondly – and an essential metaphysical claim often misunderstood or ignored altogether – though on the one hand Eckhart teaches that:

> all that is in the Godhead is *one*. Therefore we can say nothing. He is above all names, above all nature. *God works; so doth not the Godhead.* Therein they are distinguished – in working and not working. The end of all things is the hidden Darkness of the eternal Godhead and never to be known,[87]

at the same time he insists that this unknown and in principle unknowable ground of Being – the Godhead – manifests himself as 'worker' most perfectly in Christ. The connection between the Godhead and Christ is not accidental but necessary. Whereas for a non-Christian the necessary manifestation of the unknowable Godhead, e.g. the *Eyn Sof* (literally 'without end' – God before he emanates his Sefiroth) of the medieval Jewish Kabbalists, is never Christ. For Eckhart Christ is: 'the Word of the Father. In this Word the Father affirms himself, and all the divine nature of everything that God is, just as he knows it; and he knows it as it is.'[88] Even more particularly Catholic is Eckhart's belief in the Trinity, i.e. in the Trinity as the essence not only of appearances in some lower ontic realm but of the Godhead itself. Thus, in almost every one of his *Tractates* he reflects, in his extraordinarily dense, inchoate, scholastic style, on the meaning of the Triune God. Next to the Godhead, this notion is one of his recurring, and most problematic, preoccupations. For example in the *Nobility of the Soul* he writes:

Now I go on to speak about abstract knowledge of God. And I address myself to you, my brethren and my sisters, beloved Friends of God who are familiar with him and know something of the matter. I will start with the nomenclature of the holy Trinity. And here you will be called upon to follow an abstruse, technical discussion. When we speak of the Father or the Son or the Holy Ghost we are speaking of the Persons. When we speak of the Godhead we are speaking of their nature. The three Persons, as Person and essence, flow with their essence into the essence wherein they are Godhead. Not that the Godhead is other than what they are themselves: they are the Godhead in their unity of nature. The flow in essence into the essence, both Person and essence, because essence is comprehended by nothing but itself. It is fast locked in stillness, comprehending itself with itself. This influx is, in the Godhead, the oneness of the three inseparate Persons. In this same flux the Father flows into the Son and the Son again into the Father (as our Lord Jesus Christ declares, 'He that seeth me seeth my Father. My Father is in me and I in him'), and they both flow into the Holy Ghost and the Holy Ghost back to them again. (As our Lord Jesus Christ says, 'I and my Father are one Spirit.') The Father utters his Son and in his Son tells forth himself to creatures as a whole, all in this flow.[89]

Eckhart's continual talk of Jesus Christ as 'the bridegroom of the soul',[90] which draws upon the biblical–Christian sources we have already commented upon, must also be rethought in this context, for whatever Eckhart is, he is not Shankara nor, despite Suzuki, is he a Mahāyāna Buddhist.[91] He is a medieval Catholic Dominican monk, if of a special kind. We can no more correctly understand him if we stress that he was a monk of a 'special kind' to the exclusion of his Dominican piety than if we only talk of his Dominican piety without being sensitive to the reality of his unique spirituality.

There still remains much more detailed analysis of the ontological commitments of Christian mystics to be undertaken, e.g. the relation of Incarnational claims to emanationist ontologies; the specific nuances and emphases of each individual mystic's particular onto-logical understanding; the relation of Trinitarian to other trans-cendental claims; the absorptive versus the non-absorptive perspec-tives on the '*unio mystica*'; the nature of the human soul, its capacities and limitations; and so on, before we have a full conceptualization of this aspect of Christian mysticism and how it affects the particular experiences of the mystics of the Church. Nevertheless, enough has been suggested in the foregoing review to point the way towards the required sort of analysis, one which grounds the specifics of a mystical awareness in a larger ontic matrix. This situational her-meneutic is needed in order to accurately assess the Christian as well as other mystical traditions and also in order to facilitate the framing of a substantive, defensible cross-cultural phenomenology of mys-tical experience.[92] In addition, on the basis of this evidence and the work done in my earlier researches, I would like to advance the claim that the ontological structure(s) of each major mystical tradition is different and this pre-experiential, inherited structure directly enters into the mystical occasion itself.[93] As a consequence, Christian mystics, as we have shown, have Christian experiences, of Jesus, Mary, and the mysteries of the Trinity, etc., while Jewish Kabbalists meet Elijah and 'see' the *Merkabah* or God's throne. In the East Buddhists reach their goal, set by their ontology of *anitya* (imperma-nence) and suffering, of impersonal, stateless, attributeless, *nirvāṇa* or *satori*, while Hindus confirm that *Atman* is *Brahman*, as they were taught from the onset of their mystical quest by the ruling metaphys-ical presuppositions of the Hindu schools whether dualist or monist.

Nor again, are these mystic states all 'really' the same, as many would have it. The Christian *unio mystica* which finds fulfilment in Christ is *not* the Buddhist experience of *nirvāṇa*. Whereas the Christian enters a relational state, even an absorptive state in extreme cases, in which the individual soul joins with God, which John of the Cross described as 'the touch of the Substance of God in the substance of the soul,'[94] the Buddhist is 'nirvanaized', i.e. becomes a new ontic reality in which there is no place for either individual souls or a transcendent Divine Being. *Karma* not 'grace' governs the movement of the historic-transcendent situation and necessity rather than a benevolent will provides the causal power. The Kabbalistic quest for *devekuth* (adhesion to God) and the Hindu striving for

Atman are likewise not comparable to the Buddhist experience, for both affirm substantial selves. Yet, they are not really comparable to each other, or to Christianity either, for Jewish mystics work under the forms of Torah, i.e. 'Torah-power' as an ontic force, seeking to purify their souls for *devekuth*, *not* absorption, with a personal God, while Hindus seek existential confirmation that *Atman* is *Brahman*, i.e. the self is the Self, though this ultimate Self is non-personal. Then, by comparison, Christians are 'moved by the Spirit', i.e. 'grace', not the power of 'works', and seek relation with Jesus, a being to whom Jews deny any ultimate reality. In each of these, and every other mystical tradition as well, the mystical moment is the conclusion of a mystical journey. It is the solution to inherited ontological circumstances; the 'way out' of or through a prearranged ontological schema.

At this juncture and by way of conclusion what must be kept in focus is the interpenetration of relative ontological arrangements and experienced mystical states. The metaphysical naïveté that seeks for, or worse, asserts, the truth of some meta-ontological schema in which either the mystic or the student of mysticism is said to have reached some phenomenological 'pure land' in which he grasps transcendent reality in its pristine pre-predicative state is to be avoided.[95] Given the epistemic elements involved in arriving at a comprehensive phenomenology of mysticism it is wiser to stand on its head the traditional, though arbitrary, analysis of mystical experience, which contends for separable components of 'experience' and 'description', and argue that the ontological structures inherent in language and judgement pre-create the contours of experience and thus make 'pure experience' a chimera. Then, as language and judgement also belong to, indeed are inseparable from, social life, this structural matrix works to locate both experience and the experiencer (the mystic) in a given socio-historic conceptual field whose problems and problematic he or she adopts and aims to solve. For example, mystics in the Buddhist tradition seek 'release' as a result of their self-appropriation of the Buddhist non-theistic metaphysical schema of *karma* (results of action), *samsāra* (the cycle of rebirth), *duḥkha* (sorrow) and the like. As a consequence, he or she analyses the human situation in a given, Buddhist way and then seeks to overcome the pain of *samsāra* through the 'Eightfold Path'. The eight elements involved therein are: *sammādiṭṭhi* (right views); *sammàsaṅkappa* (right resolve); *sammāvācā* (right speech); *sammākammanta* (right conduct); *sammā-ājīva* (right livelihood); *sammāvāyāma* (right effort); *sammāsati* (right mindfulness); and *sammāsamādhi* (right concentration). But what is the meaning of 'right' in each of these eight contexts? What defines the 'right' is an over-arching Buddhist view of how things are. 'Right' does not mean simply or even essentially morality in the Western ethical sense but rather that which is conducive to liberation, i.e. 'right' is here to be understood as an ontologically descriptive as well as an ontologically prescriptive term. What is 'right' is what conforms to a true, i.e. Buddhist, understanding of reality complete with its illusions and traps. What is 'right' is what will lead out of the cycle of *karma*, *samsāra*, *duḥkha* and into *nirvāṇa*. The release that is *nirvāṇa* is inseparable from a larger metaphysical frame of reference.[96] The release that is *nirvāṇa* is realized as a liberation that is 'not this, not that' precisely because it is this which is anticipated and sought as the solution of the ontic, cum existential, conundrums set by Buddhist ontology. One should perhaps go further here: the Buddhist mode of knowing the world only admits of certain possible ultimate experiences – the most important of which is the experience of *nirvāṇa*. Alternatively, it does not envision even the possibility of dialogical relation with a being who approximates the character of the God of the Bible. Conversely, the indescribable presentness of *nirvāṇa* would not be a solution to the metaphysical problematic at the heart of Christianity – 'sin' and its overcoming – which is required in order for the Christian to re-establish harmonious relation to the personal God of the Bible especially as He is manifest as Jesus. Consequently, Christianity does not propose a *nirvāṇa*-like answer to her faithful. Rather, Christians are advised to 'repent' and 'seek the kingdom of God which is at hand', with mystics comprehending this classical Christian exhortation as intending the realization of some form of loving encounter or mystical union (understood both as relation and identity)[97] with Jesus or God (defined as a personal being). Therefore, Christian mystics do not, in fact, experience *nirvāṇa* but rather encounter Jesus – 'beloved bridegroom'. Make no mistake, even Eckhart's putatively attributeless 'Godhead' is *not* the Christian equivalent of *nirvāṇa* or *sūnyatā*, the metaphysical nature of the two being altogether different. Thus Christians do not envision even the possibility that Ultimate Reality is a Godless state of 'absolute emptiness', nor do they experience it as such, while Buddhists do not conceive the Ultimate as a God-like Being and do not experience it as such.

Additional examples could easily be adduced,[98] but in this context our argument seems sufficiently well documented not to require further exemplification. Instead, we conclude with the summary generalization that the experience of mystics comes into being as the kind of experience it is as a necessary consequence of the linguistic-theological and social-historic circumstances which govern the mystical ascent. And these circumstances are grounded in specific ontological schemata which shape the configuration of the quest and its goal.

IV

A third feature of mystical experience which sheds light on our 'conservative' hypothesis yet which is insufficiently studied and commented upon[99] is the role of the respective mystical 'model' in each mystical fellowship. By 'model' here I do not mean a theoretical construct as in the physical sciences, but rather the nature of 'individuals' who become *norms* for their tradition in a variety of ways. Such individuals become Ideals; their individuality becomes categorical; their biographies didactic. The normative individual is the medium of a universal teaching; the instrument for the revelation of more general truths. Every religious community, and every mystical movement within each community, has a 'model' or 'models' of the *ideal* practitioner of the religious life. These para-digmatic figures can be either human or divine and either male or female, with examples of each of these types to be found in the sources. The alternating theologies with their variant religious anthropologies reveal that the *model* plays many roles and has many functions:

(*a*) he or she provides an instantiation of the proper attitude and practice to be approximated or imitated by the faithful;

(*b*) the *model* is an existential representation of the 'tradition'. Julian of Norwich's remark after her 'Shewings' can be taken as paradigmatic here: 'For all things in this blessed showing of our Lord I beheld as one with the teaching of Holy Church . . . and never did I understand a thing therein which harms me or withdraws me from the true teaching of the Holy Church';[100]

(*c*) he or she demonstrates the lived reality of the doctrinal truth, both in showing that doctrines can be lived and more importantly in that he or she points to the dynamic *Urgrund* of the spoken and learned tradition;

(*d*) the *model* is 'proof' of the continuing presence of the Reality of the tradition, whatever this reality is understood to be;

(*e*) the *model* stands as a critique of existing attitudes and practices, setting a standard of perfection against which to measure the actions of the faithful;

(*f*) the *model* may, though need not always, bring a new revelation, e.g. Muhammad. Or he or she might bring a new doctrine, e.g. the Buddha;

(*g*) the *model* may be seen as revealing a new interpretation of an older doctrine, e.g. the claim of Jesus to 'fulfil' or rather to be the fulfilment of the Torah and especially its Messianic prophecies. Or again the claim of Isaac Luria (16th century) that he was revealing the deeper, hidden, mystical aspects of the Torah and Jewish tradition;

(*h*) the *model* often has both a temporal and trans-temporal modality imputed to it. That is, they are not just historic figures, but historic and more than historic personages at the same time. For example, Moses, Elijah, Mary, Muhammad, and Krishna, recognizing but for the moment ignoring the very different specific claims made for each of these figures, all appeared in time as temporal beings of human-like form and substance, yet each is believed in differing ways and through the support of various systematic theologies to remain contemporaneous with each succeeding generation. As a consequence, these *models* are not only *models* past, but *models* present. They are, in truth, held to be co-terminous with their contemporary disciples or devotees in every generation. Thus, Jews of every age not only constantly tell tales of Elijah's wondrous deeds in times gone by, but at the Passover *Seder*, as well as throughout the liturgical cycle, await Elijah's coming (and that of the Messiah whose 'herald' he is).[101] Another illustration is the meaning of Christ's presence in the Christian liturgical performance of the Mass as well as throughout the detailed practices and expectations of Christian life;[102]

(*i*) the *model* is often a 'Founder' of a religious community. Moses, with some qualifications regarding the Patriarchs, fits this pattern, as do Jesus, Muhammad, and the Buddha among others. As a consequence, the image of a founding 'philosopher-king' is often part of the mythic structure which surrounds, justifies, and explains the nature of the *model* (e.g. see Josephus's *Vita Moses* wherein Moses is presented as Prophet, Priest, and King.[103] And again in the *Zohar* which tells us 'no man ever except Moses was found worthy of combining the two functions of King and Prophet' (154a).) Recall also the multifarious images of Jesus as Prophet, Messiah, and King, or of Muhammad as both Prophet and Warrior King who brings men to Allah by the book and/or the sword. Likewise, Confucian tradition, with its veneration for the state and Emperor, provides a variation on this theme. Again, the Buddhist tradition not only emphasizes the Buddha's accomplishments as a religious figure but also constantly calls his royal background and even more his 'royal' achievement to the fore. The mythic qualities of kingship imputed to the Cakkavatti monarch are transferred to the Buddha who achieves this exalted state and then incorporates and transcends it in the act of becoming a Buddha;[104]

(*j*) the *model* provides an authoritative picture of 'reality'. This is done in either a radical way, departing radically from the existing communal traditions, or in an 'evolutionary' way. For example, Muhammad's message is radical for the pagan Bedouin tribes of Arabia but only a further 'evolutionary' stage of the prophetic religions, Judaism, Zoroastrianism, and Christianity; hence, Muhammad is 'The Seal of the Prophets'. Again, the Buddha's doctrines both draw upon and reject the metaphysical doctrines of his Hindu environment, while Moses' legislation in the Torah is a radical transformation of existing pre-Israelite paganism in its Egyptian, Canaanite, and Mesopotamian forms.

(*k*) the *model* shows through his or her life and being what it is to be 'human'. He or she is the *perfect one*, even if not just, only, or even truly, a human being. This is true not only of Moses and Muhammad[105] who are, despite later mythic and gnostic accretions, human figures through and through, but also operates in the case of Jesus, perfectly God and perfectly man, for Krishna in the *Gita* and later Hinduism which venerated his person, and for the Buddha who, whatever his cosmic and transmigratory status in later Buddhist metaphysical speculations, is the individual *par excellence* for all subsequent Buddhism;

(*l*) the *model* is a bridge between 'above' and 'below'. Not only is the existence of the transcendent guaranteed through his or her present being but also, and even more importantly, the existential, contemporary connection of 'above' and 'below'. The model brings together in a lived, and hence liveable, way the theory and the practice, the ideal and the real. It closes the gap between normative 'ought' and practical 'is'. The community has confidence in its ontological design because of the sureties for these schemata provided by the *model*.

(*m*) The *model* is a moral paradigm.

Even as all these aspects of the *model* personality are at work in religious bodies as a whole, they are also dynamic elements in mystical traditions, actively grounding the mystical life in the larger reality of religious communities. To indicate more specifically how these *models* function let us consider as an example, which I spell out in more detail elsewhere,[106] one major mystical tradition and the *model* operative therein. The tradition which we shall use for this purpose is Christianity, in which Christian mystics model themselves after Christ; the title of perhaps the most popular book in the whole of Christian mystical literature, Thomas à Kempis's *Imitation of Christ*, already well attesting to this widespread ambition and exhortation.[107]

In Christian mysticism the imitation of Christ is the dominant *model*, and this in two main senses. The first of these is predicated on the image of Christ as the 'Beloved' of the 'Lover' after the imagery of the Song of Songs, then reworked in various New Testament passages, discussed above. The second pattern established by the christological *model* is of the suffering Christ which leads to extreme forms of Christian mystical asceticism and mortification. Examples of the replication of these christological *models* abound in Christian mystical texts. Consider, to begin with, the climactic experience of Julian of Norwich. In her spiritual autobiography she records her intense longing to see Jesus:

> I desyrede thre graces be the gyfts of God. The fyrst was to have mynde of Chyste es passionn. The seconnde was bodelye syeknes, and the thryd was to have of goddys of gyfte thre wonndys.[108]

With these passionate desires driving her on to the brink of death she is rescued by a wondrous mystical happening:

And in this sodenly I saw the reed bloud rynnyng downe from vnder the garlande, hote and freyshely, plentuously and liuely, right as it was in the tyme that the garland of thornes was pressed on his blessed head. Right so, both god and man, the same that suffered for me, I conceived truly and mightly that it was him salfe that shewed it me without anie meane.

And in the same shewing sodeinly the trinitie fulfilled my hart most of joy, and so I vnderstode it shall be in heauen without end to all that shall come ther. For the trinitie is god, god is the trinitie. The trinitie is our maker, the trinitie is our keper, the trinitie is our everlasting lover, the trinitie is our endlesse joy and our bleisse, by our lord Jesu Christ, and in our lord Jesu Christ. And this was shewed in the first syght and in all, for where Jesu appireth the blessed trinitie is vnderstand, as to my sight. And I sayd: Benedicite dominus. This I sayd for reuerence in my menyng, with a mightie voyce, and full greatly was I a stonned for wonder and marvayle that I had that he that is so reuerent and so dreadfull will be so homely with a synnfull creature liueing in this wretched flesh.[109]

Through this revelation of Christ and the Trinity she is led to realize that 'It is gods wyll that I see my selfe as much bound to hym in love as if he had done for me all pathe hath done; and thus every soule thynke in regard to his lover.'[110] The structural elements of Julian's revelation are in accord with our explanatory thesis. Clearly she laboured to see Christ and especially to carry his suffering, his passion. With her desire to experience Christ's suffering fulfilled in a most visual way, she is content in the knowledge that the participation in this suffering leads to love of a most intimate kind. In this she is not unusual but typical, with her 'visions' drawing upon the residue of her cultural inheritance, e.g. the works of Suso; the *Priority of the Passion*; pseudo-Bonaventure's *Meditationes vitae Christi*; while in her yearning to share in Christ's passion she recapitulates the spirituality of the Franciscans and aspects of Bonaventure.[111]

This same *model* is worked in a different way by the great Spanish mystic, John of the Cross. In his description of the *Ascent of Mount Carmel* and then again in his *Spiritual Canticle*, John records:

And now, having said that Christ is the way, and that the way is to die to our natural self in all that relates to sense and spirit, I proceed to explain how it is to be done in imitation of Christ, for He is our light and our example.[112]

Christ our Lord hath said, instructing us in this way, 'Every one of you that doth not renounce all that he possesseth, cannot be my disciple.' This is plain, for the doctrine of Christ which He came into the world to teach, is contempt of all things, that we may thereby have power to receive the reward of the Spirit of God. For he who does not withdraw himself from the things of the world, is not qualified to receive the Spirit of God in the pure transformation.[113]

One desire only doth God allow, and suffer, in His presence, that of perfectly observing His law, and of carrying the cross of Christ. That soul which has no other aim than the perfect observance of the law of God, and the carrying of the cross of Christ, will be a true ark containing the true manna, which is God.[114]

Oh, that it might be perfectly understood how the soul cannot attain to the thicket and wisdom of the riches of God, which are of many kinds, save by entering into the thicket of many kinds of suffering, and by setting thereupon its consolation and desire! And how the soul that of a truth desires Divine wisdom first desires suffering, that it may enter therein – yea, into the thicket of the Cross.[115]

John of the Cross takes Jesus' crucifixion as the imitative norm for mankind; he understands the crucifixion as instructing the destruction – the crucifixion – of mankind's bodily nature so as to free its imprisoned soulful qualities. Christ teaches the way of worldly refusal and like the Master the Christian mystic must set the world aside, especially the sensual attachments of the transitory estate. To imitate Christ's passion means to crucify one's connection to creatureliness and thus crucified finding contentment in Christ's love, in being Christ-like. This carrying of Christ's cross, this crucifixion of one's human nature, however, is only important because it prepares the way for the still more ultimate moment of Christian mystical longing: the encounter of Christ as lover. This meeting is described by John in his *Canticle*, or to give it its full and usual as well as informative title: *A Spiritual Canticle of the Soul and the Bridegroom of Christ*, the autograph copy of which bears the title: 'Explanation of Stanzas treating of the exercise of love between the soul and Jesus Christ its spouse . . .'[116] In this work John of the Cross expresses the ecstatic union thus:

> O night that didst lead thee,
> O night more lovely than the dawn of light,
> O night that broughtest us
> Lover to lover's sight –
>   Lover with loved in marriage of delight.[117]

Similar images and description predicated on this christological typology abound in Christian mystical writings. One finds them in abundance in Richard Rolle,[118] who was especially known for his meditations on Christ's passion;[119] in Margaret Kempe; in Richard of St Victor; in Teresa of Avila; in pseudo-Dionysius, one of the fountainheads of the Christian mystical tradition's emphasis on love; in Francis of Assisi who perhaps of all medieval Catholic mystics most emphasized the dialectic of yearning after a share in Christ's suffering and the love of Christ; Meister Eckhart and his disciples, John Tauler and Henry Suso, the latter being one of the more excessive advocates of mortification on record. It is powerfully presented, too, in mystics of such differing times and places as Ruysbroeck, Boehme, and Fox. That is to say, it is a *formative*, indeed dominant, conceptual-structural dynamic in virtually the entire range of Christian spirituality. And, for our concerns, in addition to its intrinsic interest, it is to be noted as a powerfully *conservative* factor. That is, it shapes Christian mystical experience according to a *very* specific pattern: that of the Jesus of the Gospels and Pauline Epistles. Notwithstanding its variety of presentation this historic, 'backward looking' *model* plays a powerful role in setting the ideal behaviour after which the Christian initiate is to seek and limiting the forms Christian mysticism is to take.

What one witnesses here, as in Judaism, Islam, and elsewhere in the world's religions is the manifestation of a theological tension which exists at the heart of many religious traditions, and makes claims for the ultimacy or at least primacy of specific historical events, e.g. Sinai for Jews, Calvary for Christians, the life and work of Muhammad for Muslims. For, whatever means are used to transmute these formative historical events into happenings of contemporary significance, some friction always remains between past and present because of the claim to a once and for all historic revelation. The mystics by 'spiritualizing' history try to overcome the difficulty and they achieve remarkable success, yet still not complete success. For if history is totally spiritualized, then the claims to primacy for a given revelation are no longer sustainable; even the historicity of the revelatory event *itself* is called into question. As a consequence, the mystics of all the theistic religions of the West insist, whatever else they may insist on implicitly and explicitly as a consequence of their spiritualizing hermeneutic, that the occurrences revealed in the Torah, New Testament, and

Koran, respectively, did happen in time and space, i.e. as real historical transactions. Though Christian mystics will adopt St Paul's language and speak of being 'born again in Christ',[120] of 'suffering with Christ',[121] of 'dying with Christ',[122] of being 'burned with Christ',[123] of 'being reborn with Christ',[124] of 'rising with Christ',[125] transforming these incidents into existential experiences, this interiorizing, this contemporizing, this mystical mimetic re-enactment is possible only because of the dominant belief that there was a historic Jesus who was born of a Virgin by God, that this Jesus did suffer the torments of Good Friday described by the Synoptic authors, that Jesus did die only to be resurrected in the body on Easter Sunday, and that this Jesus then ascended to Heaven to co-rule the world with the other Persons of the Trinity. The possibility of the transformation of these events into the most intense mystical symbols is predicated initially and necessarily on their believed historic and meta-historic reality. Though their historic character does not exhaust their mystical meaning, it is necessary to it. It is precisely this common exegetical-dogmatic principle of mystical belief that makes Christian, as well as Jewish and Muslim, mysticism dialectical, i.e. alternating between past and present (as well as future), between static and dynamic, between the conservative and radical. To grasp only the present, the dynamic, or the radical is to misperceive the reality under consideration, just as apprehending only the past, the static, or the conservative would likewise be a misconceiving.

A full inventory of the notion of *model* in mystical literature would, at this juncture, go on to include the variety of religious-mystical *models* across the historical spectrum from Buddha and Muhammad to Krishna and Confucius. Such completeness, alas, is not possible here. I hope, however, enough evidence in support of our essential thesis has been adduced. There can be no doubt of the significance of *models* in mystical, as in all, religious groups. And this component tends to exert an essentially conservative influence, in the sense in which we employ that term. It is appropriate partly to repeat, partly to extend, some earlier remarks at this point. Even when the mystical emphasis with respect to these *models* is existential (which as we have seen is not always the case) this factor is not a destabilizing force. The reason this is so is straightforward: the *model* 'experienced' in one way or another is quite specific, e.g. Jesus, Moses, Elijah, Buddha,

Krishna, or Muhammad, among others. Moreover, there is a one-to-one relationship between inherited and shared doctrine and the 'model' experienced, i.e. Christians 'experience' Jesus, Buddhists the Buddha, Hindus Krishna or his colleagues in the Hindu pantheon, and Muslims Muhammad. Jesus is not 'met' by Hindus[126] or Krishna by Christians. Indeed Christians would be outraged by some of Krishna's 'loves' while pious Hindus and Buddhists often disapprove of certain actions of Jesus.

In sum, our deconstruction and re-conceptualization suggests that *models* play an important role in providing our map of reality and of what is real and, thus, contribute heavily to the creation of experience – I repeat to the *creation* of experience. This is a fact to be pondered, and pondered again.

V

The consideration of texts, ontologies, and *models* which has been started here only inaugurates the process of close textual and historical study which is required in order for a full and accurate understanding of mystical experience in both its radical and conservative modalities to emerge. In future research I hope to extend this analysis to other features of the mystical quest such as the role of Gurus, the function of 'discipleship' and the nature of mystical communities. In the interim, however, enough evidence and analysis has been introduced at least to throw suspicion on those approaches to mystical experience which treat these experiences in non-contextual ways and which choose to concentrate solely on the radical side of the phenomena. The thesis that mysticism has strong, if not dominant, conservative characteristics has at least begun to be demonstrated.

NOTES

1 Though I shall use the term 'mysticism' for convenience, readers should be forewarned that I do *not* hold that all mystical experiences are the same. Rather, readers should treat the term 'mysticism' as a shorthand for a list of independent mystical traditions, Buddhist, Hindu, Sufi, Christian, Jewish, etc. I have argued this position in detail

in my article 'Language, Epistemology and Mysticism' in S. Katz (ed.), *Mysticism and Philosophical Analysis* (London and New York, 1978), pp. 22–74.

2 This, for example, is the general view of William James as presented in his *Varieties of Religious Experience* (New York, 1902). It is certainly the contention of E. Underhill, W. Stace, R. Jones, F. Schuon, A. Huxley, and to some degree R. C. Zaehner and N. Smart. One also sees it in the influential work of Max Weber, especially in his theoretical discussion of 'charisma'.

3 On Al-Ḥallāj see Louis Massignon's classic, *La Passion d'al-Hosayn ibn Mansour Al Ḥallāj*, 2 vols. (Paris, 1922).

4 On Ortlieb see Rufus Jones, *The Flowering of Mysticism* (New York, 1939), pp. 59–60. The fate of Priscillian of Avila is discussed in H. Chadwick's study, *Priscillian of Avila* (Oxford, 1976). Eckhart's biography is described in Ernst von Bracken, *Meister Eckhart: Legende und Wirklichkeit* (Meisenheim am Glan, 1972), as well as in the standard histories of medieval mysticism, e.g. by Rufus Jones, E. Underhill, and L. Bouyer. Teresa of Avila's difficulties are reviewed in the source given in note 79 below. On Kabbalists and Hasidim see G. Scholem, *Major Trends in Jewish Mysticism* (New York, 1954); G. Scholem, *Kabbalah* (New York, 1974); and Mordecai Wilensky, *Hasidim ve-Mitnagdim*, 2 vols. (Jerusalem, 1970).

5 See especially in this context my essay 'Language, Epistemology and Mysticism', op. cit.

6 And even mystics have no privileged access to other people's experience. They too ultimately only have the reports, i.e. the texts, by which to judge what others have experienced.

7 See Carl Keller's essay on 'Mystical Literature' in S. Katz (ed.), op. cit.

8 On the *Shiur Koma* see G. Scholem, *Jewish Gnosticism, Merkabah Mysticism and Talmudic Tradition* (New York, 1965[2]).

9 *Shiur Koma*, chs. 1 and 7. Translated in D. Meltzer (ed.), *The Secret Garden* (New York, 1976).

10 For details of the medieval Kabbalistic system see G. Scholem, *Major Trends*, chs. 4–7. On the rabbinic use of the term *zivvug* see M. Jastrow, *Dictionary of the Targumim, The Talmud Babli and Yerushalmi and The Midrashic Literature* (reprinted in Israel, 1972).

11 For more details of this idea see: Moshe Idel, 'On the History of the Interdiction against the study of Kabbalah before the Age of Forty' (in Hebrew), in the *Association of Jewish Studies Year Book*, vol. 5 (New York, 1980), pp. 1–20 of Hebrew section.

12 *Zohar, Beshalaḥ* 50a–51a; translated in vol. 3, p. 155, of the Soncino English translation of *The Zohar*, (eds.) M. Simon and P. Levertoff (London, 1933).

13 This is, of course, related to a whole mystical theory of the Torah. See on this G. Scholem, 'The Meaning of the Torah in Jewish Mysticism', in *On the Kabbalah and Its Symbolism* (New York, 1965), pp. 32–86.

14 The earliest Christian commentary on the Song is that of Hyppolytus of Rome (3rd c.) rediscovered in Slavic translation and published by Bontwetsch in 1897 in the Berlin edition of the *Church Fathers*.

15 Teresa of Avila, *The Life of Teresa of Avila*, tr. D. Lewis, p. 402 (several reprints and editions).

16 Teresa of Avila, *Interior Castle*, 6th mansion, ch. 4 (available in several editions).

17 Jan van Ruysbroeck, *Adornment of the Spiritual Marriage*, tr. E. Underhill (London, 1951), pp. 4–5.

18 Julian of Norwich, *Showings* (longer version), p. 143 (many editions).

19 Catherine of Siena's own report of her experience is found in the *Dialogue of the Seraphic Virgin dictated by Herself while in a State of Ecstasy*, tr. A. Thorold (London, 1896). She is also the subject of secondary studies by I. Giordani, *St Catherine of Siena* (Boston, 1975), and R. de Vineis, *The Life of St Catherine of Siena* (London, 1960).

20 Cited in Herbert Thurston, *The Physical Phenomena of Mysticism* (Chicago, 1952), p. 131.

21 For the quotation regarding Catherine of Siena see ibid., p. 131. See Thurston's entire discussion of this remarkable phenomenon for further details on Celestine Fenouil and Marie Julie Jahenny, as well as others.

22 W. T. Stace, *Mysticism and Philosophy* (Philadelphia, 1960), p. 232. He asserts that mystics are constrained 'by the menaces and pressure of the theologians and ecclesiastical authorities'. No doubt this is sometimes true but it is too sweeping and unsupported a generalization.

23 E. Cousins (ed.), *Bonaventure, The Soul's Journey into God* (New York, 1978), pp. 54ff.

24 Ibid., p. 45.

25 Cited in H. Thurston, op. cit., p. 44.

26 H. Suso, *Little Book of Eternal Wisdom*, Pt. I, ch. 2, p. 30 (New York, 1953).

27 Ibid., p. 32.

28 Lukardis of Oberweimar's *Life* by an anonymous author was published in *Analecta Bollandiana*, vol. xviii (1899), p. 314.

29 Bonaventure, *Meditationes Vitae Christi*, ch. 13, p. 361c.

30 Cited by S. Trimingham, *The Sufi Orders in Islam* (Oxford, 1971), p. 163.

31 On this general theme see H. A. Wolfson's essay, 'The Veracity of Scripture from Philo to Spinoza' in his collected essays, *Religious Philosophy* (Cambridge, Mass., 1960).

32 The only Kabbalists to deny this were the pseudo-messianic Sabbatians and Frankists who adopted a Christian-like interpretation of 'the fulfilment of the law'. On these movements see G. Scholem, *Major Trends*, chs. 6 and 7, and his *Sabbati Sevi* (Princeton, 1973).

33 See G. Scholem, 'The Meaning of Torah' in *On the Kabbalah and Its Symbolism*.

34 See Louis Massignon, *Essai sur les origines du lexique technique de la mystique musulmane* (Paris, 1954²) and Paul Nwyia, *Exégèse coranique et langage mystique* (Beirut, 1970).

35 Louis Massignon, *Essai sur les origines*, p. 45.

36 Ibid., pp. 45–6.

37 Ibn ᶜAbraī often speaks in this way. On this issue see the pertinent remarks of H. Corbin, *L'Imagination créatrice dans le soufisme d'Ibn Arabi* (Paris, 1958), also in English tr. by R. Manheim, *Creative Imagination in the Sufism of Ibn Arabi* (Princeton, 1969), pp. 211–12.

38 On the Zaddik as a 'Living Torah' see R. Elimelech of Lizhensk, *Noam Elimelech* (Lvov, 1788). See also G. Scholem's article on the 'zaddik' in his *Collected Papers* (in Hebrew) (Jerusalem, 1976).

39 This passage is cited and discussed by H. Corbin, *Avicenna and the Visionary Recital* (New York, 1960), pp. 29ff.

40 Ibid., p. 30. See also G. Scholem, *Major Trends*, pp. 25–8 and Paul Tillich's 'Theory of Signs and Symbols' in *Systematic Theology*, vol. i (Chicago, 1951).

41 See my articles on 'Gematria' and 'Notrikon' in the forthcoming *Encyclopedia of Hasidism* (Hebrew Publishing Co., New York). See also the articles on these themes in the *Encyclopedia Judaica* (Jerusalem, 1972).

42 See Louis Massignon's classic 'La Philosophie orientale d'Ibn Sinā et son alphabet philosophique' in *Mémorial Avicenne* (Cairo, 1952). I should add that Massignon's opinion on the relation of the *Sefer Yetzirah* to 'the Arabic Jafr of extremist Islam' (p. 16), i.e. the temporal priority of the *Jafr*, is incorrect. The *Sefer Yetzirah* has its origins in a much older tradition.

43 Whether he is the author of these commentaries or only their translator into Pali is much debated. See W. Rahula, *Zen and the Taming of the Bull* (London, 1978), p. 80.

44 See Teresa's *Life* for the many detailed accounts of this sort of experience.

45 See G. Scholem, *On the Kabbalah and Its Symbolism*, p. 20.

46 On Joseph Karo see R. J. Z. Werblowsky, *Joseph Karo* (Oxford, 1962). See also S. Schechter's classic essay 'Safed in the 16th Century' in *Studies in Judaism*, 2nd Series (Philadelphia, 1908), pp. 202–306.

47 Al Ḥallāj, 'Ṭāsīn al-fahm', *Kitab at-Ṭawāsīn*, cited by A. Schimmel,

Mystical Dimensions of Islam (Chapel Hill, 1975), p. 70.

48 For more details see S. Katz, *Mysticism and Philosophical Analysis*, pp. 24–74. I have analyzed Buber's retelling of Hasidic tales in detail in my *Post Holocaust Dialogues: Studies in Modern Jewish Thought* (New York, 1983).

49 Consider W. T. Stace's use of Jewish sources as gleaned from Martin Buber, for example.

50 R. Abraham B. Isaac HaLevi Tamakh, *Commentary on the Song of Songs*, ed. Leon A. Feldman (Assen, 1970), p. 85. I have slightly emended Feldman's translation.

51 Gilbert of Hoyland, *Sermons on the Song of Songs*, I (Kalamazoo, 1978), p. 101.

52 On the issue of 'translation' see G. Steiner, *After Babel* (Oxford, 1975); R. A. Brower, *On Translation* (Cambridge, Mass., 1959); W. Quine, *Word and Object* (New York, 1960) and also his *From a Logical Point of View* (Cambridge, Mass., 1953); W. Winter, *The Craft and Context of Translation* (Austin, 1961). Compare also I. A. Richards's instructive *Mencius on the Mind* (London, 1932) for a case study of translating Chinese into English.

53 For more on this issue see G. Scholem, *Kabbalah* (New York, 1974).

54 See G. Scholem, 'The Meaning of the Torah in Jewish Mysticism' in *On the Kabbalah and Its Symbolism*.

55 The mystical treatise of the rabbinic era, the *Sefer Yetzirah*, provides a striking example of this notion.

56 See, for example, Nachmanides, 'Introduction' to his *Perush al ha-Torah*.

57 On the Sufi doctrine of the mystical significance of the Koran see A. Schimmel, *Mystical Dimensions of Islam*, appendix I entitled 'Letter Symbolism in Sufi Literature', pp. 411–25.

58 On Muhammad's 'illiteracy' see Tor Andrae, *Der Person Muhammeds* (Stockholm, 1918); see also the standard histories of Sufism and biographies of Muhammad.

59 For further details of the Sufi exegesis of Allah's name see, Leon Schaya, *La Doctrine soufique de l'unité* (Paris, 1962), pp. 83ff.

60 Yūnus Emre, *Divan*, (Istanbul, 1943), p. 308; cited by A. Schimmel, op. cit., p. 418.

61 The first chapter of the Koran.

62 The formula with which the Koran opens: 'In the name of God, the All Merciful, the Merciful'.

63 The first letter of the Koran.

64 A dot under the letter *BĀ*.

65 M. Lings, *A Moslem Saint of the 20th Century* (London, 1961), pp. 149–50. Consider his entire discussion in ch. 7 entitled 'The Symbolism of the Letters of the Alphabet'.

66 See Jan Gonda, *Vedic Literature* (Wiesbaden, 1975), p. 7 n. 2, and the whole of ch. 2. See also H. V. Glasenapp, *Die Literaturen Indiens* (Stuttgart, 1961).

67 Jan Gonda, *Vedic Literature*, p. 72. See also J. Gonda, 'The Indian Mantra' in *Oriens*, xvi (1963).

68 J. Gonda, *Vedic Literature*, p. 72. See also the sources cited by Gonda on p. 72 n. 77 of this work.

69 Ibid., p. 72.

70 *Katha Upanishad* 2 : 15–17, translated by F. Edgerton, *The Beginnings of Indian Philosophy* (London, 1965), p. 184. I have altered Edgerton's translation somewhat.

71 For problems related to translating Asian texts see the interesting essay by Gerald Larson, 'The Bhagavad Gītā as a Cross Cultural Process', in *JAAR*, xliii (1975), pp. 651–69. See also on the problems created by 'translators' and translations G. Welbon's interesting study, *The Buddhist Nirvāṇa and Its Western Interpreters* (Chicago, 1968). The entire issue has been raised afresh in a useful and direct way by K. Bolle in Part II of his translation of the *Bhagavad Gītā* (Berkeley, 1979) entitled 'On Translating the Bhagavadgītā', pp. 219–58. However, Bolle treats the problems inherent in translation of a *religious* text too lightly. On the other hand, his criticism of other translators, e.g. Isherwood, Bhaktivedanta, etc., as trying to make the *Gītā* too 'modern' and 'relevant' (pp. 234ff), is certainly correct and its warning is extrapolatable in many directions, e.g. Buber on Hasidism, I. Shah on Sufism, T. Merton on Christian mysticism, and Suzuki on Zen.

72 The fact that mantras, to be effective, must be taught directly by a Guru to his disciple also has important consequences for the study of mysticism. I intend to treat the issue of the role of Gurus in a larger future study of mysticism at which I am at work.

73 I hope to return to this issue in more detail in my larger study of mysticism.

74 Yūnus Emre, *Divan*, cited by A. Schimmel, op. cit., p. 106.

75 See G. Scholem, *On the Kabbalah and Its Symbolism*, pp. 62ff.

76 Henry Suso, *The Exemplar. Life and Writings of Blessed Henry Suso*, *O.P.* tr. M. Ann Edward (Dubuque, Iowa, 1962), vol. i, ch. 16, p. 39.

77 Ibid., vol. i, ch. 43, p. 137.

78 I have set out the relevant epistemological arguments regarding the nature of experience, including mystical experience, more fully in my essay in S. Katz (ed.), *Mysticism and Philosophical Analysis*, pp. 22–74. Here I presume the correctness of that analysis.

79 Teresa's work was briefly considered heretical and examined by the Inquisition. This event is discussed in E. Llamas Martínez, *Santa Teresa de Jesús y la Inquisición Española* (Madrid, 1972).

80 See Bernard's *Sermons on the Canticles*, 2 vols. (Dublin, 1920). This edition is to be used with care. The new edition, On the Song of Songs, tr. K. Walsh, 2 vols (Washington, D.C., 1971–76), is now the preferred translation. See also for a brief discussion of this work and its love theme, C. Butler, *Western Mysticism* (London, 1927²), pp. 139ff. By 'Western' Butler means early and medieval Christian! For a more general treatment see J. Leclercq, *Bernard of Clairvaux and the Cistercian Spirit* (Kalamazoo, 1976), and E. Gilson's *The Mystical Theology of Saint Bernard* (New York, 1955). M. Ratisbonne's *Histoire de Bernard et son siècle*, 2 vols (Paris, 1903), is still a standard work.

81 Though it may sound strange to many, mystics do have disciples, and this is an important fact.

82 John of the Cross, *The Living Flame of Love*, tr. David Lewis (London, 1934), pp. 31ff.

83 Ibid., pp. 146–47.

84 See, for example, the use of Eckhart by R. Otto in his *Mysticism East and West* (New York, 1960) and by D. T. Suzuki in his *Mysticism, Christian and Buddhist* (New York, 1957).

85 Meister Eckhart, *Die lateinische Werke*, ed. E. Benz *et al.* (Stuttgart, 1938 and subsequently), iii, 4.

86 Ibid., iii, 295ff.

87 Cited in Rufus Jones, *Studies in Mysticism* (London, 1923), p. 225.

88 Meister Eckhart, *Die lateinische Werke*, ii, 38.

89 Meister Eckhart, *The Nobility of the Soul*, tr. C. De B. Evans (London, 1924), pp. 282–83. See for more on this theme, for example, Eckhart's treatise, *The Kingdom of God*, pp. 267ff., as well as his *The Three Creations*, pp. 382–89, both of which are also in the Evans volume.

90 Meister Eckhart, *The Rank and Nature of the Soul*, tr. C. de B. Evans (London, 1924), p. 299.

91 See D. T. Suzuki, *Mysticism: Christian and Buddhist* (New York, 1957), ch. 1. Suzuki is wrong in his judgement (p. 16) that: 'Eckhart is in perfect accord with the Buddhist doctrine of sūnyatā, when he advances the notion of Godhead as "pure nothingness" (ein bloss nicht)'. The verbal similarity conceals a radical ontological disparity.

92 On the many serious problems with the existing cross-tradition phenomenologies, e.g. Stace, Zaehner, and James, etc., see S. Katz (ed.), *Mysticism and Philosophical Analysis*, pp. 25–32 and 46–57.

93 In *Mysticism and Philosophical Analysis*, pp. 33–40, I have further filled out this picture of ontological variety by sketching the outlines of the Jewish and Buddhist ontologies as relevant to Kabbalists and *Bhikkhus*.

94 John of the Cross, *Collected Works*, tr. A. Peers (London, 1934–35), vol. iii, p. 49.

95   For a more detailed discussion and defence of this position, see my
     essay in *Mysticism and Philosophical Analysis* referred to above.
     Husserl and his students, as well as students of mysticism such as
     W. Stace and F. Schuon, are guilty of harbouring this illusion and
     fostering it in others.

96   For a more detailed description of the totality of the Buddhist ontology
     see: S. C. Chatterjee, *An Introduction to Indian Philosophy* (Calcutta,
     1939), pp. 145–53; S. D. Dasgupta, *A History of Indian Philosophy*, 5
     vols (Cambridge, 1922–55); Karl Potter, *Presuppositions of India's
     Philosophies* (Englewood, New Jersey, 1963); Th. Stcherbatsky, *The
     Central Conceptions of Buddhism* (Calcutta, 1956²); Paul Hacker,
     Vivarta (Wiesbaden, 1953); E. Conze, *Buddhism: Its Essence and
     Development* (New York, 1965); and W. Rahula, *What the Buddha
     Taught* (New York, 1962). See also R. Gimello's article in S. Katz, op.
     cit.

97   See our discussion above, pp. 11–12.

98   I plan to provide an exhaustive inventory of the alternative ontological
     schema of the world's major mystical traditions in the larger study on
     which I am presently at work. It should also be noted that the relation
     of morality to mystical experience, in the context of mystical onto-
     logies, is also apposite to this analysis. I have begun to analyze this
     relationship in my 'The Relationship of the Ethical and the Mystical' in
     the 1980–81 papers of the Boston University colloquiam on the
     Philosophy of Religion to be published under Leroy Rouner's
     editorship by Notre Dame University Press in 1983, exact title as yet
     undecided. It is also my intention to use the occasion of the *David
     Baumgardt Memorial Lectures* under the sponsorship of the American
     Philosophical Association, which I shall deliver at Harvard in the fall of
     1983, as an opportunity to develop my views on this theme.

99   Among all the issues treated in this paper this was the subject on which
     my bibliographical researches turned up the *least* amount of serious
     secondary material. The role of *models*, along with that of holy men,
     Gurus, etc., is clearly a subject requiring further study.

100 Julian of Norwich, *Showings* (shorter version), ch. 6, pp. 17–18.
     Available in many editions.

101 On the role of Elijah in Jewish tradition and liturgy see
     M. W. Levinsohn, *Der Prophet Elia nach den Talmudim –
     und Midraschimquellen* (1929); E. Margoliot, *Eliyahu ha-navi be Sifrut
     Yisroel* (Tel Aviv, 1960). See also the Index for 'Elijah' in Louis
     Ginzberg, *Legends of the Jews*, 6 vols (Philadelphia, 1909–28).

102 See here M. Eliade's remarks in *Myths, Dreams and Mysteries* (New
     York, 1967), p. 30. Kierkegaard's position on what it means to be a
     Christian is a paradigm of this argument in modern Christian

literature. See, for example, his discussion in *Concluding Unscientific Postscript*, trs. D. F. Swenson and W. Lowrie (Princeton, 1944).

103 On this and related themes see John Gager's study, *Moses in Greco-Roman Paganism* (Nashville, 1972).

104 See, for example, the biography of the Buddha as drawn in the *Ṇiddānakatha*, tr. T. W. Rhys David as *Buddhist Birth Stories* (Boston, 1880). E. J. Thomas's *The Life of the Buddha* (New York, 1927) is also a valuable early study of the Buddha's 'life'. Of the more recent contributions, the study by Frank E. Reynolds, 'The Many Lives of the Buddha' in F. E. Reynolds (ed.), *The Biographical Process* (The Hague, 1976), pp. 37–61, is helpful. See also Etienne Lamotte's seminal essay, 'La Légende du Bouddha', in *Revue de l'histoire des religions*, vol. cxxxiv (1947), pp. 37–71, and his larger, more recent study, *Histoire du Bouddhisme Indien* (Louvain, 1967). A. Foucher's *La Vie du Bouddha d'après les textes et monuments de l'Inde* (Paris, 1949) is another important discussion of the issue. An abridged English translation of this work is available as *The Life of the Buddha* (Westport, Conn., 1972). Some further useful comparative material is provided by Joseph Campbell, *The Hero with a Thousand Faces* (Princeton, 1946). However, care must be taken when using this, or any other, of Campbell's work.

105 On Muhammad see R. E. Nicholson's fine paper, 'The Perfect Man', in his *Studies in Islamic Mysticism* (Cambridge, 1967²), pp. 77–161. See also A. Schimmel's remarks on this theme in her *Dimensions of Islamic Mysticism* (Chapel Hill, 1975), and Earle Waugh's, 'Following the Beloved', in F. E. Reynolds, op. cit., pp 62–85.

106 See my 'Models, Modeling and Mystical Training', in *Religion*, vol. 12 (July 1982), pp. 247–75.

107 Thomas à Kempis only edited this work, he did not write it as is usually thought. On the problems concerning the literary history and traditions of this work, see R. Jones, *The Flowering of Mysticism* (New York, 1939), pp. 238–44.

108 Julian of Norwich, *Showings* (shorter version), ch. 1.

109 Julian of Norwich, *Showings* (longer version), ch. 3j.

110 Ibid., ch. 65–Revelation 15.

111 These influences are discussed in E. Colledge and J. Walsh's excellent new edition of *The Book of Showings to the Anchoress Julian of Norwich* (Toronto, 1978). On the relation of Julian's desire to see Christ's passion and the authentic corpus of Bonaventure's writings, see Colledge and Walsh's article, 'Editing Julian of Norwich', in *Medieval Studies*, xxxiv (1972), pp. 422–34.

112 John of the Cross, *Ascent of Mount Carmel*, chs. 2, 7, 8 (many editions).

113 Ibid., chs. 5, 2.

114 Ibid., chs. 5, 8.

115 John of the Cross, *A Spiritual Canticle*, 36:13 (many editions).

116 Cited in the 'Introduction' to *A Spiritual Canticle* by its editor B. Zimmerman (London, 1919).

117 Cited by E. Underhill, *Practical Mysticism* (London, 1914; New York, 1918), p. 133.

118 See, for example, Rolle's *Incendium Amoris*, (ed.) M. Deansley (Manchester, 1915), chs. 8 and 9 on 'Scourings' and chs. 24 and 25 on 'Love'. The best, though not always accurate work on Rolle is still H. E. Allen, *Writings Ascribed to Richard Rolle* (New York, 1927).

119 Rolle's 'meditations' are printed in H. E. Allen (ed.), *English Writings of Richard Rolle* (Oxford, 1931). For a more recent study of this work see M. M. Morgan's article 'Meditations on the Passion ascribed to Richard Rolle', in *Medium Aevum*, xii, 2 (1953), pp. 93–103.

120 Gal. 4.17.

121 Gal. 4.7; Col. 1.24.

122 Rom. 6.6.

123 Rom. 6.4.

124 Rom. 6.4.

125 Col. 3.1.

126 Some Christian 'apologists' like Raymundo Panikker think otherwise; see, for example, his *The Unknown Christ of Hinduism* (London, 1964).

STEVEN T. KATZ (editor): Ph.D. (Cambridge University, England). In addition to editing the present volume Dr. Katz's other works include: *Jewish Philosophers* (1975); *Jewish Ideas and Concepts* (1977); *Mysticism and Philosophical Analysis* (1978) and *Post-Holocaust Dialogues: Studies in Modern Jewish Thought* (1983). He is a member of the editorial team of the *Cambridge History of Judaism* and the *History of Nineteenth Century Religious Thought*, being published by the Cambridge University Press, and is Editor of the journal *Modern Judaism*, published by the Johns Hopkins University Press. He has also published several dozen articles and reviews in leading philosophical and religious journals. He held the Burney Studentship in the Philosophy of Religion at Cambridge University from 1970 to 1972 and has been a visiting Professor at the Hebrew University of Jerusalem, King's College, University of London, the University of Lancaster, the University of Toronto, Harvard University and Yale University. He will give David *Baumbardt Memorial Lectures*, sponsored by the American Philosophical Association, at Harvard in 1983. At present he is Professor of Religion at Dartmouth College, Hanover, New Hampshire, U.S.A.

Mysticism in Its Contexts

ROBERT M. GIMELLO

I

It is the purpose of this essay to call into question an assumption which I detect in the very inception of the modern study of mysticism and which I believe continues to dominate and to hamper that study even now. I refer to the assumption that mysticism constitutes an autonomous and self-contained realm of human experience, that it is essentially separate from the contexts of culture, history, tradition, and discipline in which it is found and that it is possessed of its own independent rules, values, and truths.[1]

Corollary to this approved dogma of mystical autonomy – and wedded to a certain pervasive intolerance of, or inability to cope with, genuine diversity among religions – is the belief in the essential sameness of mysticism. Such differences as may seem to distinguish mystics one from another, e.g. profoundly different beliefs about the existence and nature of God, dissimilar evaluations of the reality and worth of 'this world', sharply contrasting regimens of practice, discordant anthropologies, discrepant moral attitudes and rules, etc., are commonly judged to be superficial when compared with the alleged experiential similarities uniting all mystics. The latter include unitive experiences, unargued convictions of the truth thereof, transports beyond the range of discourse and conventional thought, coincidence of opposites, paroxysms of emotion frequently combined with recessions of serenity, and so forth. These are held to be the true inviolate substance of mysticism which, the argument continues, has been subjected through history to a variety of extra-mystical and *ex post facto* interpretations. The distance said to separate the mystical experience from its subsequent and diverse interpretations is precisely the distance which is believed to separate the autonomy of mysticism from any and all possible contexts. In the typical exposition of this view, the claim of mysticism's autonomy is the premise from which is drawn the conclusion of mysticism's cross-cultural invariance.

Recently several studies have appeared which, on both general philosophical and specific historical grounds, have demonstrated that the varieties of mysticism cannot be reduced to a single common core of pure, undifferentiable experience, nor even to only two or three basic types of such experience. The view that they can be so reduced has been shown to rest on the naïve and false assumption that the so-called interpretations of mystical experience are mere extrinsic templates of meaning which have no roles to play in the experience itself but are only applied to it, usually after its actual occurrence. But both Steven Katz and Peter Moore, in arguments that need not be reconstructed here, have shown that what is perhaps mislabelled 'interpretation' is actually ingredient in and constitutive of mystical experience.[2] All mystical experiences, like all experiences generally, have specific structures, and these are neither fortuitous nor *sui generis*. Rather they are given to the experiences, at their very inceptions, by concepts, beliefs, values, and expectations already operative in the mystics' minds. Nor are these structures of meaning mere 'forms' which the discrete 'content' of mysticism may happen to take. They are more immanent than that. They are of the essence of mystical experience. They engender it. They inform its very identity. Were one to substract from mystical experience the beliefs which mystics hold to be therein confirmed and instantiated, all that would be left would be mere hedonic tone, a pattern of psychosomatic or neural impulse signifying nothing. Surely such mindlessness is not what those who take the matter seriously mean by mystical experience. Mystics themselves portray their experiences as powerful moments of knowing. The knowledge gained thereby is admittedly not merely conceptual in character. It does not consist only in, or go no further than, intellectual understanding of religious doctrine, for example. But concepts certainly do contribute to it in essential ways. They inform it, giving it shape and meaning as it emerges, however, difficult of description that shape and meaning may be. In turn, they are themselves experientially enhanced, amplified, clarified, intensified, animated, transfigured so as to become concrete and palpable, and generally rendered more compelling.

This is not to say that mystical experience may never be the occasion for the dissolution or alteration of prior beliefs. Mystical terminology like 'enlightenment', 'insight', 'gnosis', etc., implies that the mystic is liberated by his experiences from false views which he may previously have held. But even this, the critical and revolutionary dimension of mysticism, serves to confirm the conceptual particularity of mystical experience because in these cases such experience provides the refined interior forum in which correct views are enabled, as it were, to contend with and to vanquish false views. In my own previous work, on epistemological premises much like those argued by Katz and Moore, I have analyzed a particular example of this, one drawn from the Buddhist meditative tradition wherein the ecstatic and unitive experiences of the contemplative (i.e. *śamatha*, *samādhi*, etc.), which are just the experiences usually cited by those who aver the essential identity of Buddhist mysticism with the mysticism of other traditions, are shown to have no liberative value or cognitive force in themselves but to be only the psychosomatic circumstances in which one can exercise discernment (*vipaśyanā*) of the truth of Buddhist doctrine. This, in turn, leads to insight (*prajñā*) into the true nature of things, thence to compassion (*karuṇā*), the latter being the final goal of Buddhist practice.[3] Buddhist mystical experiences, then, are precisely *experiences of* emptiness (*śūnyatā*), *of* dependent origination (*pratītyasamutpāda*), *of* the buddha-nature (*buddhatā* or *buddhagotra*) of all sentient beings, *of* the merely representational character of reality (*vijñapitmātratā*), etc. These are in no sense the same as the Christian mystic's experience of the Trinity, Christ, or the Godhead; nor the same as the Jewish mystic's experience of *En-sof*; nor even the same as the Vedantist's experience of the identity of *ātman* and *brahman*.[4]

The thesis I would here propose in opposition to the claim of mystical autonomy and its corollary claim of mystical sameness may be stated briefly as follows: Mysticism is inextricably bound up with, dependent upon, and usually subservient to the deeper beliefs and values of the traditions, cultures, and historical milieux which harbour it. As it is thus intricately and intimately related to those beliefs and values, so must it vary according to them. Evidence in support of this thesis is abundantly available, to all who are able and willing to seek it out. It is not to be found in the features of mysticism which most scholars have been disposed exclusively to consider, viz. its phenomenological and allegedly experiential commonalities. Rather it is to be found amidst the multiplicity of specific means which traditional sponsors of mysticism have provided for the achievement of mystical experiences, and among the various strategies they have developed for harnessing the power of those experiences so that it may be directed towards ends which they have deemed proper.

II

The few examples I shall now offer in support of the arguments sketched above are drawn from the pan-Asian Buddhist tradition, because this is the subject in which I have whatever expertise I can lay claim to and because Buddhism offers us an especially vast array of elaborate and technically explicit accounts of its mystical paths. All of the cases to be presented will be dealt with very briefly, because of constraints of space and in consideration of the fact that the general tenor of my argument has already been expounded in the above section.

The following is a short quotation from the *Contemplations of the Dharmadhātu*, a very brief text from the Chinese Buddhist canon attributed to the monk Tu-shun (557-640 A.D.) and quite possibly the earliest and the fundamental document of the Flower Garland (Hua-yen) school.[5] The author is here concluding an exposition of a sequence of meditations on emptiness (Skt.: *śūnyatā*, Chin.: *k'ung*) in which the meditator is urged to envisage from several perspectives the mutual identity and interpenetration of emptiness and material form (Skt.: *rūpa*, Chin.: *se*). The character of the exposition is rather abstract and theoretical. To make it clear that these contemplations are not merely food for the intellect but are to be *realized* in experience of a kind we may call mystical, the author declares that his final concern is:

> . . . the correct establishment of the essence of practice. If one does not understand the prior theoretical explanations, then he has not the means with which to pursue and accomplish this practice. But, if one does not understand this to be finally a practical teaching, quite beyond the reach of theoretical explanations, then he has failed to grasp the true import of those explanations. And if one continues to adhere to the explanations, and does not finally relinquish them, then he will fail to enter into practice. Thus, one must realize both that practice is formed upon the basis of theoretical understanding and that, when practice is achieved, theoretical understanding is transcended.[6]

This passage may stand as a concise statement of the classical Buddhist position on the relation between doctrinal conceptualization and liberating experience. It concludes with an assertion widely acknowledged in standard treatments of mysticism, viz. that transformative mystical experiences and the patterns of practical life which they engender do not consist merely in intellectual assent to certain concepts and beliefs. In this case, an abstract understanding of the emptiness or insubstantiality of all things is distinguished from the immediate intuitive perception of things as empty and from the compassion toward all sentient beings that is possible only for those who have actually seen, felt, touched, and tasted emptiness. But note that there is more to the relationship than this. The text clearly maintains also that the desired experience is unattainable without correct prior theoretical understanding. Such understanding is to be relinquished in practice, but only after it has itself enabled practice. This, the mystical efficacy of concept and belief, is not so well attested in the interpretative literature on mysticism. As a later commentator on this passage put it, theoretical explanations of the way things are, together with the intellectual understanding thereof, are to the confirmatory practical experience of reality as a man's eyes are to his feet. Without the former, he walks blindly, stumbling over obstacles and with little chance of reaching his destination. Without the latter, however, he does not proceed at all. He can at best only dimly descry his destination from afar.[7] The more traditional Buddhist rubric for such concepts as guide or give sight to practice thereby helping to shape its outcome is that of *samyagdṛṣṭi*, 'right view' (Chin.: *cheng-chien*), which is one (traditionally the first) element of the Noble Eightfold Path. Buddhists have always held that practice of any other element of the path, even practice of something so seemingly aconceptual as 'right concentration' (Skt.: *samyaksamādhi*, Chin.: *cheng-ting*), is sure to go awry if not based on 'right view'. Thus Bhikkhu Nyanatiloka, summing up volumes of scripture, says:

It is true that a really unshakable and safe foundation to the path is provided only by Right View which, starting from the tiniest germ of faith and knowledge, gradually, step by step, develops into penetrating insight (*vipassanā*) and thus forms the immediate condition for the . . . realization of *Nibbāna*. Only with regard to this highest form of Supermundane insight, we may indeed say that all the remaining links of the path are nothing but the outcome and the attendant symptoms of Right View.[8]

Other Buddhist labels given to this same thing are 'correct concept' (Skt.: *samyaksaṃkalpa*, Chin.: *cheng ssu-wei*) and 'notion associated with insight' (Skt.: *prajñāsaṃprayuktasaṃjñā*, Chin.: *chih-hui hsiang-ying hsiang*). An example of the latter, taken from the *Mahāpra-jñāpāramitāśāstra* ('Treatise on the Great Perfection of Insight') attributed to Nāgārjuna, is the 'notion of impermanence' (Skt.: *anityasaṃjñā*, Chin.: *pu-ch'ang hsiang*), of which that text says, 'it is but a synonym for the noble path itself'.[9] This last is a very interesting and apposite remark. It tells us not only that the concept of impermanence is necessary to liberating insight but also that it is somehow tantamount to the whole course of practice which Buddhists call the Path. Liberation is possible only if one follows the Path, and must therefore be quite impossible unless one fully grasps impermanence. This in turn must mean that the concept of imperma-nence, together with the other concepts and beliefs which make up 'right view', is essential to the Buddhist mystic's ultimate experiences. And since enlightenment is, among other things, the living apprehen-sion of impermanence, it seems quite reasonable to conclude that the *notion* of impermanence, though no substitute for the claimed *reality* thereof, does inform the Buddhist's mystical experience of reality. The wonder of Buddhist mysticism, to be sure, is its capacity to quicken such concepts, to transform them into the stuff of vivid and immediate experience, but such transformations cannot be said to count against the crucial importance of what is so transformed. This is why Buddhist mystics tell us that what they experience is the radical transience, the utter instantaneity, of all things. It is also why they do not tell us that they experience the eternality of *Ātman-Brahman*, or of God. It is not because they must rely on such inherited Buddhist notions to describe their essentially indescribable realizations, but because those notions actually determine the kinds of realizations they have. That 'right view', with all that it implies in Buddhism, is held to be a *sine qua non* of Buddhist enlightenment I take to be strong evidence for the general claim that mystical experiences are essen-tially informed by their conceptual contexts.

However, the processes by which concepts generate and shape particular kinds of mysticism are not simple or direct. All mystical traditions testify that the transformation of belief into intense, confirmatory, and liberating experience requires a practical disci-pline. Even the most potent and fertile ideas would remain inert if concrete steps were not taken to bring them to life, to activate them. Buddhism offers for our investigation a virtually inexhaustible store of specific practices for accomplishing this task. Included among them are moral precepts (*śīla*), monastic regulations (*vinaya*), and of course, the great variety of undertakings which are generally called meditation (*dhyāna, yoga, samādhi, bhāvanā,* etc.). Without hoping even to suggest the wealth and diversity of this practical Buddhism, we can at least select a representative example that will allow us to follow one Buddhist concept, through the practical course of its cultivation, to its realization as an ingredient of mystical experience. Under the same general rubric of 'right view', and thus ranged together with the primary notions of impermanence and suffering, is the Buddhist master-concept of 'selflessness' (*nairātmya*).[10] Buddhists believe, in fact, that the impermanence of things is a function of their insubstantiality. All persons and things, because dependently originated, are devoid of independent, substantial identities. In this sense they are said to lack 'selves' or to be essentially marked by the characteristic of 'non-self' (*anātman*), and are thus held to be incapable of duration. In one way or another, every component of the Buddhist path, every technique of meditation, is a means of demonstrating or verifying this basic teaching. Contemplation of one's body as a composite of elements all subject to decay; contemplation of one's feelings or sensations of pleasure, pain, and indifference as mere autonomic reactions to sense impressions; contemplation of the mind as a faculty wholly vulnerable to agitation from within and distraction from without; and contemplation of the objects or contents of the mind (*dharmas*) as unstable objects of clinging – all of these devices serve to disabuse the meditator of any confidence he may once have had either in his own integral identity as a separate, perduring personal entity or in the purported substantiality of things in the world.[11] As enlightenment, the mystical goal of Buddhism, is said to be in part a triumph over attachment to ego, made possible by the perception that ego does not exist, so the notion of insubstantiality and these means of contemplating it may be said to share in the constitution of enlightenment.

But this is one of the comparatively obvious practical consequences of the notion of selflessness. There are more subtle ramifications to be considered. Prominent among the schemes of meditation advocated in Buddhism is 'cultivation' (*bhāvanā*) of the four 'divine abodes' (*brahmavihāra*), otherwise known as the four 'immeasurables' (*apramāna*). These are contemplations, respectively, on benevolence (*maitrī*), compassion (*karuṇā*), sympathetic joy (*muditā*), and equanimity (*upekṣā*). Traditionally these four, taken as a group, have been identified as preliminary practices, as part of 'the' moral foundation of the religious life'.[12] They were not held to be among the proximate causes of enlightenment itself. One of them, however – compassion – came to have a separate and amplified significance in certain later Buddhist traditions and therefore merits special attention. In its standard formulation, the cultivation of the immeasurable thought of compassion begins with the arousing of sympathy in one's mind for the plight of obviously unfortunate persons or for miscreants who may seem now to be enjoying good fortune but who are doomed to dire future suffering because of their current evil conduct. The meditation then proceeds to the extension of such sympathy first to loved ones, whose suffering evokes immediate distress, next to those toward whom one is indifferent, and finally to hostile enemies. Its general objectives are to develop a disposition to share vicariously in the inevitable suffering of all sentient beings and to inspire actual kindness toward them. The virtue of non-violence (*ahiṃsā*) is its expression in conduct, and among its effects is a loosening of attachment to deeply ingrained notions of discrete and independent selfhood. Such notions are thought to dissolve in the bond of empathy with all beings which is forged by compassion. All of these are major contemplative achievements. Nevertheless, as one of the four 'divine abodes', compassion is usually seen only as an antidote to specific spiritual ills, e.g. a penchant for cruelty, which impede one's progress toward higher attainments. Moreover, many texts advocate this theme of meditation in a spirit of religious pragmatism, stressing its beneficial effects for the meditator (e.g. deep and restful sleep, absence of nightmares, the good will of other human beings, protection of deities, serenity of countenance, etc.).

In Mahāyāna Buddhism, however, compassion – or, more precisely, 'great compassion' (*mahākaruṇā*) – is elevated to a more exalted status. It ceases to be only a preliminary and antidotal practice, a mere means to higher ends, and is acknowledged as an end in itself. Indeed, it comes to be regarded as one of the two major components of enlightenment coequal with that destruction of all delusions which is insight (*prajñā*) into the way things really are. Liberation, therefore, cannot be conceived in Mahāyāna as a private goal; it must encompass all sentient life. The *bodhisattva* ('being of enlightenment'), who is the Mahāyāna ideal, consecrates his virtually endless career as much to compassionate action in the world as to contemplative perception of the radical interdependence, emptiness, and illusory nature of that world. Thus the paramount mystical attainment of Mahāyāna Buddhism comprises love, as well as gnosis. Another way of putting this, by borrowing the polemical language of Mahāyāna, is to say that the *bodhisattva*, unlike the practitioner of lesser vehicles (the *śrāvaka*, *arhat*, or *pratyeka-buddha*), does not enter *nirvāṇa*, or that he enters only the '*nirvāṇa* without fixed abode' (*apratiṣṭhita nirvāṇa*) wherein he finds himself to be still very much *in* – though not at all *of* – the world. One of the most eloquent Mahāyāna proponents of enlightenment as the perfection of compassion is the eighth-century poet and mystic Śāntideva. In his famous *Bodhicaryāvatāra* ('Entrance into the Career of Enlightenment'), in the course of celebrating the 'perfection of meditation' (*dhyāna-pāramitā*), he urges practice of contemplative identification with other beings. This he calls either meditation on the 'sameness of self and others' (*parātma-samatā*) or the 'transference of self and others' (*parātma-parivartana*):

> Primarily one should zealously cultivate the equality of other and the self. All joys and sorrows are equal, and I am to guard them like my own. . . .
>
> All sorrows, without distinction, are ownerless; and because of misery they are to be prevented. Why then is restriction made?. . .
>
> Because of habit, the concept of an 'I' becomes located in drops of semen, in blood, and in things belonging to another, although in reality the concept is false. . . .
>
> So why should the body of another not be taken as my own? It is not difficult, because of the remoteness of my own body. . . .
>
> Whoever wishes to quickly rescue himself and another, should practise the supreme mystery: The exchanging of self and other.[13]

We must bear in mind that such identification with others – like immeasurable compassion, the four foundations of mindfulness, the meditative concept of selflessness, etc. – is not a mere abstract ideal designed for intellectual edification. Rather, it is a practice, a particular pattern of interior effort every bit as practical as the postures, breathing rhythms, and physical austerities which make up the visible surface of the contemplative life. In this meditative exercise of compassionate transference and in the relationship between it and the culminating mystical goal of Mahāyāna, which is an enlightenment comprised of compassion as well as of insight, we have, I think, a good example of the ways in which the practical contexts of mysticism consort with its conceptual contexts to shape both mystical experience and mystical conduct. The sequence of its development, broadly and unhistorically sketched, is as follows: The concept of non-self, initially only a datum of belief for the aspirant, predisposes him to expect final experiential confirmation of the insubstantiality of all persons and things, including himself. It also leads to the selection of such particular practices as would seem to corroborate it. Especially interesting among these is the meditative extension of compassion to all sentient beings, which serves initially to free the meditator of certain of the passions associated with attachment to false notions of selfhood and substance, e.g. mental dispositions of selfish indifference to or cruel delight in the suffering of others. Yet the relation of compassion to the perception of selflessness proves to be deeper and more essential than that of means to end. It is discovered, in such meditative refinements of the theme of compassion as the 'transference of self and others', that selflessness and compassion are mutually entailed. One cannot help but extend compassion to all beings once one has seen that no being, least of all oneself, exists independently of all others. Insubstantiality is but the 'substance', as it were, of that one reality whose 'function' is empathy and altruism.[14] On the other hand, Buddhists hold that the perfection of compassion, conversely, requires acceptance of the truth of selflessness. Were any person or thing found to have separate substantial existence, his or its status as a discrete entity would stand as a barrier to the full communion of all beings in suffering. In appreciation of this deeper affinity between compassion and insight into selflessness, the Mahāyāna tradition alters its definition of final mystical attainment so as further to exalt compassion, raising its position from that of a mere means to that of an essential ingredient in enlightenment itself. All of this I take to be further evidence of the contextuality of mysticism, specifically of the formative and constitutive influence of mystical practice on mystical experience and on post-experiential mystical behaviour.

It was asserted in the previous section of this essay that discourse, i.e. language and its products, is yet another important determinant of mysticism. Now, if one were to attend only to its typical strictures against language, to its repeated warnings that language is one of the more pervasive and insidious manifestations of the inveteracy of ignorance, one might suppose that Buddhism contradicted my assertion. It is true, after all, that Buddhist texts do often treat language as primarily a medium for *prapañca*, for that tendency of the mind to grow 'diffuse' and 'expansive' in the 'proliferation' of concepts.[15] (Interestingly the Chinese translated this word as *hsi-lun*, literally 'vain discourse'.) Then too, Asaṅga's choice, in his *Compendium of Mahāyāna* (*Mahāyānasaṃgraha*), of the term *mano-jalpa* (i.e. 'mumblings of the mind', Chin.: *i-yen*) as a label for our habit of naming things and then constructing propositions about them is hardly atypical.[16] The capacity of language to snare the mind and divert it from reality is widely acknowledged, and feared, in Buddhism. There is no denying this. To speak, Buddhists hold, is necessarily to err or to lie, even if this be only because language consists in good measure of nouns, which purport to be the names of discrete things and thereby misrepresent reality in so far as no discrete things actually exist.[17] And yet one must note that there is in Buddhism a compensatory appreciation of the spiritual utility of language. Even Nāgārjuna, who was perhaps Buddhism's most incisive analyst of the pathology of language, observed that 'ultimate truth is not taught except upon the foundation of conventional usage' (*vyavahāram anāśritya paramārtho na deśyate*).[18] He also acknowledged, as did all other Buddhists, that utterances may have at least 'conventional truth' (*samvṛti-satya*), even though they can never express 'ultimate truth' (*paramārtha-satya*). Focusing on such positive, if qualified, evaluations of language, and yet not lapsing into naive assumptions of its definitive referential capacity, we can get some purchase on the mystical efficacy Buddhists are willing to attribute at least to the judicious use of discourse, notwithstanding their sense of its limitations.

Buddhist mystics, like all others, insist that language is valueless as a means of literally and truthfully describing the real world. But they also insist that it does have other kinds of value. The proper use of words can effect certain changes in the mind; it can instigate alterations in the user which in turn will allow him, not to *say*, but to *see* how things really are. Its function is not descriptive or cognitive but connative, corrective, performative. Buddhists claim, that is to say, to know how to do with words other things than try to depict the world. Consider, for example, their classical distinction among the three kinds of insight: insight born of learning (*śrutamayī-prajñā*), insight born of reflection (*cintamayī-prajñā*), and insight born of cultivation (*bhāvanāmayī-prajña*).[19] The second and third of these are, respectively, the degree of insight achievable by the logical or rational analysis of teaching and the higher degree of more direct insight that is possible as a result of meditation. But the first of the three, insight through learning, is of special relevance to the subject at hand. This is the kind and measure of insight attainable in the study of scripture or in attendance upon the instruction of a teacher. It is held, admittedly, to be by itself quite insufficient for liberation. But as often and as strongly as its sufficiency is denied, its necessity is affirmed. It is regarded as an essential precondition for success in those higher exercises of insight which are proximate causes of liberation. Without it, one's ventures beyond the realm of ordinary experience into the higher and radically altered states of mind that meditation can effect would be blind and perilous. And it is in the practice of this insight through learning that the practitioner of Buddhist mystical disciplines intentionally submits himself to the tutelage of canon and renders himself susceptible to its formidable powers of suggestion.

It has occasionally been assumed, e.g. by some whose perceptions of Buddhism have been distorted by their mistaken notions of mysticism, that the recommendation of the study of scripture in Buddhism is but a pious nod to tradition, a piece of mystical condescension. But consider the following claim of the Yogācāra tradition of Mahāyāna Buddhism. In his *Mahāyāna-saṃgraha*, in response to a question concerning the means by which the liberating 'transformation of fundamental consciousness' (*āśrayaparāvṛtti*) is effected, Asaṅga says that enlightenment or the attainment of a 'supramundane mind' (*lokottaracitta*) is brought about precisely by the 'influence (literally: the impregnation) of an ample hearing of Mahāyāna doctrine' (*bahuśrutavāsanā*). In other words, doctrine, as conveyed in the words of scripture, inserts itself like a seed (*bīja*) into the defiled mind of one so supremely fortunate as to hear it and there fructifies to become the 'counter-agent' (*pratipakṣa*) of the mind's normal impurities (*āsrava*). The purification which it then effects as it grows under cultivation is just the ultimately sought transformation from ignorance and defilement to enlightenment. Clearly, under this description (by a recognized mystic), the study of scripture is much more than only an incidental practice, and it is not at all a mere recourse for those in need of figures of speech to use in post-experimental interpretation. Rather it is the very germination and gestation of enlightenment itself. Canon, 'heard' or studied, is said actually to suffuse the mind, to unite with it as does 'milk with water', and so eventually to alter its essential character.[20] Thus, when we are faced with the task of evaluating typical similarities between the locutions of Buddhist scripture and the reports of Buddhist mystics about their experiences, we ought to pause before leaping to the conclusion that such similarities are the result simply of a docile disposition to 'translate' the ineffabilities of mystical transport into the linguistic conventions of available canonical tradition. It would appear that there is strong reason to hold, on the contrary, that mystical experience displays the sort of similarity to its scriptural context that progeny bears to its parentage. To draw out the metaphorical implications of Asaṅga's language we may say that in Buddhism scripture, or canonical discourse, is recognized as the 'father' of mystical experience. And the faithful piety a Buddhist demonstrates when, in accord with Buddhist scripture, he describes his transforming experiences as insights into the dependent origination, emptiness, and transience of all things (rather than, for example, as loving unions with God, etc.) is a kind of filial piety.

The formative influence of scriptural discourse upon mystical experience is a function not only of the content of the texts, their doctrinal formulations, dominant images, etc.; it may also flow from their form, from their styles and manners of discourse. Virtually since its inception Buddhism has shown a discriminate sensitivity to the modal differences among its canonical texts. Among the consequences of this was the early development of a sophisticated genre theory. The distinctions among the 'three baskets' (*tripiṭaka*) of the canon, or among its ten or twelve 'members' (*aṅga*),[21] are evidence of the Buddhist perception that scripturally authoritative language operates in differing ways according to, among other things, its tropic character. Consider, for example, the scriptural genre of *abhidharma*. Whereas the most familiar texts in the Buddhist canon are the sermons or conversations of the Buddha (*sūtra*), the narratives of his earlier lives (*jātaka*), the ecstatic proclamations of his gnosis (*udāna*), the lyrical expressions of the faith of his disciples (*gāthā*), etc., the *abhidharma* texts are dry, exceedingly prosaic and meticulous categorizations of doctrine. They constitute the analytic and scholastic component of Buddhist scripture and offer to their readers only the most austere and detailed taxonomies of religious experience. It is in these texts, for example, that one finds fully wrought the various renditions of the *dharma* theory, that strategy of Buddhist thought – and meditation – whereby the comfortable structures of normal experience are shattered and reduced to their minimum constituents; whereby, for example, the 'self' (*ātman*) which would seem to preside over all experience is shown to be not a whole personal entity but only an ever-shifting assemblage of fleeting sub-personal events (*dharma*) arrangeable into five categories, the five 'aggregates' (*skandha*) of 'material form' (*rūpa*), 'feeling' (*vedanā*), 'perception' (*saṃjñā*), 'karmic disposition' (*saṃskāra*), and 'consciousness' (*vijñāna*). This doctrine is to be found in other kinds of Buddhist scriptures too, but what distinguishes the *abhidharma* versions of it is their manner of discourse. Whereas other canonical genres like *sūtra* consist in 'conventional discourse' (*vyavahāra-vacana*), i.e. in ordinary language, the *abhidharma* books are said to have been written in a 'discourse of ultimate truth' (*paramārtha-vacana*), a technical and disciplined language held to be relatively free of the distortions implicit in everyday usage.[22] It is difficult to characterize this mode of discourse briefly, but among its salient features are a tendency to periphrasis and to the use of a technical rather than a common nomenclature, a preference for intransitive over transitive verbs and for the passive rather than the active voice, and a consistent avoidance of personal pronouns. The result of all of this is an oddly flat, abstract, detached, and circumlocutory prose. As literature it is quite unpalatable, some would say downright repellent. Nevertheless, it is a deliberate style, and its features, such as they are, are consciously chosen in the conviction that they serve certain spiritual ends, most particularly the end of depersonalization of experience. For example, the sort of experience which one might report in ordinary language by saying simply, 'I hear beautiful music', would in the language of *abhidharma* be described in something like the following manner: 'There arises in an aural perception (*saṃjñā*) an impulse of auditory consciousness (*vijñāna*) which is produced in dependence upon contact (*sparśa*) between the auditory faculty (*indriya*) and certain palpable vibrations emanating from a material (*rūpa*) instrument; this impulse of consciousness, in concert with certain morally conditioned mental predispositions (*saṃskāra*), occasions a feeling or hedonic tone (*vedanā*) of pleasure which in turn can produce attachment (*upādāna*)', and so on.[23] This sort of description, which shows experience to be very complex and particulate, is, of course, quite consonant with the Buddhist notion of no-self; it is in fact an exercise therein. Just as there is no sovereign 'self' to do the experiencing, so is there no word for such a self, no pronoun 'I'. In place of the ego and the 'I' there is a congeries of objective psychomatic events, each one labelled with a specific *terminus technicus*. Clearly, language has been artificially constrained here so that it might better intimate the nature of a selfless and insubstantial reality. But it is important to note too that abhidharmic language is held to be as much prescriptive as it is descriptive, that it is said not only to reflect reality but also to shape one's experience thereof. Deliberate and extended exposure to the rigorously de-personalized discourse of *abhidharma* (which is but an extreme example of the relative impersonality of most canonical Buddhist discourse) conditions the mind to relax its hold upon deep-seated notions of selfhood. It obstructs the kind of reinforcement that conventional language can give to such false concepts. Thus, when the more advanced disciplines of meditation are undertaken, the mind of the canonically informed practitioner is all the more receptive to their granulating, deconstructive effects and is led to have corroborating experiences precisely of the selflessness, the linguistic expression of which is the style of the texts he has studied.

In the twelfth century, the Christian mystic Saint Bernard of Clairvaux proclaimed, '*Mea grammatica Christus est.*'[24] His inten-tion, surely, was to distinguish personal communion with a loving God from the mere study of languages and literatures (even though such study was an important part of his monastic culture). Our Buddhist example of *abhidharma*, however, may allow us to give a new twist to this motto, to read it as saying not that experience should replace language but that the object of one's mystical experiences, be it Christ or emptiness or whatever, is constituted at least in part by the rules and patterns of one's discursive world. Such an interpretation might offend a Saint Bernard, but I doubt that a Buddhist student of *abhidharma* would object to it.

Another example of Buddhism's appreciation of the consequential role of discourse in the mystical life is to be found in a pair of discursive categories formulated in medieval China and employed in the serious task of sorting out and ranking the varieties of Buddhism then available. The following is a passage from Tsung-mi's (780–841) 'General Preface' to his lost or never completed *Ch'an Sourcebook* (*Ch'an-yüan chu-ch'üan-chi tu-hsü*). Tsung-mi, who was recognized as a 'Patriarch' of both the Hua-yen and the Southern Ch'an (Zen) traditions of Buddhism, was concerned in this work to distinguish between those kinds of Buddhism, traceable back to the great Indian sage Nāgārjuna, which emphasized to the virtual exclusion of all else the doctrine of emptiness, from those other kinds which stressed the 'Buddha-nature' inherent in all things and beings. The former, which he called the 'emptiness lineage' (*k'ung-tsung*), was profoundly negative in tone, so negative in its unremitting denial of substantiality, selfhood, permanence, etc., that it verged on nihilism or at least laid itself open to such a misinterpretation. The latter, which he called the 'nature lineage' (*hsing-tsung*), was far more positive in character, more inclined to affirm the truth than simply to deny falsehood. Among the ten distinctions he makes between these two general modes of Buddhism is a distinction of discourse. The terms he uses to draw this distinction are not unlike pseudo-Dionysius' 'apophasis' and 'kataphasis' or '*via negativa*' and '*via positiva*'. Here is the relevant passage:

> The two lineages differ from one another as regards their use of negative (i.e. apophatic) discourse (*che-ch'üan*) and expressive (i.e. kataphatic) discourse (*piao-ch'üan*). 'Negative' means rejecting what is not the case. 'Expressive' means manifesting what is the case. That is to say, negation is the denial of all things other than the real, whereas expression is the direct revelation of the very substance of the real. Consider for example the scriptures' exposition of the true and marvellous principle of Buddha-nature. All the scriptures say that neither is it born nor does it perish, that it is neither soiled nor pure, that it is without either cause or effect, that it is neither characterizable nor conditioned, that it is neither common nor noble, that it is neither essential nor accidental, etc. This is all negative discourse. In the scriptures and authoritative treatises the phrase 'is not' (*fei*) is used to negate all existents. It may appear as many as thirty to fifty

times in a single passage. The same is true of the phrases 'not have' and 'no' (*wu, pu*). Thus does one speak of the 'hundredfold negation'. But when the scriptures speak of 'the illumination of insight and enlightenment', of 'the mirror-like radiance of the spirit', of 'brilliant refulgence', of 'universal repose', etc., then they are using expressive discourse.

Now, if there were not such substantial realities as 'insight', what could be revealed as the Buddha-nature, what could be said 'neither to be born nor to perish' and so forth? One must recognize that understanding in the very perception of what is presently at hand is precisely the Buddha-nature of the mind. Then can one say that such understanding 'neither was born in the past nor will perish in the future', etc. It is like speaking of salt. To say that it is not sweet is negation, whereas to say that it is brackish is expression. Or, in the case of water, to say that it is not dry is negation, but to say that it is wet is expression. The 'hundred negations' mentioned in all the doctrinal systems of Buddhism are all negative locutions, but the direct manifestation of the one truth is accomplished by expressive discourse.

The discourses of the emptiness lineage are exclusively negative, but the discourse of the nature lineage partakes of both negation and expression. Exclusive negation is incomplete [i.e. its meanings are not explicit, not fully realized – *neyārtha*], but the combination of negation with expression hits the mark exactly. Men of these days [i.e. ninth-century China] all regard negative discourse as profound and expressive discourse as shallow. Thus they set store only by such phrases as 'neither mind nor Buddha', 'neither conditioned nor characterizable', and finally 'all is ineffable'. This is all due to their mistaking purely negative discourse for profundity and to their failure to aspire after an intimate personal realization of the substance of the truth.[25]

Apart from the light it sheds upon questions of Buddhist hermeneutics, this passage is valuable for the glimpse it provides us of Buddhist views on the mystical efficacy of language. So crucial is discourse to the mystical pursuit, it implies, that the success in mystical attainment hangs by a thread of rhetoric. An inappropriate verbal strategy, e.g. the adoption of the mock profundity of unqualified apophasis, can skew an aspirant's practice and deflect him from his true goal. Clearly the misuse of language could not have such dire consequences unless its proper use had inversely proportionate beneficial results. There must then, as we have suggested, be some deep and necessary connection between discourse and experience. It must be that Buddhist mystics have the kinds of transforming experiences they have in part because of the kinds of discourse they learn and use.

Tsung-mi's assertion of the superiority of a flexible discourse which can balance negation with affirmation over an inflexibly negative discursive disposition is connected, in ways we have not the space to explore here, with Buddhism's transmission from India to China, especially with its translation from Sanskrit to Chinese. Both Chinese culture in general and its literary traditions in particular favour judicious affirmation over relentless negation. The '*neti . . . neti . . .*' ('not this, not that') of Indian mysticism did not sit well with the Chinese, and it rang false in their tongue. The mysticism of a Tsung-mi, shaped as it was not simply by Buddhist discourse but by the discourse of a Sinified Buddhism, must count, on the premises I have argued, as Chinese mysticism, as a mysticism that is at least as Chinese as it is Buddhist. The process of the Chinese or East Asian transformation of Buddhist mysticism in which Tsung-mi played so important a role reached a kind of culmination in Ch'an or Zen Buddhism. And Ch'an in turn provides us with further evidence of the discursive contextuality of mysticism. I refer to the *kung-an* (Japanese: *kōan*, literally: 'public case') or the *hua-t'ou* ('verbal theme') which became a standard device in Ch'an. The core of any *kōan* is a paradoxical, apparently senseless statement or a literally unanswerable question, which is used in Zen as an object of meditation. Its function generally is to irritate the mind and to confute its conventional rationality by instigating what is called 'the great doubt'. Here we have language acting homeopathically to cure the ills inflicted on man by language itself. The *kōan* does not yield to rational analysis; it does not bear exegesis. Rather it baffles normal thought procedures and thereby disabuses those who use it of confidence in such procedures. Because it is meant to be used only in the course of meditation, it is designed to launch its assault on the mind at just that time when the mind has been made vulnerable, through quiescence and concentrated introspection, to its influence. Whatever else it may be, the *kōan* is surely one of the most effective and cunning linguistic instruments in the arsenal of mysticism.

One of the more recent additions to the canonical *kōan* repertory, the *kōan* of 'the sound of a single hand' (*sekishu no onjō*), has become so well known as to be made the butt of vulgar humour. But note what its author, the Japanese monk Hakuin (1686–1769), says about it:

Five or six years ago I made up my mind to instruct everyone by saying, 'Listen to the Sound of the Single Hand'. I have come to realize that this koan is infinitely more effective in instructing people than any of the methods I had used before. It seems to raise the ball of doubt in people much more easily and the readiness with which progress in meditation is made has been as different as the clouds are from the earth. Thus I have come to encourage the meditation on the Single Hand exclusively. . . .

What is the Sound of the Single Hand? When you clap together both hands a sharp sound is heard; when you raise the one hand there is neither sound nor smell. . . If conceptions and discriminations are not mixed within it and it is quite apart from seeing, hearing, perceiving, and knowing, and if, while walking, standing, sitting, and reclining, you proceed straightforwardly without interruption in the study of this koan, then in the place where reason is exhausted and words are ended, you will suddenly pluck out the karmic root of birth and death and break down the cave of ignorance . . . At this time the basis of mind, consciousness, and emotion is suddenly shattered; the realm of illusion with its endless sinking in the cycle of birth and death is overturned. . .

How worthy of veneration it is! When the (Sound of the) Single Hand enters the ear to even the slightest degree, the sound of the Buddha, the sound of the gods, the sound of the bodhisattvas, *śrāvakas, pratyeka-buddhas*, hungry ghosts, fighting demons, the sound of beasts, of heaven and of hell, all sounds existing in this world, are heard without exception. . .

I urge everyone to labour and strive and before this dew-like life is ended and the physical body disintegrates, to stand in fear and trembling and seek to hear from himself the Sound of the Single Hand.[26]

Paradoxical and inimical to conventional discourse though the *kōan* may be in effect, it is nevertheless itself a piece of language. Indeed it may be fairly described as a very unusual kind of trope. Therefore Hakuin's celebration of it must stand, whether or not he so intended it (though I think he did), as a tribute, if not to language generally then at least to the spiritually canny use of language. Even the capacity for paradox, the essence of the *kōan*, is a property of language. To the degree that the paradox of the *kōan* is essential to *satori*, to that degree does language shape even the ultimately translinguistic character of Zen mystical experience.

In his advocacy of *kōan* practice, Hakuin, like many Zen masters before him (a notable early example being the great Chinese monk Ta Hui, 1089–1163), took pains to criticize quite harshly what was known as 'the Zen of silent illumination (Chin.: *mo-chao ch'an*, Jap.:

mokushō zen). This sort of Zen, which sought enlightenment in wordless quiescence and made a fetish of ineffability, Hakuin regarded as bogus. What its practitioners attained, he believed, was not an enlightenment beyond language; it was mere aphasia. The following is typical of his condemnation:

> At times one hears people, from the vantage of a one-sided view, say: 'The place that I stand facing now is the mysterious, unproduced pre-beginning where the Buddhas and the Patriarchs have yet to arise. Here there is absolutely no birth, no death, no nirvāna, no passions, no enlightenment. All the scriptures are but paper fit only to wipe off excrement, the bodhisattvas and the arhats are but corrupted corpses. Studying Zen under a teacher is an empty delusion. The koans are but a film that clouds the eye. Here there is nothing; there there is nothing. I do not seek the Buddhas. I do not seek the Patriarchs. In starvation and sleeplessness what is there lacking?'
>
> Even the Buddhas and the Patriarchs cannot cure an understanding such as this. Every day these people seek a place of peace and quiet; today they end up like dead dogs and tomorrow it will be the same thing. Even if they continue in this way for endless kalpas, they will still be nothing more than dead dogs. Of what possible use are such people![27]

Like all Buddhists, Hakuin recognized the limitations of conventional language, but he also valued and revered the special kinds of language found in scripture and in the recorded sayings of the Patriarchs (the source of the *kōan* genre). Therefore did he rail so harshly against those who chose to dismiss or defame them. In so doing Hakuin has again warned us against succumbing to the hackneyed and unreflective invocation of ineffability. Ineffability *is* a nearly universal feature of mystical experience. There can be no doubt that such experiences *are* indescribable in language. Neither can it be denied that such experiences *do not* consist only in the apprehension of language. But none of this, as Hakuin suggests, can count against the efficacy that language *does have*, its real power to generate and inform the goal of mystical practice. Concerning the *kōan* specifically we must attend not only to its discursive abnormality but also to the more obvious fact that it is itself a locution. Then, noting that it is a paradoxical locution, we should not be surprised to discover that the enlightenment which its proper use can yield is also said to be paradoxical in nature, to be in fact the embodiment of paradox. Again we have, even at these frontiers of both language and experience, an instance of the capacity of the former to shape and determine the latter.

Hakuin's remarks on the value of the *kōan*, particularly the last passage quoted above, lead directly to a brief consideration of the last of our four major contexts of mysticism, viz. its institutional context. We note that Hakuin had as low an opinion of the rejection of teachers as he had of the rejection of canon. In this he echoes a constant refrain of Buddhism. One of the more general terms for teacher or spiritual adviser in Buddhism, particularly in the Mahāyāna, is *kalyānamitra* (literally: good friend). The presence of such spiritual friends in the life of a Buddhist is regarded as essential. They are held to be sources of the inspiration that one needs to generate that 'aspiration for enlightenment' (*bodhicitta*) which marks the inception of the *bodhisattva* path. Once one has set out upon that path, however, he finds himself in even greater need of them, for the path is said not to be traversable alone. As they provide the novice *bodhisattva* with the more intimate kinds of guidance and support in study and meditation that he needs as he progresses on the path, these spiritual friends assume the more specific roles of preceptor (*upādhyāya*), instructor (*ācārya*), *guru*, Zen master, etc., in which they are charged with the tasks of actually moulding the aspirant's eventual enlightenment. The following, from *The Jewel Ornament of Liberation* of the great Tibetan Kagyü-pa (*bKaḥ-brgyud-pa*) teacher Gampo-pa (*sGam-po-pa*) is typical of the Mahāyāna estimation of such companions of the spirit. He says, on the topic of spiritual friends as contributory causes of enlightenment:

> Although you may possess the most perfect working basis, but are not urged on by spiritual friends as a contributary cause, it is difficult to set out on the path towards enlightenment, because of the power of inveterate propensities due to evil deeds committed repeatedly in former times. Therefore you have to meet spiritual friends. . . .
>
> Spiritual friends are like a guide when we travel in unknown territory, an escort when we pass through dangerous regions and a ferry-man when we cross a great river.

They are like guides through dangerous territory, he continues, because the regions of practice are difficult and hostile:

> When we go there without an escort, there is the danger of losing our body, life or property; but when we have a strong escort we reach the desired

place without loss. So also, when we have set out on the path towards enlightenment, accumulated merits and spiritual awareness and are about to go to the city of the Omniscient One, if there is no spiritual friend to act as an escort, there is danger of losing our stock of merits either from within ourselves, by preconceived ideas and emotional instability, or from outside, by demons, wrong guides and other treacherous people, and there is also the danger that we may be robbed of our life which is approaching pleasurable forms of existence.[28]

It is this sort of crucial guidance to which I referred above when I discussed the authority with which mystical traditions often invest their teachers, an authority actually to decide which spiritual achievements are true or ultimate and which are false or only preliminary. Buddhism achieved the status of a continuous tradition precisely because it did not leave this crucial office to chance or to the vagaries of custom. Rather, it formalized and rationalized it in the development of monastic societies, teaching lineages, hierarchies, councils, ceremonial calendars, etc. Buddhism has, after all, been more a cenobitic than a purely eremitic tradition virtually since its beginnings. The Buddhist monk may in some sense depart from the institutions of the mundane world, he may therefore be called 'one who has gone forth' (*parivrājaka*), but he also 'takes refuge' (*śaraṇaṃ gacchati*) in the *Saṅgha*. That brotherhood is the very matrix of Buddhist mysticism. Even lay Buddhism, which has also harboured mystics, is a part of it, or of the 'Greater *Saṅgha*' which includes it. The elaborate rules governing life in the *Saṅgha*, the formal bonds of respect and mutual concern which bind it, even the minutiae of its daily routine are all in their own way as much of the essence of Buddhist mysticism as are its most profound doctrines and its most sublime transports. We do our subject serious injustice, and are guilty of a kind of intellectual condescension, if we only notice the experiential flower of Buddhism and ignore its institutional leaves, branches, trunk, and roots.

One of the more delightful, and informative, books published recently on Zen Buddhism is a work called *Unsui: A Diary of Zen Monastic Life.*[29] It consists of a series of ninety-six charming colour drawings by the late Giei Satō, a Zen monk of the Rinzai sect. To each is attached a brief and simple commentary by the Reverend Eshin Nishimura. The drawings depict with touching humour scenes in the daily lives of Zen monks in a typical Japanese monastery. The more solemn activities of the monastery, e.g. 'Chanting the Scriptures',

'Meeting with the Zen Master', 'Individual Meditation at Night', etc., are well represented, but most of the drawings are of such things as 'Going to Bed', 'Taking a Bath', 'Shaving the Head', 'Begging in the Streets', 'Cooking', etc. The artist has succeeded, as seems to have been his intention, in capturing the texture of Zen life, in evoking its sounds, smells, rhythms, and colours. The Zen he portrays is no ethereum of sages; it is a very down-to-earth sort of mysticism indeed. However, included among the drawings, is one of enlightenment itself (*kenshō*, literally 'seeing one's nature'). It shows a slightly comic monk seated in the palm of a gigantic Buddha, laughing uproariously. As this drawing is neither the first nor the last in the series, as it is preceded by a picture of a kind of *sūtra*-title shouting match and followed by another depicting the reassignment of housekeeping chores, and as it is done in the same droll style, one cannot but be impressed (paradoxically) by the inconspicuousness of enlightenment amidst the details of Zen monastic life. There is, I assume, a serious message in this bit of whimsey, a message I take to support my general thesis. Mysticism is in the end a quite ordinary thing. As Zen monks are wont to say of Zen in particular, so may we say of mysticism in general, it is really nothing special. It is a very human phenomenon. It emerges within the confines of human life, and although it enriches that life with moments of joy and with more lasting qualities of spiritual poise, integration, and generosity, it none the less partakes of the banality, the prosaicness, even the tedium of the quotidian. It is as much a matter of mending a torn robe as it is an intuition of the emptiness or oneness of things; as much a matter of obedience to one's monastic superiors as it is a vision of the face of God; as much a matter of the rules, norms, proprieties, and priorities of human intercourse as it is a coursing in the void. Again Hakuin has summed it up well:

If you think that dead sitting and silent illumination are sufficient then you spend your whole life in error and transgress greatly against the Buddha Way. Not only do you set yourself against the Buddha Way, but you reject the lay world as well. Why is this so? If the various lords and high officials were to neglect their visits to court and to cast aside their governmental duties and practise dead sitting and silent illumination; if the warriors were to neglect their archery and charioteering, forget the martial arts, and practise dead sitting and silent illumination; if the merchants were to lock their shops and smash their abacuses, and practise dead sitting and silent illumination; if the farmers were to throw away their ploughs and hoes, cease their cultivation, and practise dead sitting and silent illumination; if craftsmen were to cast away their measures and discard their axes and adzes, and practise dead sitting and silent illumination, the country would collapse and the people drop with exhaustion. Bandits would arise everywhere and the nation would be in grievous danger. Then the people, in their anger and resentment, would be sure to say that Zen was an evil and an ill-omened thing.

But it should be known that at the time that the ancient monasteries flourished, old sages . . . heaved stones, moved earth, drew water, cut firewood, and grew vegetables. When the drum for the work period sounded, they tried to make progress in the midst of their activity. That is why Po-chang said: 'A day without work, a day without eating.' This practise is known as meditation in the midst of activity, the uninterrupted practise of meditation sitting.[30]

Mysticism does not stand apart from 'the lay world' of duty, station, prudence, 'law and order', labour, etc. It is woven together with all of these things into a whole pattern or 'form of life', and the institutions *within which* it flourishes help to give it its particular character. If the study of mysticism is to advance, then it must not shy away as it has in the past from the 'thick description' of those social, political, economic, and legal contexts which have nurtured mystics in all cultures and at all times.

The examples we have now considered of the formative influence of conceptual, practical, discursive, and institutional contexts upon mystical experience have all been drawn from the Buddhist tradition. But what they illustrate is not some peculiar characteristic of Buddhism; it is the general principle of mysticism's essential contextuality. That principle, as was argued in the previous section, governs all mysticism. Thus, similar examples could no doubt be adduced from other traditions. The piquant conclusion to be drawn from this, it is worth repeating, is that what various mysticisms have most in common is a fidelity to their respective traditions, and precisely in this lies their basic difference one from another.

III

Throughout this essay, I have tended to speak more of 'mystical experience' than of 'mysticism'. In bringing my remarks to a conclusion, I wish to make it clear that my repeated references to the experiential component of mysticism, to those extraordinary intensities of knowing and feeling by which we seem to recognize the phenomenon, ought not to be taken as implying that mystical experience is all there is of mysticism, nor even that it is its most important component. Indeed, my intention is precisely the opposite. Ecstasies, intuitions, sudden insights, epiphanies, transports of union, disenthralments, and the like may be necessary to the definition of mysticism, in the sense that there is nothing which can reasonably be called mystical that does not include such things, but there is much more to the matter than that. The mysticism of any particular mystic is really the whole pattern of his life. The rare and wonderful 'peaks' of experience are a part of that pattern, but only a part, and their real value lies only in their relations to the other parts, to his thought, his moral values, his conduct towards others, his character and personality, etc. The modern study of mysticism has, I believe, tended to overlook those relations. My own emphasis on the historicity and contextual character of mystical experience – the deep and formative connections between it and the systems of concept, practice, discourse, and institution which produce and contain it – is meant to redress this current imbalance of scholarly attention.

But the consequences of such a redress for our understanding – and, more importantly, for our evaluation – of mysticisms are quite serious. If it can be shown, as I have tried to show, that the mysticism of a Buddhist mystic is essentially informed by his Buddhism, i.e. by his Buddhist beliefs, his Buddhist habits of action and speech, his Buddhist communities, then our judgement of his mystical attainments must depend upon and conform to our judgements of his Buddhism. The study of mysticism can no longer serve as a means of circumventing the hard conceptual and historical issues that the diversity of man's religions presents. To state the case in a somewhat different and more eristic way, we may say that acceptance of the dependency of mysticism upon its contexts, together with the entailed acceptance of the fundamental differences among varieties of mysticism, lends support to a view repugnant to many enthusiasts, viz. that mystical experience is simply the psychosomatic enhancement of religious beliefs and values or of beliefs and values of other kinds which are held 'religiously'. But such a view of mystical experience should be disturbing only to those who set little store by religious beliefs and values. Herein, I suspect, lies much of the real resistance to the notion of mysticism's essential contextuality. Here is a hidden source of the claim that mysticism is everywhere alike and wholly autonomous. Both spring from a curious and seldom acknowledged antipathy toward or suspicion of religion. Mysticism has become fascinating to many of its students exactly because it has seemed to them to be an alternative to religion. It has come to be viewed as a repository of all that is best and still admirable in religion but one that is free from such no longer acceptable elements as dogma, authority, discipline, respect for tradition, etc. I hold no particular brief for any of these things as they exist in any particular religion, but in the interests of sound scholarship, not to mention philosophical coherence, I do hope that the arguments and examples presented above will give some pause to those who are inclined to such assumptions of the separability of mysticism from religious traditions.

NOTES

1   In a study which was originally to have been the opening part of this essay, but which because of its length will be published separately elsewhere, I trace the origins of this view of mysticism to certain currents of late nineteenth- and early twentieth-century European opinion on religion. I argue that the authors of some of the earlier classical studies of mysticism (e.g. Underhill, Inge, Leuba, Maréchal, Poulain, Otto, Von Hügel, Massignon, etc.) fashioned a rather romantic and reactionary view of mysticism in which mystics are seen to stand aloof from and independent of the religious traditions 'of the masses' and to comprise a universal religious elite, a transcultural aristocracy of *illuminati*. The basis of this view, I suggest, was a widespread loss of confidence in, in some cases a disdain for, traditional institutionalized religion. I further argue that this view, long influential in the study of mysticism, slights the genuine eminence of mystics *within* their traditions and impedes the search for an adequate definition of mysticism.

2   Steven T. Katz, 'Language, Epistemology, and Mysticism' and Peter Moore, 'Mystical Experience, Mystical Doctrine, and Mystical Technique' – both in Steven T. Katz (ed.), *Mysticism and Philosophical Analysis* (London and New York, 1978), pp. 22–74 and 101–31.

3   Robert M. Gimello, 'Mysticism and Meditation', in Katz, op. cit., pp. 170–99.

4   Hindu, particularly neo-Vedantist, appropriations of Buddhism are among the more common examples of the homogenization of mysticism. The work of Ananda Coomaraswamy on Buddhism is a case in point. One of the few modern scholars of mysticism who does not

explain away the genuine plurality of religions and mysticisms is Gershom Scholem. Perhaps this is because, as a Jewish scholar, he had personal experience of the intolerance of religious 'otherness'. See the Introduction to his *Major Trends in Jewish Mysticism*, 3rd ed. (1961; New York, 1974), pp. 1–18.

5 For a sustained analysis of this text see R. M. Gimello, 'Apophatic and Kataphatic Language in Mahāyāna: A Chinese View', *Philosophy East and West*, 26 (1976), 117–35.

6 T1878: 45.652c. Note that quotations from the Chinese Buddhist canon are from its *Taishō shinshū daizōkyō* ed. (abbrev. 'T'), cited by serial no., vol., page, and column. Note too that unless otherwise stated all translations from Asian languages are my own.

7 Ch'eng-kuan, *Hua-yen fa-chieh hsüan-ching*, T1882: 45.676a.

8 Nyanatiloka, *Buddhist Dictionary*, 3rd rev. ed. (Colombo, 1972), p. 93.

9 *Ta-chih-tu lun*, T1509: 25.229c.

10 Two versions of this teaching are found in Buddhism. One is personal selflessness (*pudgala-nairātmya*), the doctrine that sentient beings lack souls. The other, dharmic selflessness (*dharma-nairātmya*), holds that even those sub-personal elements which make up what appear to be whole sentient beings lack substantiality.

11 These four themes of meditation, the four 'stations of mindfulness' (*satipaṭṭhāna*), constitute one of the classic meditation curricula of Buddhism. For an admirable treatment of them, including translations of their scriptural expositions, see Nāṇaponika Thera, *The Heart of Buddhist Meditation* (1962; rpt. New York, 1971).

12 Paravahera Vajirañāṇa, *Buddhist Meditation in Theory and Practice* (Columbo, 1962), p. 263.

13 Marion L. Matics (tr.), *Entering the Path of Enlightenment: The Bodhicaryāvatāra of the Buddhist Poet Śāntideva* (New York, 1970), pp. 202–4. The verses here quoted are nos. 90, 102, 111, 112, 120 of chpt. VIII.

14 I am employing here the conventional Chinese distinction between '*t'i*' (the substance, inner structure, or 'whatness' of a thing) and '*yung*' (the function, pattern of behavior, or 'how' of a thing). These are a very useful pair of terms for discussing things mystical and were commonly so used by the Chinese.

15 See Bhikkhu Nāṇananda, *Concept and Reality in Early Buddhist Thought* (Kandy, 1971). This is an extended study of the term *prapañca* (Pāli: *papañca*) in the early Buddhist canon.

16 *She Ta-ch'eng lun*, T 1593:31.118a.

17 An intriguing literary experiment with language consisting only of verbal forms, an experiment inspired I suspect by Buddhism, is Jorge Luis Borges's 'Tlon, Uqbar and the Third World' in his *Ficciones*.

18 *Mūlamādhyamikakārika*, 24:9, T1564:30.33a.

19 For a classical statement of this three-fold insight see Kamalaśīla's *Bhāvanākrama*, Tucci's ed. *Minor Buddhist Texts*, Pt. II (Rome, 1958), p. 187, *et seq.* Kamalaśīla's treatment is influenced, I suspect, by Asaṅga's in his *Mahāyānasaṃgraha*.

20 Asaṅga, *Mahāyānasaṃgraha*, 1:46, *She Ta-ch'eng lun*, T 1594:31.136c.

21 For an expert treatment of the nine and twelve genres of Buddhist scripture see Étienne Lamotte, *Histoire du Bouddhisme Indien des origines à l'ère Śaka*, Bibliothèque du Muséon, Volume 43 (Louvain, 1958), pp. 154–63.

22 See Nyanatiloka Mahāthera, *A Guide Through the Abhidhamma-Piṭaka* (Kandy, 1971), p. 2, *et passim.*

23 I am here following the excellent model of explanation provided by the late Edward Conze in his *Buddhist Thought in India* (London, 1962), p. 98.

24 A discussion of this motto is to be found in Jean Leclercq, O.S.B., *The Love of Learning and the Desire for God* (New York, 1961), pp. 309–29.

25 I have translated this passage from Shigeo Kamata's ed. of the Chinese text – *Zengen shosenshū tojo*, Zen no goroku 9 (Tokyo, 1971), p. 167.

26 Philip B. Yampolsky (tr.), *The Zen Master Hakuin: Selected Writings* (New York, 1971), pp. 163–69.

27 Yampolsky, *Hakuin*, pp. 114–15.

28 Herbert V. Guenther (tr.), *sGram.po.pa: Jewel Ornament of Liberation* (London, 1959), pp. 30–31.

29 Bardwell L. Smith (ed.), *Unsui: A Diary of Zen Monastic Life* (Honolulu, 1973).

30 Yampolsky, *Hakuin*, pp. 51–52.

ROBERT M. GIMELLO, Ph. D. in Buddhist Studies and East Asian Languages and Cultures (Columbia University). Professor Gimello has taught at Columbia, Dartmouth College, and the University of California at Santa Barbara. He is now Head of the Department of Oriental Studies and Professor of Oriental Studies at the University of Arizona. He is the author of *Chih-yen and the Foundations of Hua-yen: A Study in the Sinification of Buddhism* and has published a number of articles on the history and philosophy of Asian religions.

The Mystical Illusion

HANS H. PENNER

The basic assumption of this essay is that there are no direct experiences of the world, or 'between individuals except *through* the social relations which "mediate" them'.[1] Once this principle has been granted, it does not make much sense to speak of states of 'pure consciousness' or experiences not constituted from within a linguistic framework. The principle is not revolutionary or new. It is, however, often forgotten when scholars focus their attention on religion and mysticism. If the principle is firmly held it will follow that, *if* mystical experiences have any significance, in order to explain their significance it will be necessary to locate and explicate the set of relations which mediate them.

The thesis of this essay is that 'mysticism' is an illusion, unreal, a false category which has distorted an important aspect of religion. This is not to imply that the assertions made by yogis, Śaṁkara, St John of the Cross, or Eckhart are unreal or illusory. It is precisely such puzzling data that have led scholars to construct so-called mystical systems and, in turn, to see 'mysticism' as the essence of religion.

It would be an awkward exercise to set quotation marks around, or apply the adjective 'so-called' to, the term "mysticism" every time it is used in this essay. It is nevertheless important to remember that the adjective or quotation marks are understood whenever the term 'mysticism', or 'mystical experience' appears.

I

I would like to begin my substantive discussion by offering a few comments on the essays in *Mysticism and Philosophical Analysis*, edited by Steven T. Katz, which represent an excellent review of contemporary scholarship on mysticism. The basic texts dealing with mysticism which are evaluated by the contributors to that symposium are those written by such scholars as E. Underhill, W. Stace, R. C. Zaehner, and R. Otto.[2] Although there are significant differences between these classical approaches to mysticism, we can summarize the goal of each as an attempt to locate and describe the essence of mysticism. The emphasis is on mystical experience as expressed by mystical language. The experience is described as an ultimate experience, an experience of the absolute, numinous in quality, transcending self and world. The various mystical languages are explained as symbolic expressions of a basic, universal, experience.

If, however, Otto, as one example, is correct in his assumption that there is an experience which is *sui generis* and identical across mystical traditions, then he must produce a well-formed set of rules explaining how it is possible to treat as synonymous mystical statements which at least on the surface are clearly dissimilar. However, we are never provided with such rules by any scholar who believes that mystical languages, or types of languages, express an identical experience. Of course Otto, Stace, Underhill, and Zaehner were not primarily interested in the semantics of the language of mysticism; their concern was the mystical experience as such. And once this experience is defined it is mapped on to the different mystical languages as so many representations of *mysticism*. Thus, once Otto posits the essence of mysticism as both subjective and theistic he will find both qualities in the mystical language of Śaṁkara and Eckhart.

The language of mysticism thus becomes secondary to the experience itself for most scholars of mysticism. Mystical languages are viewed as variations on an essential experience common to most if not all mystics. Underhill expresses this notion as follows: mysticism is 'the expression of the innate tendency of the human spirit towards complete harmony with the transcendent order; *whatever be the theological formula under which that order is understood*'.[3] Clearly, it is not the 'formula' or the language used that is essentially important, but the experience of 'mystic union' or 'contemplation' that is the proper subject of mysticism. Otto and Zaehner would find Underhill's definition far too broad, in light of their classification of mystical types. Nevertheless, both would affirm the *a priori* nature of the mystical experience as represented across religious traditions in various formulas or types.

I suggest that we must reverse such approaches to the study of mysticism. We must remember that all we have for understanding mysticism is language, not experience. It is not mystical experience which explains mystical traditions or languages, rather it is mystical language which explains mystical experience. In fact it is useless to appeal to mystical experience as the basis of our explanation because it is precisely this experience that needs to be explained. Mystical experience, among other experiences, is one of the most obscure aspects of religion and scholars are often tempted to use it as the basis for an explanation. But, they forget, as Lévi-Strauss has reminded us about the use of affectivity, 'that what is refractory to explanation is *ipso facto* unsuitable for use in explanation. A datum is not primary because it is incomprehensible; this characteristic indicates solely that explanation, if it exists, must be sought on another level. Otherwise, we shall be satisfied to attach another label to the problem, thus believing it has been solved.'[4]

Lévi-Strauss has given us sound advice on what to avoid in the study of religion and mysticism. The advice, however, has had little effect, and this is especially true with regard to scholarship on mysticism. The first essay in *Mysticism and Philosophical Analysis*, for example, is 'Understanding Religious Experience'.[5] In that essay Ninian Smart is not satisfied with Otto's and Zaehner's classification of mysticism. He proposes that we divide religious experience into 'numinous' and 'mystical'. However, it is anything but clear how such a classification advances our understanding of mysticism or how it accounts for such experiences. What we are given are new sets of labels with the belief that the problem has now been solved. But the problem remains unsolved precisely because mystical experience continues to resist explanation and is therefore unsuitable for use in our explanations.

What I find most interesting in Smart's paper is that all of his examples are taken from either the world of ordinary language and linguistics or from statements which invoke beliefs, thought, and theory. Clearly, the inference to be drawn from these examples is that an explanation of mystical experience must be sought on another level. Yet, we are never told what the significant relation is between language, belief, theory, and mystical experience.

It would be an over-simplification and distortion to leave the impression that the work of Otto, Stace, Zaehner, and Smart are the only possible approaches to the study of mysticism. There are alternatives and one of them is easily predictable. If some of us are convinced that emphasis on the essence of mystical experience is misguided, one option is to study the varieties of mysticism in their historical contexts. As Gershon Scholem expressed it: 'There is no mysticism as such, there is only the mysticism of a particular religious system, Christian, Islamic, Jewish mysticism and so on.'[6] Scholem, unlike some others who take this position, added the remark that it would be absurd to deny the common characteristics of mystical systems which are described in comparative analysis. He did, however, deny the reality of an abstract mysticism which, for many scholars, had become the basis or essence of all religions.

Scholem was certainly correct in challenging the reification of abstractions which are produced in the minds of scholars. We must, however, proceed with caution. Once we are aware of the trap into which the search for the essence of mysticism leads, we must take care lest we stumble into a second methodological pit. The advice that there is no mysticism as such, only the mysticisms of particular religions, can lead us very quickly into the incoherence of what I shall call 'mystical relativism'. Let us pause for a moment in order to understand why this is so.

Most relativists think that scholars of mysticism such as Otto, Stace, and Zaehner are wrong. Why do they think they are wrong? In some instances we find that they are wrong because they were biased, dogmatic, ethnocentric, or metaphysical in their analysis of mysticism. I shall choose a different perspective in order to get at the heart of the disagreement. My choice is guided by the judgement that I do not think such accusations are very helpful. I do not think that such scholars were intentionally dogmatic, biased, or ethnocentric – who is? They did not simply misread the same texts we use. They were not, from what I can tell, poor translators or dilletantes, but respected scholars in the study of religion.

From a relativist point of view, scholars such as Otto or Zaehner are wrong because they assumed that mystical languages as types of religious language mean the same thing. Not only that; they also must have believed, perhaps naïvely, that, if religious mysticism entails truth, truth is one. Mystical relativism is in sharp opposition to this position. The basic assumption of the mystical relativist can be described as follows: what is meaningful, what is in accord with reality and not in accord with reality, shows itself in the *context* that a mystical system has. If this is not the basic assumption dividing the two fundamentally different approaches to the study of mysticism, then it is not clear to me what the debate is all about. I shall assume that I have stated it correctly.

A relativist approach to mysticism is not simply concerned with demonstrating that mystical traditions differ from each other. Every scholar, including Otto and Zaehner, is well aware of that fact. The relativist is opposed to positions such as Zaehner's because Zaehner believes that he can not only compare different mystical systems, but also judge which systems are valid, genuine, or true. For Zaehner, monistic mystical systems are not in accord with Reality.

The relativist will dispute Zaehner's conclusion not simply because it is theologically biased or because mystical statements are incapable of being verified. Zaehner's conclusion is incorrect because what is in accord and not in accord with Reality shows itself in the *context* that a mystical system has. The central point is that mystical languages cannot be thought of as referring to the same Reality, because Reality is relative to a language system. Different mystical languages, therefore, represent or express different mystical worlds.

Zaehner's mistake, from a relativist's point of view, should now be clear. His judgements about monistic mysticism were made from within the context of a theistic mystical system. What he did not perceive is that the two systems are incommensurable.

The relativist position appears to furnish a powerful critique. It is also a valuable corrective or warning with regard to ethnocentricism. Furthermore, it forces us back to a more careful reading of texts and traditions. However, we must carefully reflect upon some of the consequences of this position before wholeheartedly endorsing it. We must notice, first of all, that strict adherence to mystical relativism entails rejection of the notion that a neutral explanation or under-standing of mysticism by which the various mystical systems can be described is possible. This is ruled out because every explanation or description of the world entails some conceptual system, and since this is the case it is logically impossible to step outside of every conceptual system, which is what a neutral explanation entails. It would seem, therefore, that the only option we have for understand-ing a mystical system is to 'adopt' the context or language of the mystical system we wish to understand. Just how we are to go about this is never made clear, but what is clear is that we would have to 'adopt' each system one at a time because we cannot 'adopt' two systems simultaneously.

Strict adherence to the relativist position also leads to the conclusion that debate between a Christian and Buddhist mystic would be impossible or nonsensical. Furthermore, how would we explain a mystic's conversion from one mystical system to another? It would also seem impossible, from a relativist position, to translate a Sanskrit mystical text into English. And finally, one of the most difficult problems confronting this approach is drawing the boundaries between mystical systems. Do Buddhist, Hindu, Islamic, Jewish, and Christian mystical traditions constitute five systems? Two? And how do we go about drawing the boundaries without stepping outside our own conceptual system?[7]

If Otto and his fellow travellers have not provided us with an adequate method for understanding mysticism, then, I would suggest, we must proceed with great caution in order to avoid the alternative methodological dilemmas presented by mystical relativism. It might be best to start all over again. I may be wrong, but I think the study of mysticism, as it has been carried on to this point, has been basically misconceived.

II

The diagnosis of the problem with studies of mysticism is simple; the cure, however, may take time and patience. When we review the history of texts on mysticism we observe that at the beginning mysticism was defined in rather straightforward terms. With the passage of time and greater attention to the subject things have changed; now mysticism eludes all attempts at definition. The various attempts at defining mysticism clearly suggest that there simply is no identifiable subject for study. The reaction to this state of affairs has been the development of studies in particular mysticisms.

The following statement is an excellent example of the present situation with regard to the study of mysticism:

> Attempts to define mystical experience have been as diversified and as conflicting as attempts to interpret and assess its significance. . . Some discriminations are possible, even if exact definition is not. Mystical experience is religious experience, in a broad but meaningful sense of 'religious'. It is sensed as revealing something about the totality of things,

something of immense human importance at all times and places, and something upon which one's ultimate well-being or salvation wholly depends. More specifically, a mystical experience is not the act of acquiring religious or theological information but is often taken to be a confrontation or encounter with the divine source of the world's being and man's salvation. An experience is not held to be mystical if the divine power is apprehended as simply 'over-against' one – wholly distinct and 'other'. There must be a unifying vision, a sense that somehow all things are one and share a holy, divine, and single life, or that one's individual being merges into a 'Universal self', to be identified with God or the mystical One. Mystical experience then typically involves the intense and joyous realization of oneness with, or in, the divine, the sense that this divine One is comprehensive, all embracing, in its being. Yet a mystical experience may be given much less theological interpretation than this description suggests. A mystic may have no belief whatever in a divine being and still experience a sense of overwhelming beatitude, of salvation, or of lost or transcended individuality.

Some mystical experiences occur only at the end of a lengthy, arduous religious discipline, an ascetic path; others occur spontaneously (like much nature-mystical experience); others are induced by drugs such as mescalin or take place during the course of mental illness.[8]

It is clear from this attempt at describing the nature of mysticism that mysticism does not refer to any particular kind of system or experience. In fact, the term mysticism now covers a host of beliefs and experiences which have no relation to each other whatsoever.

This situation is not unique. There is a striking parallel to be found in the history of the study of totemism. Since the details of scholarship on this subject are well known, I will not rehearse them here.[9] Let us simply recall the important point that totemism was once upon a time thought of as the origin, the basis, or foundation of religion. Totemism was thought of as an institution with specific properties. It did not take very long for criticism and detailed comparison of the data to discover that there were severe problems which simply could not be solved by this explanation of the fascinating phenomena.

I will now be satisfied if the reader has gone on to predict the alternative approach for solving the problem before I have had the opportunity to state it. The alternative route which scholarship on totemism took was to assert that there is no such thing as totemism as such, there is only the totemism of a particular social system, Australian, Ojibwa, Tikopian, and so on.

The consequences of this alternative for the study of totemism were the same as for the study of mysticism. Instead of continuing on with totemic studies, I will simply substitute the word 'mysticism' for 'totemism' in the following quotation, which will serve as a perfect description of the contemporary state of studies in mysticism:

> It will be seen that the term 'mysticism' has been applied to a bewildering variety of relationships. . . For this reason it is impossible to reach any satisfactory definition of mysticism though many attempts have been made to do so . . . All definitions of mysticism are either so specific as to exclude a number of systems which are commonly referred to as 'mystic' or so general as to include many phenomena which cannot properly be referred to by this term.[10]

We have ended up with formal definitions which contain nothing with regard to the *content* of mysticism. What we find instead is a list of 'salient features' which are not necessarily the only features of mysticism, to which we can add or subtract if the evidence so indicates.[11]

Lévi-Strauss, in his study of totemism, has also summed up the results for scholarship on mysticism when he asserts that

> this caution with regard to a notion which can be retained only after it has been emptied of its substance and, as it were, disincarnated, does no more than underline the point of Lowie's general warning to the inventors of institutions: 'We must first inquire whether . . . we are comparing cultural realities, or merely figments of our logical modes of classification'.[12]

We can now raise a question which will become crucial for the next section of this essay. If mysticism as such is an abstraction, a figment of our logical modes of classification, why does it become less problematic when carried over into particular religious systems?

III

The mystical illusion is the result of an abstraction which distorts the semantic or structural field of a religious system. As such it is a false category, unreal, regardless of whether it is taken as the universal essence of religion or as a particular feature of a religious system. The chimera is produced by focusing upon certain elements of the system.

And once these elements have been selected they seem to take on 'an originality and a strangeness which they do not really possess; for they are made to appear mysterious by the very fact of abstracting them from the system of which as transformations, they formed an integral part.'[13] The results of this process can be illustrated by a brief summary of scholarship on the religious tradition of India.

Scholarship on the religions of India has focused primarily upon the 'mystical' element in both Hinduism and Buddhism. The 'wisdom of the East' is 'mystical wisdom', the wisdom of the yogi and the Buddhist monk. I think that when most people think of India's religion they think of the ascetic, the person who renounces the world in order to seek his own liberation.

Most texts on either Hinduism or Buddhism reinforce this point of view. Pick up any book on either religion and you will find that the primary emphasis is on the ascetic; the mystical element has become the 'essence' of both Hinduism and Buddhism. Hindu art, Indian architecture and mythology have become totally 'mystified' as representations of India's 'ascetic philosophy'.[14]

The distortion which this emphasis produces can be seen very quickly once we remember that there is more to India's religion than asceticism. In fact, when we single out the 'mystical element', India's religious tradition becomes incoherent. For example, if India's greatest contribution to the history of religion is the wisdom of the renouncer, then India has not made use of that wisdom in her own religion. Alongside the ascetic life and the wisdom of renunciation we find affirmation, passion, worldliness, and eroticism. Once the 'mystical element' is extracted as the essence of this religion it becomes impossible to explain the coherence, the rationality, of India's religious tradition as a religious system. Hinduism is a religion which *encompasses* Yoga Sūtras and Dharma Shastras, Brahma Sūtras and Kama Sūtras.

When the mystical element of the Hindu religious system is singled out, the part that is substituted for the whole takes on an originality and strangeness which it does not really possess. The ascetic tradition is made to appear mysterious by the very fact of abstracting it from the system of which, as a transformation, it originally formed an integral part. The effect is to distort not only the significance of the mystical element in Hinduism, but also the total semantic field of the system. It effects our understanding both of the Indian renouncer and of the Hindu who follows his *Dharma*. The fragmentation of the system which results is often 'corrected' by the creation of labels such as, 'elite' *v.* 'popular' religion, 'great' *v.* 'little' tradition, 'aryan' *v.* 'indigenous' religion, 'sanskritization' and so on, and the problem is then thought to be solved.

It is important to pause here for a moment to consider *why* we have perceived Hinduism as essentially ascetic and mystical. The overwhelming emphasis on the great renouncer traditions of India and the effect this has had on our understanding of India cannot be due to sheer accident, or the whim of scholarship. More research on Western scholarship of India's religion might show that we have selected the one element which reflects our own perception of what is of value in life: individualism, and the quest for individual salvation. Thus the quests of both the Hindu yogi and the Buddhist monk are taken as analogous to the Christian pilgrim's progress. Such an account of scholarship on India remains to be written.[15] Suffice it to say, I shall not attempt to explore this possibility here; instead, I will attempt to counter this mistaken emphasis by placing the ascetic tradition of India back into its proper semantic field.

IV

Let us begin this section by recalling a principle set forth at the beginning of this essay; if mystical experiences have any significance, it will be necessary, in order to explain that significance, to locate the set of relations which mediate them. In order to explain one element or unit in a system we must first of all discover the relations which define it within the system. The significance of an element lies in its relation with other elements in the system; it is the relations between elements which generate what I have called the semantic field. The significance of a term in a sentence, for example, is its functional relation with other terms in the sentence. It is of fundamental importance to remember that the functional relations between terms of a system, whether linguistic, social, or religious, cannot be found by observing the empirical surface or by an appeal to the history of the system.

This principle has important implications for the study of India's religious tradition, including its so-called mystical element. It implies, first, that any attempt to explain this element by extracting it from the system of which it is a part will be misguided; it will produce what I have called the mystical illusion. It further implies that we will be unable to describe the functional relations of the element in the Hindu religious system simply by observing the performance of the Hindu whether renouncer or follower of *Dharma*. Finally, we will be unable to explicate the mystical element by describing the history of yoga, because the history of yoga cannot explain the meaning of yoga. It should also be obvious that we cannot determine the significance of this mystical element by studying the etymology or historical development of the term. Change and development must be accounted for as transformations within a system.

Let us examine a slightly different aspect of scholarship on India in order to illustrate my basic argument. A review of most books on India's mythology reveals that the predominant approach is to single out individual deities for examination and explanation. We have numerous texts which examine individual Vedic gods and goddesses, Vishnu, Shiva, Pārvatī, and Lakshmī. Creating a list of gods and goddesses has become the traditional mode of presenting India's rich and complex mythology.

Anyone teaching Hinduism or introductory courses on religion in the past four years has undoubtedly welcomed the appearance of two excellent anthologies of Hindu myths.[16] Although the collections of myths were assembled by different authors, the organization is almost identical; myths of origin, of Vishnu, Krishna, Shiva, and then a section on the goddess.[17] The significance of the myths and deities is usually presented by a quasi-historical and etymological account of the stories. The artificial nature of these classificatory schemata becomes evident when we reach the short section on the goddess in each volume, for she has in fact been present throughout most of the selections. What we need in order to understand Hindu polytheism is a new systematic analysis of the deities as elements of a system. The significance of a deity would be analysed as a functional relation with other deities in the system. Hindu polytheism is a complex set of relations which scholarship has dismembered under the illusion that the examination of individual elements will somehow explain the system. Once again, the deities appear more mysterious by the very fact of abstracting them from the system of which they formed an integral part. And their mysteriousness is compounded once they are 'mystified' as symbolic representations of the ascetic tradition; the sexual union of Shiva and Pārvatī, for example, becomes the symbolic expression of the 'mysticism' of the Upanishads or classical yoga.

The first step towards overcoming this error is to define the semantic system in which the renouncer or ascetic is an element. We may begin by postulating that Indian asceticism, in both its Hindu and Buddhist forms, is in oppositional relation with what it has renounced. We may designate the distinctive feature of Indian asceticism as 'other-worldly'. The significance of this feature is its functional relation with what is 'this-worldly'. What is important for this distinctive feature is the vocation described by the Eightfold path of classical yoga and Buddhism. It is the Eightfold path in each of these renouncing traditions which describes the renouncer in his opposition to 'this world'.

In our haste to unlock the meaning of *saccidānanda, samādhī, mokṣa,* and *nirvāṇa,* we often overlook the context in which these terms are found. We need to do more than simply look up the terms in a lexicon or trace their historical usage. The terms are found in a specific vocation, the life of an ascetic. If *samādhi,* the eighth stage in classical yoga, is the ascetic goal, then the necessary condition for attaining that goal is the fulfilment of the very first stage. In fact, the eight stages of yoga can be viewed as the definition of liberation. In this sense a great deal of what has been written about the ascetic's mystical experiences becomes irrelevant because concentration on the last three or four stages of yoga produces a distortion of its significance. The point of departure for any yogi is not meditation. The necessary condition for 'liberation' requires the renunciation of caste.

A brief review of Patañjali's *Yoga Sūtra,* will illustrate my point. *Yoga Sūtra,* II.29, defines asceticism as constituted by eight limbs: 1. Abstention (*yama*), 2. Observance (*niyama*), 3. Bodily postures (*āsana*), 4. Breath control (*prāṇāyāma*), 5. Sense withdrawal (*pratyāhāra*), 6. Concentration (*Dhāraṇā*), 7. Meditation (*Dhyāna*), and 8. Contemplation (*samādhi*). Now if you are familiar with this eightfold definition of classical asceticism in Hinduism you are also aware of the fact that most scholars describe them as 'techniques' for reaching the mystical goal. Eliade, for example, calls his chapter on the eight limbs of yoga, 'Techniques for Autonomy' and states that, 'the first two groups, *yama* and *niyama,* obviously constitute the

necessary preliminaries for any type of asceticism, hence there is
nothing specifically yogic in them', that 'these restraints can be
recognized by all systems of ethics and realized by an apprentice
Yogin as well as by any pure and upright man'.[18] This view is as
mistaken as it is popular. First of all, the eight limbs of yoga are no
more 'techniques' than marriage is a 'technique' for reproduction.
Second, a brief description of the first limb of yoga, abstention,
should correct the notion that 'any pure and upright man' can realize
it.

   Yoga Sūtra, II.30, describes abstention as consisting of five parts:
1. Non-violence (*ahiṃsā*), 2. Truth (*satya*), 3. Not stealing (*asteya*),
4. Chastity (*brahmacarya*), and 5. Non-possession (*aparigraha*).
Commentaries on the *Sūtra*, such as Vyāsa's, make it clear that the
five abstentions are not simply moral rules which can be realized by
any upright man. They are not prescribed for any pure and upright
man, they are rules for the ascetic who has renounced caste. No
upright *Kṣatriya*, for example, could follow non-violence, for this
would violate his *dharma* as a warrior, which, as Arjuna is told in the
Bhagavadgītā, is to fight. And no one in caste could follow the rule of
non-possession. It should be obvious that no upright member of the
caste system could follow the rule of chastity—complete abstention
from sexual activity in speech, thought, and act.

   Yoga Sūtra, II.31, calls the five rules of abstention the 'supreme
vow' (*mahāvrata*), which is to be followed without regard to caste,
place, or time. In other words, the ascetic breaks away from the
practice of caste rules, and the observance of rituals (chastity, for
example), at particular sacred places, such as pilgrimage sites or
temples, and sacred times, such as a particular time of the month or
year. To undertake the supreme vow is to renounce caste, and the
renunciation of caste *is* liberation from *karma*.

   Buddhism in India follows the same path. To gain release from
suffering, one must become an ascetic, follow the eightfold path. To
become a monk is to 'fare lonely as a rhinoceros', giving up
companionship, the ties of kin, son, wife, father, mother, and wealth.
The monk roams free as an untethered deer, beyond joys and pains,
delights and sorrows. The *arhat* who has done what is to be done, who
has laid down the burden and knows *nirvāṇa* as *nirvāṇa*, 'does not
think of *nirvāṇa*, he does not think of himself as *nirvāṇa*, he does not
think of himself in *nirvāṇa*, he does not think "*nirvāṇa* is mine", and

he does not think of himself in *nirvāṇa*, he does not rejoice in *nirvāṇa*' (*Majjhima-Nikāya*, I.4).

The significance of Indian Buddhism is not to be sought primarily or essentially in contemplation or the meaning of the term '*nirvāṇa*'. The central significance of Indian Buddhism is to be found in the oppositional relation of the eightfold path to 'this world' (caste). It is the oppositional relation of both elements which defines them and provides us with the semantic field of India's religion.

Now the distinctive feature of 'this world' in India is caste. Thus, the semantic field which constitutes Indian religion as a rational system, which defines the elements of the system, is the relation asceticism–caste. And when we break this relation by singling out *either* of the bipolar elements as the essence of Hinduism we distort the semantic field and hence the reality we are trying to explain.

Once the relation ascetism–caste is broken, Indian asceticism appears to take on a life of its own. Yoga becomes a subject of study in itself or it is compared to other 'mystical techniques'. Given the postulates of this essay such approaches to yoga become impossible. The *Yoga Sūtras* as one element in India's religious system have no significance as such. The semantic field of such *Sūtras* as well as their commentaries is not mysticism, but the *Dharma Sūtras* and *Shastras* of caste which stress the life of the householder as the supreme stage in life. This does not mean that comparison is impossible. However, when we do begin to compare, the analysis will have to involve the comparison of the semantic fields, of the different religions rather than certain elements in each of them. It may well be the case that once we begin this kind of analysis we shall discover that there are a finite set of rules which constitute the religious systems of the world. But be this as it may, one thing does seem clear. Once we place yoga back in its proper setting as an element in a system the mystic illusion disappears.

The fact that this has been overlooked in our quest for the meaning of Indian mysticism is confirmed by text after text which omit caste as an essential element for our understanding of the meaning of yoga and Buddhism. It is precisely this distorted understanding of yoga and Buddhism as semantically independent of the world of caste which perceives yoga or Buddhism as the paradigm of the religious life in India. A few examples will suffice to illustrate the widespread assumption that caste is not of primary significance in our understanding of Indian mysticism.

Let us begin with a popular text which has been read by literally thousands of undergraduates. In what must be one of the most successful texts on the religions of mankind, Noss has this to say about caste:

> And now [after the Aryan occupation], though the separation between classes was not hard and fast, there were definitely coming into being four distinct social groups – the Kshatriyas or nobles, the Brahmins or priests, the Vaisyas or Aryan common people, and last the enslaved Shudras or non-Aryan blacks . . . There also existed a struggle for social prestige between the ruling nobles and the Brahmins; each group, in the name either of use or wont, or of religion and supernatural prerogative, claiming final and supreme authority.[19]

Ringgren and Ström are more sophisticated. They do not view caste as the result of a power struggle between upper castes. They describe caste as 'primarily a social system based on division of labour', caste 'takes on a decisive religious significance by the fact that the individual is believed to be able to change his caste through piety and good morals in a future existence'.[20]

R. N. Dandekar divides the tradition in the following way: 'Hinduism as a religion must be distinguished from Hinduism as a social organization'.[21] Later on in the essay Dandekar admits that one of the distinctive features of Hinduism is the 'belief in the ideological complex of *karma-saṃsāra-mokṣa* on the metaphysical-ethical plane and the acceptance of the caste system on the socio-ethical plane'.[22] In other words, Hinduism *as a religion* does encompass both asceticism and caste.

According to Noss, caste is the result of exploitation which is then rationalized by the doctrine of *karma*. For Ringgren and Ström, caste is primarily a division of labour, that is to say, it is basically an economic and political system, a judgement in which Dandekar seems to concur. Noss represents the well-known view of religion as an ideology for the exploitation of labour. From this point of view religion is artificial; it can, perhaps should, be overthrown by the working class. The perplexing question is, how have millions of Hindus been duped by this ideology for over two thousand years?

If we take the more modern view of caste as represented by Ringgren, Ström, and Dandekar, then the decisive significance of Hinduism as a religion is its function in maintaining the caste system as a division of labour. For what the Hindu believes does not change the economic system represented in caste, it reinforces it. The Hindu believes that if he lives a pious and moral life he can change his caste status in a *future* existence. It is not true, therefore, that religion explains the caste system. On the contrary, Hinduism as a set of religious beliefs is explained as a function of the caste system. The effect of such religious beliefs is to satisfy certain needs produced by this particular economic/political system.

I shall not repeat the criticism which has demonstrated the basic weakness of functionalism.[23] What is important for my argument is that, even when caste is mentioned in texts on Indian religion, the system is not viewed as an essential aspect of religion. And the crucial point of this essay is that none of the texts I have reviewed includes the caste system as a necessary element for understanding the mystical tradition. The relation, asceticism–caste, is broken apart into two separate elements and the mystical element, the ascetic tradition, then appears to take on a life of its own. Hinduism becomes the history of the ascetic tradition from the Upanishads to Bhaktivedanta's commentary on the *Bhagavadgītā*. I can think of no example which illustrates more clearly the larger thesis of this essay.

We can now specify another reason for the predominant emphasis on mysticism in scholarship on India's religion. Most, if not all, historians of religion have accepted the sociological premise; caste is primarily a division of labour, an economic/political system. Caste is a species of class.

V

The task in this final section of the essay will be divided into three parts. First, I shall demonstrate that the social scientific view of caste which historians of religion have accepted is false. Secondly, I shall briefly describe caste as a religious system. We shall then be in a position to understand how the ascetic, Indian mysticism, can only be fully explained as one of the bipolar elements in the totality of Hinduism as a religious system.[24]

As we have seen, for at least fifty years caste has been described as social class. We have known, since the discovery of India by the West, that caste is a hierarchical system comprised of four units: *Brahmans* who are ritual specialists, *Kṣatriyas* who are political/military specialists, *Vaiśyas* the merchant specialists, and *Śudras* who are service specialists. The primary task in the study of the caste system has been the differentiation of this hierarchy along economic and political lines, showing that there is a correlation or congruence between wealth, power, and ritual status. This explanation assumes that ritual rank follows economic rank; ritual validates the political/economic system. This assumption, however, breaks down when it is applied to the caste system. Although the problem is a complex one, the breakdown of the explanation can be easily demonstrated. The two extremes of the caste system, the *Brahmans* and *Śudras*, contradict the explanation. *Brahmans* are not necessarily wealthy or powerful and yet they are the highest unit in ritual rank in the hierarchical system. Furthermore, it is the *Kṣatriya*, not the *Brahman*, who has consistently been defined as wielding political power in the various Shastric texts. And the *Kṣatriya* is always placed below the *Brahman* in the hierarchical system; ritual status is placed above political status. Conversely, *Śudras* are lowest in ritual rank and are not necessarily powerless or poor. Moreover, regardless of the accumulation of wealth or power, the ritual status of *Brahman* and *Śudra* always remains the same. Thus the assumption that ritual status follows economic rank is refuted by the extreme ends of the system.[25] The caste system cannot be explained by a political/economic class theory. Such explanations fail because they cannot account for the extreme ends of the system, the *Brahman* and *Śudra*. Ritual status, therefore, *is not* congruent or correlative to the division of labour in economic or political terms.

Caste is an essentially religious system. Dumont has, I believe, convincingly demonstrated that the basic set of oppositions which constitute the caste system is a complementary ritual relation between the pure and the impure. The basic structure of the caste system is neither economic nor political, but religious. The principle of pollution constitutes the *form* of the system in both theory and practice.

The complementary set of relations based upon the principle of pure/impure can be analysed on several levels (see figure). One of the more interesting is that both *Brahmans* and *Sudras*, who constitute

The Structure of India's Religious System

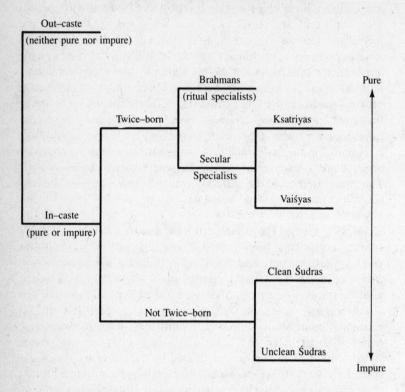

the extreme limits of pure/impure, are both service castes. Furthermore, it is this extreme set of relations which encompasses the 'political' (*Kṣatriya*) and 'economic' (*Vaiśya*) elements of the system. Finally, we cannot account for the system by focusing upon one element in it. It is the relations between the elements which give them their significance. The *Brahman* is pure and his rituals purify *because* of the relation which defines him in hierarchical opposition to the *Śudra* who is impure and pollutes.

Dumont has provided an extremely important conclusion grounded on his analysis of caste as a hierarchical system based upon the bipolar relations pure/impure: 'To say that the world of caste is a world of relations is to say that the particular caste and the particular man have no substance: they exist empirically, but they have no reality in thought, no Being.'[26] The importance of this conclusion for our analysis of the ascetic tradition will become clear later in this essay.

We are now in a position from which the significance of the mystical element of India's ascetic tradition can be fully perceived. The Indian ascetic is in opposition to caste. The renouncer is out-of-caste (see figure). The ascetic, the mystical element in India's religious history, is a transformation of a hierarchical system based upon the pure and impure into its opposite. The basic relation, in-caste/out-of-caste (caste/asceticism) can be described as a relation between 'pure/impure' (caste) and its opposite, 'neither pure/impure' (asceticism). Thus, just as the pure is in opposition to the impure in caste, the ascetic is in opposition to caste, or pure is to impure as asceticism is to caste.

Some descriptions of the renouncer as in opposition with caste – as out-of-caste – will illustrate the basic structure of this religious system. First, anyone has the right to renounce caste and become an ascetic.[27] The significance of this rule of *Dharma* has been overlooked in most of the publications on modern reform movements in India. Gandhi's 'asceticism' and Ambedkar, an untouchable who 'converted' to Buddhism in 1956, involve much more than political reform.[28] Both followed the ancient rule in their battle to liberate untouchables. The millions of Hindus who followed Ambedkar into Buddhism also put into practice this rule of *Dharma*. To become out-of-caste is to become neither pure nor impure.

As we shall see in a moment, caste as a set of relations between the pure and impure affirms *karma*. The renouncer, out-of-caste, eliminates *karma* altogether. Although anyone has the right to renounce caste (a rule put to brilliant use by Ambedkar), we must remember that to move out-of-caste does not eliminate or abolish caste, since the one is a necessary condition for the existence of the other. By renouncing caste the ascetic gives away all his goods and loses all rights to family property. He owns nothing, produces nothing, and is entirely dependent upon what he has renounced. He 'draws his fire into himself', that is to say, he completes his own funeral rites.[29] He is not touched by impurity, which is to say that he is not touched by purity either, he is neither pure nor impure. He is buried not cremated.[30] To be out-of-caste is to be in opposition to the in-caste cosmological system in which death is transformed into a transition ritual which recreates a person into an ancestor at death. Thus, to be out-of-caste is to *be* immortal; caste affirms *karma*, the renouncer negates it.

It is a mistake to view *karma* as something negative, something which we must struggle to overcome. This distortion of the meaning of the term is a consequence of the over-emphasis upon Indian asceticism. *Karma* is related to *Dharma*. Good *Karma* is good *Dharma*. And, as Krishna instructs Arjuna in the *Bhagavadgītā*, 'it is better to perform one's own *dharma* though imperfectly, than another's well performed' (III. 35). Action in the world of caste is always translated as performing one's duty (*dharma*). Although one's duty varies within the caste system, the *Dharma Sūtras* often describe this complex notion as consisting of three debts which all twice-born Hindus at least must pay. The first is to the sages by means of the study of the *Vedas*. The second is to the gods by the performance of *pūjā* or sacrifice. The last is to the ancestors by founding a household. The duty to these three classes of beings is fully described in the ritual texts called *Gṛihya Sūtras*. It is man, through karmic action, that is, ritual action, who sustains and mediates between sages, gods, and ancestors through the performance of his *dharma*.

The rites of passage from birth, initiation into caste and the study of the *Veda*, marriage, and death, affirm *karma* as the threefold mortal condition of all things, which is birth, death, and rebirth. And it is important to note that in this ritual system it is marriage, the establishment of a household, that mediates or establishes the relation between birth and death. Moreover, it is the establishment of a household that provides the necessary condition for paying the threefold debt to the sages, gods, and ancestors. It is in marriage that sons are born who will in turn study the Veda and perform the necessary rituals for the ancestors upon the death of the father.

This brief description of life in caste is sufficient to confirm the striking opposition of the renouncer. The renouncer negates *karma* by taking one simple but awesome step; he renounces the life of the householder. To renounce marriage entails the renunciation of *dharma* and the debt that is owed to sages, gods, and ancestors. The *Bṛihadāranyaka Upanishad* makes this very clear:

> Such a one [the unborn *atman*] the Brahmans desire to know by repetition of the Vedas, by sacrifices, by offspring, by penance, by fasting. On knowing him, in truth, one becomes an ascetic. Desiring him only as their home, medicants wander forth.

Verily, because they know this, the ancients desired not offspring, saying: 'What shall we do with offspring, we whose is this Soul, this world?' They, verily, rising above the desire for sons and the desire for wealth and the desire for worlds, lived the life of a mendicant. For the desire for sons is the desire for wealth, and the desire for wealth is the desire for worlds; for both these are desires.   (4.4.22, tr. R. E. Hume)

If once having renounced caste a person should decide to return to caste as a householder, he and his children shall be considered to be untouchable.[31] And Śaṁkara, one of the greatest of India's classical renouncers, asserted that, if twice-born, a person must give up the sacred thread upon becoming an ascetic.[32] The sacred thread is bestowed upon a young boy in the rite of passage called the *Upanāyana* ritual, or the *dvija* (twice-born) ritual.[33] It is the ritual which marks the transition from childhood into caste and study of the Veda. It is the prerequisite for the ritual which follows it–the rite of marriage. Nothing signifies the opposition of in-cast/out-of-caste in a more striking fashion than parting with the sacred thread and the vow of celibacy.

If you have patiently followed the development of this essay I am certain that you have also become somewhat impatient. After all, when we think of mysticism we think of mystical teaching and experience. What does all this have to do with the Hindu mystics claim that *atman* is *brahman*? That the world is *maya*, neither real nor unreal? What does any of this have to do with the Buddhist notion that there is no self? That all things are impermanent?

Such questions are entirely legitimate. However, they could not be raised until the semantic field, in which they are expressed, was described, albeit briefly. The basic postulates of this essay imply that, whatever the answers to the above questions, they must be derived from within the encompassing structure.

We can now begin to answer the questions raised above, and I believe that we can do so in a way that does not render the initial problem we are trying to resolve more mysterious and incomprehensible rather than less; i.e., we can attempt to explain the ascetic from within the semantic field of Hinduism. Let us begin by again recalling Dumont's conclusion with regard to the caste system: 'To say that the world of caste is a world of relations is to say that the particular caste and the particular man have no substance: they exist empirically, but thay have no reality in thought, no Being.'

If Dumont's assertion appears somewhat mysterious, it is because we of the modern West think of society and religion in different terms. Our ontology is the reverse of India's. Dumont clarifies his statement in another context: 'With us, modern Westerners, the ontological unit is the human *indivisible* being. In traditional India it is always a whole, whether big or small, an entirety embodying relations, a multiplicity ordered by its inner, mostly hierarchical, oppositions, into a single whole. But let us not forget that over this complex being hovers the great shadow of the renouncer.'[34] It is the renouncer tradition that has provided the bridge between two contrasting ontologies. However, as I have already pointed out, we have viewed the renouncer from our own ontological point of view. He has become our own self image, an *indivisible* being, 'free from dependence on the wills of others, . . . the proprietor of his own person and capacities, for which he owes nothing to society.'[35]

This view of the ascetic in India is mistaken. For, although the ascetic is in opposition with caste, the conceptual framework of his contemplation does not *contradict* caste as a hierarchical 'world of relations' in which the individual, existing empirically, has no reality in thought or being. A few examples will suffice to illustrate this point.

A review of asceticism in India from the Upanishads to Śaṁkara confirms that the individual (i.e. the parallel of the 'mystic' in the West) in the ascetic tradition has no ontological significance. The well known *Katha Upanishad* describes the 'wise one' as 'not born, not coming from anywhere, not becoming anyone, neither slaying nor slain' (2.18). And after the well-known description of the Self as a rider in a chariot in which the chariot, driver, reins, and horses are described as the parts of individuality, the *Katha Upanishad* arranges those parts in a hierarchical order:

> Higher than the senses are the objects of sense.
> Higher than the objects of sense is the mind.
> And higher than the mind is the intellect.
> Higher than the intellect is the great Self.
> Higher than the Great is the Unmanifest.
> Higher than the Unmanifest is the Person.
> Higher than the Person there is nothing at all.
> That is the goal. That is the highest course.[36]

The *Sāṁkhya* system employs many of the terms in the passage quoted above in its description of the evolution of nature (*prakṛiti*).

One important term in the *Sāmkhya* system, however, is missing in the passage from the *Katha Upanishad*. The term is *ahamkāra*, often translated as 'ego-maker' or "self-formation'. The term has often been given a psychological interpretation.[37] Yet it seems clear that *ahamkāra* is not a psychological ego in *Sāmkhya*, it is cosmological in meaning. It is the evolution or formulation of 'name and form' from which mind, wind, fire, earth, and so on evolve.[38] We must also remember that *puruṣa*, translated as 'person', does not act, will, or possess self-interest. It is inactive. What we have in the *Sāmkhya* system, a very important part of India's ascetic tradition, is a set of hierarchically ordered terms, which, when taken as a set, leave no room for individuality. It also should be pointed out that the term *karma* does not appear in the *Sāmkhya-Kārikā*. This should come as no surprise since, as we have seen, the renouncer has negated *karma* by becoming an ascetic.

When we turn to the *Bhagavadgītā*, the most popular of all Hindu texts, we find that the categories of *Sāmkhya* are used to express a concept of deity in the framework of a hierarchy.[39] Many commentaries, in quest of the mystical experience, trap us into singling out what the *Gītā* has to say about the 'highest abode' or 'highest nature' of Vishnu. This emphasis distorts a complex text. It is the *relation* between Vishnu's highest nature *and* lower nature, the relation between *puruṣa* and *prakṛiti*, which encompasses the universe. The *Gītā* never negates or denigrates the lower nature of Vishnu. If Arjuna has singled out Vishnu's lower nature as all there is, the mystical illusion commits the reverse error by singling out Vishnu's highest nature as of 'ultimate' significance. Arjuna's final vision is a vision of Vishnu in his totality.

Buddhism, born in India, is the tradition which most strikingly confirms that the renouncer does not contradict Dumont's central thesis with regard to the nature of the caste system. It is precisely the desire for immortality and self-interest which cause desire. The self is but a name for a set of *dharmas* which are defined as a function of their relations. Nāgārjuna in his *Madhyamaka-Kārikās* drives this point home when he asserts that it contradicts the teaching of the Buddha to speak of a *dharma* as having its 'own-being' (svabhāva).[40]

For Śamkara, the great *advaitan* ascetic, individuality, the individual, is neither real nor unreal (*maya*). For Śamkara, the individual, existing empirically, has no reality in thought, no being.

Fascination with mystical experiences, with mysticism, has often led scholars into explaining what Śaṁkara meant by the 'Real' (*nirguṇa brahman*). The results of this fascination are more mysterious and incomprehensible than the massive commentaries of Śaṁkara. Investigations of what he meant by 'the Real' are not very helpful because Śaṁkara's system becomes intelligible only when we remember that the core of his argument assumes a set of relations. Śaṁkara speaks of the Real (*sat*) as in *opposition* to the unreal (*asat*). The Real is the relation of identity, the unreal is the relation of contradiction.[41] And the empirical world, the world of *maya* (*saguṇa brahman*) mediates the opposition, for *maya* is neither identity nor contradiction; it is therefore neither real nor unreal.

Eliot Deutsch, in an excellent study on the reconstruction of *advaita vedānta*, has this to say about western resistance to the doctrine of *karma*. One reason for the resistance is that 'Indian philosophy has failed to make explicit and clear just what the status of the idea of *karma* is. Indian philosophers, including *advaitan* thinkers, in short, have neglected to approach the doctrine of *karma* critically.' Deutsch concludes that for *advaita vedānta, karma* is a 'convenient fiction'.[42]

The first part of Deutsch's assertion strikes me as rather odd. If *karma* is basic to Indian philosophy, that is to say, the ascetic tradition, then why the failure to make it explicit and clear? If the doctrine of *karma* is basic, then why did Śaṁkara simply pass it by in his massive commentary on the *Brahma Sūtras*? Deutsch does not answer this question. I would suggest, following the principles with which I have been working, that the answer is as follows: the doctrine is *not* basic to the ascetic tradition. It is indeed a 'convenient fiction' because, as we have seen, the ascetic in renouncing caste also negates *karma*. The silence with regard to *karma* is overwhelming in the various commentaries and *sutras* on the ascetic tradition in both the Hindu ascetic tradition and in Buddhism.

The ascetic tradition does not address itself to the 'doctrine' in any critical or analytic way. I have found only two places where Śaṁkara addresses himself to the question; both are in the context of discussion of the various stages of the person in caste. In one, Śaṁkara affirms that 'The wandering ascetic, with colourless dress, shaven, wifeless, pure, guileless, living on alms qualified himself for knowledge . . . which is independent of work (*karma*).'[43]

The present essay is not to be seen as asserting that the ascetic tradition of India's religion can be 'reduced' to the structure of caste. There is simply no sense in which India's 'mystical' tradition can be explained as a symbolic representation or an ideology of the caste system. On the contrary, caste is in opposition to asceticism. What we must remember is that to be in opposition is not the same as to be in contradiction; black is in opposition to white, but this does not mean that black contradicts white. What I have attempted to demonstrate is that, once we perceive the semantic conditions of India's religion, we shall be able to see that, although the relation between in-caste/out-of-caste is one of opposition, the doctrines of the ascetic tradition do not contradict, but complement the structure of caste. The meaning of India's ascetic tradition must be discovered in the totality of the system. The significance of Indian mysticism is its relation to caste.

Whether one element of this complex structure, the element of asceticism, can be lifted out of the system and transplanted into another cultural system, is a question which deserves the space of another essay. On the surface at least, it would seem that Western modes of Indian contemplation have reversed the ascetic tradition of the East in the continued quest for Western individual identity.

NOTES

1 Maurice Godelier, *Rationality and Irrationality in Economics* (New York, 1972), p. xvii.
2 See the essays in *Mysticism and Philosophical Analysis*, ed. Steven T. Katz (London and New York, 1978).
3 Evelyn Underhill, *Mysticism* (New York, 1955), pp. xiv–xv (italics mine).
4 Claude Lévi-Strauss, *Totemism* (Boston, 1963), p. 69.
5 See Ninian Smart, 'Understanding Religious Experience', in *Mysticism and Philosophical Analysis*, pp. 10–21; also, 'Mysticism, History of', *Encyclopedia of Philosophy* (New York, 1967), vol. v, pp. 419–20. Robert Gimello, in what is in other respects a brilliant essay on Buddhist meditation, thinks that Smart's classification is 'a breakthrough in the study of religion'; the breakthrough, however, soon breaks down. See 'Mysticism and Meditation', in *Mysticism and Philosophical Analysis*, pp. 172ff.

6 Gershom G. Scholem, *Major Trends in Jewish Mysticism* (New York, 1941), p. 6.

7 One of the best accounts of the problems inherent in cultural and conceptual relativism can be found in Roger Trigg's book, *Reason and Commitment* (Cambridge, 1973); some of the essays in *Rationality*, ed. Bryan R. Wilson (New York, 1970), are also directly relevant to the problem; see also Steven Lukes, *Essays in Social Theory* (London, 1977), Part 2, 'Rationality and Relativism'.

8 Ronald W. Hepburn, 'Mysticism, Nature and Assessment of', *Encyclopedia of Philosophy*, vol. v, p. 429.

9 See Lévi-Strauss, *Totemism*, for an excellent account of the history of totemism, together with the relevant bibliographies. I have reworded 'The Totemic Illusion' (ch. 1) for the title of this paper.

10 *Totemism*, p. 9. The actual quotation reads as follows: 'It will be seen that the term "totemism" has been applied to a bewildering variety of relationships between human beings and natural species or phenomena. For this reason, it is impossible to reach any satisfactory definition of totemism, though many attempts have been made to do so . . . All definitions of totemism are either so specific as to exclude a number of systems which are commonly referred to as "totemic" or so general as to include many phenomena which cannot properly be referred to by this term.'

11 For totemism, see Lévi-Strauss, *Totemism*, p. 10. For mysticism, see *Mysticism and Philosophical Analysis*, pp. 13, 97, 178; also, N. Smart, 'Mysticism, History of', *The Encyclopedia of Philosophy*, vol. v, pp. 419–20.

12 *Totemism*, p. 10.

13 *Totemism*, p. 18.

14 A few examples should confirm this judgement. See H. Zimmer, *Myths and Symbols in Indian Art and Civilization* (New York, 1946); S. N. Dasgupta, *Hindu Mysticism* (New York, 1927); Ananda K. Coomarswamy (New York, 1957); Thomas J. Hopkins, *The Hindu Religious Tradition* (Belmont, Calif., 1971); Richard H. Robinson, *The Buddhist Religion* (Belmont, Calif., 1970); John B. Noss, *Man's Religions* (New York, 1974); *Religions of Mankind*, ed. H. Ringgren and Ake V. Ström (Philadelphia, 1967); and the relevant essays in *Historia Religionum*, ed. C. J. Bleeker and Geo. Widengren (Leiden, 1971), vols i and ii. The list is virtually endless.

15 Louis Dumont has provided a framework for this account in *Homo Hierarchicus: An Essay on the Caste System* (Chicago, 1970), ch. 1. See also, Dumont's 'The Functional Equivalents of the Individual in Caste Society' and 'The Modern Conception of the Individual', in *Contributions to Indian Sociology*, vol. viii (1965), pp. 85–9 and 13–61.

C. G. Macpherson's *The Political Theory of Possessive Individualism* (London, 1962) is an excellent account of the ideology of individualism in Western philosophy and its consequences for political theory. See also John M. Steadman, *The Myth of Asia* (New York, 1969), and K. M. Panikkar, *Asia and Western Dominance* (London, 1969).

16 Wendy Doniger O'Flaherty, *Hindu Myths: A Sourcebook Translated From the Sanscrit* (Penguin Books, 1975), and Cornelia Dimmitt and J. A. B. van Buitenen, *Classical Hindu Mythology: A Reader in the Sanskrit Puranas* (Philadelphia, 1978).

17 For similar classifications compare A. L. Basham, *The Wonder that was India* (New York, 1954), and Sukumari Bhattacharji, *The Indian Theogony*, (Cambridge, 1970).

18 Mircea Eliade, *Yoga: Immortality and Freedom* (New York, 1958), pp. 49, 50.

19 J. B. Noss, *Man's Religions*, 5th edn. (New York, 1974), p. 94, also 103.

20 H. Ringgren and A. Ström, *Religions of Mankind* (Philadelphia, 1967), pp. 313, 354.

21 *Historia Religionum*, ed. C. J. Bleeker and G. Widengren (Leiden, 1969), vol. ii, p. 239.

22 *Historia Religionum,* vol. ii, p. 241.

23 See Hans H. Penner, 'The Poverty of Functionalism', *History of Religions*, vol. xi (1971), pp. 91–7; Hans H. Penner, 'Commentary [on Spiro]', *Science of Religion: Studies in Methodology* (Proceedings of the Study Conference of the International Association for the History of Religions (Turku, Finland, 1973)), (The Hague, 1979), pp. 345–51; I. C. Jarvie, *Functionalism* (Minneapolis, 1973), and Anthony D. Smith, *The Concept of Social Change* (London, 1973).

24 The argument of the last two sections is completely indebted to the works of Louis Dumont. In addition to the texts already cited in n. 15, see *Religion/Politics and History in India* (The Hague, 1970).

25 See Dumont, *Homo Hierarchicus*, pp. 75ff.

26 Dumont, *Religion/Politics and History*, p. 42.

27 P. V. Kane, *History of Dharmashastra* (Poona, 1974), vol. ii, Pt. II, pp. 944–5.

28 See Eleanor Zelliot, 'Gandhi and Ambedkar – A Study in Leadership', and Owen Lynch, 'Dr B. R. Ambedkar – Myth and Charisma', in *The Untouchables in Contemporary India*, ed. J. Michael Mahar (Tucson, Arizona, 1972). Neither Zelliot nor Lynch places these movements within the structural framework of caste/asceticism.

29 *History of Dharmashastra,* vol. ii, Pt. II, p. 958.

30 Ibid., vol. iv (1953), p. 231.

31 Ibid., vol. iv, p. 113.

32 Ibid., vol. ii, Pt. II, pp. 963–4.

33 For a description of this ritual see Hans H. Penner, 'Creating a Brahman', in *Methodological Issues in Religious Studies*, ed. Robert D. Baird (Chico, Calif., 1975).

34 Louis Dumont, 'The Functional Equivalents of the Individual in Caste Society', p. 99 (italics mine), see also 'The Modern Conception of the Individual', pp. 13–61, and Dumont's *From Mandeville to Marx* (Chicago, 1977).

35 For the assumptions which comprise possessive individualism, see C. B. Macpherson, *The Political Theory of Possessive Individualism*, pp. 261f.

36 *Katha Upanishad*, 3.3–4, 10–11(tr. R. E. Hume).

37 See H. Zimmer, *Philosophies of India* (Princeton, 1969), pp. 314ff., and Gerald J. Larson, *Classical Sāṃkhya* (Delhi, 1969), p. 200.

38 See J. A. B. Van Buitenen, 'Studies in Sāṃkhya', *Journal of the American Oriental Society*, Part I, vol. lxxvi (1956); Parts II and III, vol. lxxvii (1957).

39 See the *Bhagavadgītā*, especially chs 6 and 10.

40 See Nāgārjuna's *Madhyamakārikās*, ch. 15.

41 See Śaṁkara's Commentary on III.2.22 (*The Vedānta-Sūtra with the Commentary of Śaṅkarācārya*), tr. G. Thibaut, *Sacred Books of the East*, vol. xxxviii.

42 Eliot Deutsch, *Advaita Vedānta: A Philosophical Reconstruction* (Honolulu, 1969), pp. 68–9, also 73.

43 *Vedānta Sūtra*, III.4.20.

HANS H. PENNER, Ph. D. (Chicago). Professor Penner has published many articles and reviews on methodological problems in the study of religion. He is Professor of Religion and Dean of the Faculty at Dartmouth College, Hanover, N. H., U.S.A.

The Purification of Consciousness and the Negative Path

NINIAN SMART

I

The use of negatives, or words which have a negative feel, is common in mystical literature. We hear of the unconditioned, the empty, the cloud of unknowing; we are reminded of the limits of language by such locutions as the inexpressible, the ineffable, the incomprehensible; and we tread that highway to the Beyond known as the *via negativa*.[1] Why should such blankness figure, so to speak, at the heart of mysticism? It may be useful to say something by way of analysis of the void, for even the empty can be analysed, since its context and meaning are not themselves opaque or simple.

Briefly, the reason for much of this language has to do with the purification of consciousness – the attainment of a kind of consciousness-purity. Why should such purity be thought valuable? And what questions can be raised about its viability as a source of knowledge? I shall add some remarks about these issues too. In concentrating here on that aspect of the mystical which is found in consciousness-purity I neglect external visions, interior images, numinous experiences, shamanism[2] – though I do not wish to undervalue such phenomena. But I voyage here more in the cloud of unknowing.

II

One aspect of consciousness-purification is the use of a kind of yoga or system of contemplation which allows a person to wash images, whether external or internal, from his mind. This is well delineated in Buddhist texts concerning the *jhanas*; but can be found elsewhere in manuals of the contemplative life. Thus a state of mind is arrived at which cannot in one ordinary sense of 'describe' be described, even though as we shall see the negative terminology does itself constitute a kind of description. It is common that when we close our eyes we still see things, as the metaphor has it, in the mind's eye. It is indeed quite difficult *not* to 'see' something or other, whether an after-image, or a scene from our lives or some figment. There is a strangely compelling way in which our mind wanders through slices of actual and possible perceptual experience, mimicked internally – pictures and yet they are not pictures. Such mental simulacra of outer experience are also woven into the threads of thought which tend to run like a silent dialogue through our darkened heads. No time is all this more apparent to a person than when he/she is trying to fall asleep. Thus if we define one aspect of purity of consciousness by saying that it contains no such images, no such flow of meandering thoughts, no such pictures strung on experimental threads – then we can understand one use of the whim of blankness: the purity of consciousness is empty, void; and we cannot describe it in usual ways.

For in so far as we describe our inner flow it is in such ways as the following: that 'I can see the beach at Santa Barbara where we often go' or 'I was thinking just now about the time when the children were small' or 'I was day-dreaming about Italy'. Such musings also can be summoned up somewhat at will. 'Imagine a white plate with a tomato resting on it'; and sometimes they remain consciously plastic 'I remember roughly what she looks like but I really can't visualize her features clearly'. Colours, shapes, sounds, smells, feels – all these can be called up. And we thus use their words to describe an inner simulacrum and the foci of thought, memory, fantasy, hope, fear and so on. So these are descriptions of inner experience which act by analogy with descriptions of the outer world. But if the normal flow of inner experience is replaced by a blank state, then that state is not ordinarily describable; that is, not describable in the ordinary way. But nevertheless to say 'Awake, and conscious, but not having an ordinarily-describable flow of experience' is to offer a description. Blankness is itself a property, and not nothing. Thus we may formulate a first paradox (a paradox, I say, but not a contradiction): to say that a mental state is blank and thus not to be described is to describe it.

The reason why this is not a contradiction is simply that in the ordinary sense of description – where details can up to a point be given – a blank is indescribable. But to be consistent rather than conventional a blank is, as I have said, something not nothing, and to use words about it (like 'a blank') is to describe it.

But of course it is not clear that, even though the contemplative experience may be blank, a kind of cloud of unknowing, it is *only* blank. For one thing it is a blank in context – the context of feelings and a kind of exalted serenity: and the context too of the whole search, e.g. the search for God, the return to God, the path to *nirvāṇa* and so on. It has, that is, an emotional context and in the broadest sense a conceptual context.

Still, the purity of consciousness is remarkable in itself. It is unusual and difficult – a certain heroism of yoga seems to be required. But there are many difficult and unusual events and achievements in this world. What makes consciousness-purity especially remarkable is that it acquires by blankness a number of (so to speak) metaphysical qualities. For one thing it, by its transcendence of distractions and appetites beyond ordinary feelings whether positive or negative, and by being so serene, has its own kind of bliss, as mystics so frequently testify. Not the bliss of supreme conjugal love; nor the bliss of heady worldly achievement; but the rapture of great music or great painting. All these may serve sometimes as images of the mystical. But rather it is the bliss of a kind of unshakeable consciousness, because there is no 'because'. For normally when I count myself overjoyed it is in nature of some outer good fortune or achievement, some good thing. The contemplative void is so to speak blissful (and yet not in a worldly sense blissful) in itself.

Note, incidentally, that the line between the transcendental and the worldly (the this-worldly) is not drawn between experience and what lies beyond, or between the empirical and the non- or trans-empirical. It is a line drawn between sublime and ordinary experience. That is it is a line drawn *within* the realm of experience.

Another remarkable 'metaphysical' quality of the void is that because it does not involve mental images it does not involve even make-believe time. When I daydream of Gileta Beach and what we did there in sunny days gone past, the luminescent shadows in my mind which picture the scenes contain time in hours or minutes, vague sketches of time – these are there implicitly, and slip by in a kind of make-believe and a kaleidoscopic memory. But a blank is timeless. 'I saw Eternity the other night'!, but how long did that take? Thus *nirvāṇa* is seen as a deathless place.

One can dimly picture the bright light within the mystic's skull and as he comes out from his rapture the way the world seems suddenly soaked in time and therefore in a kind of impermanence. The doctrine of impermanence in Buddhism is a sort of mirror image of the experience of the timeless.

So the blank consciousness implies a timeless serenity. The context of feeling – that somehow serenity lies beyond joy and so is paradoxically a kind of bliss, but one not to be measured by ordinary reasons – introduces a different way in which the mystical void lies beyond word.

For expressive ineffability is involved – that which operates performatively. In saying that no words of mine can adequately express my profound gratitude I am, after all, expressing (albeit inadequately) gratitude. The very use of 'ineffable' or 'I cannot say how grateful . . .' is itself a method of alleviating inadequacy. Tone of voice matters too. But leaving that on one side, the use of 'ineffable' makes the performative expression of gratitude less inadequate than it would otherwise be.

There is then a *performative* as well as a *descriptive* or constative ineffability about the supremely serene blank of consciousness-purity. This, by the way, does not distinguish mysticism from other aspects of religious experience and practice. After all, the overwhelming theophany of Vishnu in the *Gītā* left Arjuna partially speechless. But being thus struck dumb is very different from adumbrating the bliss of a bright inner void. [3]

There is, however, a set of considerations as to why an expression of feeling or of value should be inadequate. One consideration just has to do with intensity, and another relatedly with the erosion of force. Thus expressive language has its gradations, corresponding to the intensity of feeling. We might think of it as a range of superlatives: 'happy', 'very happy', 'supremely happy' . . . But 'I can't convey how supremely happy I feel' is not so much an account of failure as a way of going beyond 'supremely happy', and on the same scale. So from one point of view 'indescribably . . .' is an intensifier on a performative continuum in which feelings, etc., are ranged in a fervidity scale. Secondly and connectedly a perceptual proneness to erosion affects the force of expressive terms – for instance expletives. A previous generation's bad words become small change the next: 'bloody', 'damn', 'hell of a', for instance, have almost entered the polite tea party and the drawing room. Thus restlessly society keeps creating new superlatives to try to keep up with the processes of erosion. And so, in so far as the language of expression is faded, there is pressure to signal its inadequacy as part of the very task of expressing feelings. So there is here a reinforcement of the disclaimer of expressibility as itself a means of expression.

In short if we combine consciousness-purity with a sense of the sublime intensity of feeling we produce a double ineffability – the one the indescribability of what is abnormally blank, the other the inexpressibility of what is performatively beyond ordinary scales of feeling.

This analysis may be open to the objection that it fails sufficiently to take account of a paradoxical aspect of the cloud of unknowing namely that it is in so much literature pointed to as the locus of a kind of knowing, *prajña*, *vidya*, gnosis, knowledge.[4] It is paradoxical perhaps not only because it is 'knowledge but not knowledge'. Maybe it is also paradoxical because it is somehow in defiance of logic, beyond reason, etc.[5] I have said above that the noetic quality represents an objection to my analysis so far, i.e. it is an omission. This has to be taken in if the account is to be complete. But first a point about paradox and the transcendence of logic.

First, paradoxes are often rhetorical – constructive Irishisms as it were. Thus 'The only difference between children and adults is that adults never grow up', 'Sometimes the only way to get a cork out is to push it in', 'He who loses his life will save it' . . . They are intelligible challenges to assumptions: the assumption that adults are not deeply childish and vice versa; the assumption that opening a bottle implies extraction, the assumption that living can be quantitatively measured . . . and so on. Sometimes too paradoxes are not so much rhetorical as almost forced breaches of rules, though not contradictory ones. Thus some descriptions of strange perceptual states seem to break the rules, as when a migraine is described as including a blank in the field of vision, but not a grey or colourless patch – a real blank without any measurable width, etc. Again radio waves – waves with nothing for them to be waves of – were once thought somewhat of an effrontery to our usual talk and thought. Such paradoxes are not so much *rhetorical* as *categorical* or *analogical*. By these labels I merely mean that because a migraine blank is in a different category from the blankness of a blank wall it only has an *analogy* not a strict resemblance to the ordinary blankness. Likewise the concept *wave* in the radio case differs from the ordinary (ocean) concept and so is a wave by analogy, embedded in a different conceptual scheme from that of water and seas. It sometimes takes time to discover this: the ether hypothesis stands as witness.

Now it would not be at all surprising if mystical states were described by paradoxes either rhetorical or analogical; for the inner life is liable – especially this heroic, transcendent-gleaming sort of inner life – to issue in states which are only by *analogy* describable in quasi-visual terms. Thus the inner light. (Though I do not deny that mystics may also see lights, that is mental images of light, etc.)

Such paradoxes are not contradictions: just peculiarities, or rather, ways of stating peculiarities. Mystical states are relatively rare: if they were commonplace – and religious experiences of various life-enhancing and prayer-oriented sorts are much more frequent than the hopeful rationalist and 'ordinary man' might expect – then we would lose the sense of paradox, as has now happened with radio waves.

But what about dialectical paradoxes, the breaking down of thought, the avoidance of categorization in relation to the mystical or to the transcendent? Not either this or not-this, or both this and not-this, or even neither this nor not-this – the tetralemma seems to close off all avenues of affirmation, a *via negativa* with a vengeance. It would be hard, even with sensible brevity, to deal properly with this problem here, but let me make a few points.

First, dialectical negation has a certain direction – this being indicated in Dionysius (for example) by his use of 'super-', to suggest a negation *beyond* ordinary essences, or in other words a trans-cendental direction towards which the *via negativa* tends; and likewise it is indicated by the differing-level of truth theory in Nāgārjuna, etc. There is in brief something being pointed to. As it were: dialectics here has a denotation but no connotation (its meanings self-destruct).

Second, naturally the dialectical negations do not work unless the principle of non-contradiction holds. Whatever is done, *logic* is not what is destroyed. But it does not have any purchase on the Beyond or the Void, a different thing.

Third, we should see the dialectical process, and indeed the whole process of philosophizing as existential, and so itself, in the context of mysticism, as a form of askesis.

But let us now return to the question of the noetic aspect of the cloud of unknowing.

The fact that it is not propositional knowledge, i.e. it is not directly knowing that something or other is the case,[6] is less transparent than one would expect; because the mystic, out of trance and out of heaven (so to speak), when she has climbed down the *jhānas* and re-emerged into the cheering light of day, no longer sees that cheer, that light, that day in the same way. The higher illumination itself becomes applied to the discursive circumstances of the world and by consequence forms the basis for what might be considered to be propositional knowledge, for instance the Four Aryan Truths. Even here we should note that the supposed propositional knowledge has an existential aspect. You do not realize the truth of impermanence simply from a textbook or a scripture. It is something to which experience and impact have to be added. Or rather, they are already ingredients of the truth to be conveyed, and so the statement is abortive unless it has such impact.

That the Brahman or the Void or God is experienced in some direct way in the state of consciousness-purity is a claim which already imparts tremendous noetic power to the experience or experiences involved. Mysticism thus involves a kind of knowledge by acquaintance which is ultimate. But this 'ultimacy' again must have an existential force. Is it not because the consciousness-purity seems itself to contain something of sublime importance, even of salvific power, that it is so staggering as an intuition? And yet how could something ineffable be so rich in suggestion?

An answer seems to emerge from a number of observations, and since these deal with questions of value and validity I shall present this part of my discussion in a separate section. But first let me sum up.

The indescribability of the pure state of consciousness which I postulate to be at the core of mysticism is not *strict* indescribability. For to call consciousness-purity 'blank', 'empty', 'indescribable' is to say that it cannot be described by any of the usual terms to signify items in or phrases in the *usual* flow of consciousness, which teems with thoughts and feelings and inner and outer pictures. Second, such

terms as 'indescribable', 'ineffable' and so on are themselves per-
formatives also, and help to *express* an off-scale sublimity beyond the
usual rungs of the ladder of value and joy. There is nothing specially
mysterious in all this; limitations on description and expression are
widespread: how do you describe the sublime taste of artichokes?

III

We may approach the question of the noetic power of consciousness-
purity by considering whether so much weight can be attached to
interpretation that the character of the experience essentially ceases
to matter. We must not, however, suppose that the experience of
consciousness-purity is characterless. Moreover, it generates certain
suggestions. As we have noted, a kind of transcendental bliss (which
yet is not bliss) and a kind of timelessness adhere to the blankness of
it. Thus though in no way does such experience verify or prove that
there is a timeless Ultimate, a *nirvāṇa* or God beyond God, these
qualities may be said to harmonize with that thought and are
therefore *suggestive* of the claim that in the experience there is an
'apprehension' of the Ultimate as described in a given scheme of
things, namely the doctrinal scheme of the person involved. Eternity
is ascribed to God; timelessness characterizes *samādhi*; it is not too
outré to think of *samādhi* as thus a kind of realization of the divine.

This is not saying that anyone who had the experience would
recognize God there – he would have to have the concept *God* for a
start.[7] Of course this is not to say that the experience might not
change his conception of God. Indeed, the very impact of the
unknowing knowing would make it probable that his beliefs about
God would be changed, emphases altered, everything seen in a new
(inner) light.

Also, consciousness-purity implies the apparent elimination of the
typical subject–object polarity, and so would tend to favour an
interpretation involving unification of the inner self and God (but not
in Buddhism which, because not postulating a Being out there nor
indeed one 'in here', can economically disperse with the talk of unity,
union, and so forth which is often taken to be typical of the mystical
experience). There is plenty of evidence of the tension between the
dualism which God-as-focus-of-worship implies and the unity which
the washing away of subject and object in consciousness-purity

suggests. Thus it is a hypothesis of some interest that, (*a*) where the mystical is combined with theism, union becomes an organizing concept; (*b*) where it is combined with a notion of a Ground of Being not so strongly perceived as Other, identity is a natural notion; and (*c*) when there is neither God nor Ground, you have neither union nor identity nor their negations (as in Buddhism and in a differing way in Jainism): isolation is the motif where souls are neither, so to speak, rising to a God nor descending to a Ground. Also, of course, where there is no Ground or God but many souls, then plurality in liberation is natural. But where there is a Ground and identity becomes central, the many souls (of course) disappear. There can only be one – the Self. In brief, one does not need much to be able to infer patterns of interpretation of the subject–object disappearance. Thus consciousness-purity itself can in differing contexts lend credence to such varying doctrinal interpretations.

It is of the essence of these remarks that the relationship of relatively unramified descriptions of mystical states to doctrines is one of *suggestion*. The fit is loose but credence-generating. We are of course used to such a loose fit in a whole range of human experience. But because of the aura of sanctity surrounding the topic, and the perhaps necessary reliance on gurus and other spiritual directors, who are typically (perhaps by definition) authoritarian, it is easy to suppose that what the mystic claims on the basis of his own experience must be the right interpretation – and this tends to introduce plurality into categories or types of experience. Though it is quite obvious that there are different varieties of religious experience; and though it is quite obvious that interpretation gets so to speak built into experiences – thus making experiences of the same type different in particular ways – it does not follow that there does not exist a type to be identified cross-culturally as 'consciousness-purity' or as 'mystical'. Such a view has the merit of making sense both of the facts the perennialists point to and of the undoubted differences of exposition, flavour, and significance as between the various traditions.

Before we go further into this question of the 'contextual value' of mysticism in a given tradition, there remains a difficulty, perhaps, in my doctrine of the *suggestion*, i.e. the view that though an experience of consciousness-purity does not entail or overwhelmingly imply a doctrinal interpretation it can be suggestive of it. Such 'looseness of fit' may not itself fit with the fact that a noetic quality is so often assigned to the higher experience, as we have seen. Is it then not knowledge after all? By acquaintance of a sort, it is, yes: but this is not to say that the doctrines and the scheme in which the ultimate presents itself in experience are necessarily as they are claimed to be.

If one takes the world view context as defining truth and falsity for those who hold it – if, that is, one holds that the claim to knowledge is internal to the system and makes no real sense outside it – then maybe the knowledge-claim can be preserved. But such a fideistic stance rests on a half-truth and the other half is that faith-systems come to confront one another in the world. In any event, even in a culture in which a system is dominant there are other strata of experience, belief and knowledge to which religion stands in some kind of cognitive relationship. When the Pope says 'I know p', we think of the Ayatollah's 'I know otherwise'.

Such mystical noesis is actually rather more like 'I knew what my duty was', even if we also know that such matters are debatable. Existential certitude can live still within the wider context of epistemological uncertainty.

But certitude is partly related to context, and to sureness about the way the world is to be diagnosed. Consequently bare consciousness-purity is not enough: it is its tie to, for example, worship of Christ or to Buddhist intellectual analysis which gives it meaning and, so to speak, direction. This is where we arrive at the question of why consciousness-purity, or any other remarkable experience, should have more than passing value. Briefly, we may see the wider importance under three heads. First, there is the impact of the experience itself, its intrinsic impressiveness, so to speak. It has a wider effect, for any really biting or solemn or deep or traumatic experience changes a person. Other experiences, other interests, look different after a glorious trip, after torture, after a sublime dive into serenity, etc. This change may itself be reinforced, in the case of mysticism, by the fact that there is an askesis used to train mind and body towards consciousness-purification. The fact that such askesis has a theory round it, normally, must be taken into account also. It may be remarked too that, if a stunning experience occurs but is not integrated into the rest of life, it is just isolated, changing tone for other experiences, but remaining a surd. It is usual for people to try to weave it into an intelligible framework. A doctrinal or other framework is to give meaning to the impact of such an experience.

Second, the characteristics of consciousness-purity have a special existential relevance. The sense of timelessness to which we have referred may give a sense of invulnerability – having tasted the eternal I may feel that life's vicissitudes cannot touch me now, for I have known a kind of completeness. The fact that we have a purity of consciousness makes us feel we have reached the soul-essence (a non-self essence!), which in other words is the pure form of the person: it is consciousness which differentiates the higher animals from the rest of creation, and the capacity to know that one is conscious differentiates men from all others. So the mystical experience is somehow a descent into the essence, perhaps even the ground of all existence, for what is the world without anything to be aware of it? Also, the mystic sacrifices her (daily) self, tames her passions, rises to a kind of objectivity of feeling, a sublime peace. It is thus not inappropriate to interpret this sublime and superior indifference as a kind of transcendence of ordinary concerns, a rising therefore above what is worldly. Thus it is valuable on a kind of superscale, beyond ordinary computations of satisfaction and dissatisfaction. As a failure of words may actually be a powerful use of language, so a disappearance of emotions may be the most potent feeling. The mystical experience is rather like the monk who in withdrawing from the world transcends worldly status – a status beyond status; the serenity of consciousness-purity is as it were above the most intense of worldly feelings. The characteristics of the experience point to the transcendent and the timeless, and thereby to a higher level of existence. The meaning of the experience can thus be thought of as giving access to something beyond. It is not just that it has a noetic flavour, but also that the noesis is of the transcendent. (But the 'metaphysical' quality of the mystical experience here is not in a positivistic sense metaphysical, for the 'transcendent' here has meaning in relation to a particular sort of human experience.)

Third, the consciousness-purity has significance in so far as it is already contextualized in a way of life, a system of doctrines, and so forth. Thus the transcendent to which consciousness-purity may be thought to give one kind of access is not 'bare' but typically embedded in a world view and milieu of practice, which means that the experience is widely connected to a web of meanings. Thus *nirvāṇa* is embedded in a milieu in which the *Sangha* mediates the message, Christian mysticism has a sacramental ambience and so forth. The characteristics of the experience affect the way the ambience is interpreted. So the noetic quality of consciousness-purity may suggest new insights or what are taken for such. Thus mystical union gives a new sense to doctrines of Christ's two natures fused into one, etc.

IV

The ineffability of mystical experience is as I have argued intelligible within the context of consciousness-purification. Perhaps it is a pity that we have to use the term 'mysticism'. For though some of the classical mystics East and West have pursued such a path to a kind of inner emptiness – also a fullness in its own way – there are many other kinds of experience which are loosely termed 'mystical'. And those who aspire to consciousness-purity may have various other visionary adventures. An inventory of religious experiences seems necessary.

NOTES

References are all to *Mysticism and Philosophical Analysis*, ed. Steven T. Katz (London and New York, 1978).

1 See p. 119: Peter Moore attacks the exclusion of visions, locutions, and similar phenomena from the philosophical study of mystical experience. He is right. But still, we can distinguish. Since one can have what I refer to as consciousness-purity without these other phenomena and vice versa, we can treat them separately. But the inmost rapture which is imageless and locutionless is in my view the heart of mysticism, and correlates with some main uses of negative language and theology. But 'the heart of' may be too much of an evaluation. Never mind. Leaving aside evaluations we can still treat consciousness-purity separately.

2 P. 114: Moore refers to Paul's Damascus road experience, which cuts across such divisions as 'mystical/numinous, natural/cultivated, individual/communal and even Jewish/Christian'. As I use the term mystical it does not cut across the numinous/mystical. It just is not mystical. It is more in the numinous category, from which I think it wise to exclude consciousness-purity. The latter may be marvellous, but it is not outside and disturbing. Hair does not stand on end – for one thing it may have been shaved off.

3   P. 211: Renford Bambrough says that the silences beloved by Otto belong to the *via negativa*. Perhaps. But the *via negativa* belongs primarily to the neo-Platonic tradition rather than the prophetic. But the speechlessness of being struck dumb with astonishment can meet with the speechlessness of the *yogin* expressing his inner insight and peace. The blend of the two forms of religion is not necessary, but can be fruitful.

4   Excellently discussed in Robert M. Gimello's 'Mysticism and Meditation', especially pp. 180ff.

5   See Steven Katz's discussion, pp. 50ff. and Peter Moore's, pp. 106–7. However, often the paradoxicality of mysticism may arise through a doctrinal and living intertwining of differing motifs of belief rather than in the experience itself.

6   But see Nelson Pike's example, p. 215.

7   See the excellent exposition by Moore of distinctions among retrospective, reflexive, incorporated, reflected, and assimilated interpretation. Here, we deal with incorporated interpretation primarily. See also Steven Katz's important remarks, pp. 22–46 and 62–66, on the epistemological character of mystical experience and especially on how the pre-experiential context of the mystic influences the mystical experience itself. See also S. Katz's paper in the present volume for further details of this phenomenon.

NINIAN SMART, M.A., B. Phil. (Oxon), D.H.L. (Loyola). Professor Smart is the author of numerous publications, among which the most important are: *Reasons and Faiths* (1958); *Philosophers and Religious Truth* (1964); *Doctrine and Argument in Indian Philosophy* (1964); *The Religious Experience of Mankind* (1976²); *The Concept of Worship* (1972); *The Phenomenon of Religion* (1973). He has also published several dozen articles and reviews in such leading philosophical and religious journals as *Mind*, *Philosophical Quarterly*, *Religion*, *Religious Studies*, and *Philosophy*. He was Professor of Theology at the University of Birmingham from 1961 to 1967 and then became the first Professor and Chairman of the Department of Religious Studies at the University of Lancaster, England, a post he held from 1967 to 1975. He has also been a visiting Professor at Princeton, University of Wisconsin, and Benares Hindu University. At present he holds two chairs, one at the University of Lancaster and the other at the University of California at Santa Barbara, spending half a year at each.

Sufism and the Islamic Tradition

ANNEMARIE SCHIMMEL

'Sufism is a foreign plant on the sandy soil of Islam' – this statement was made in mid-nineteenth-century Europe and since then repeated time and again by both historians of religion and general writers. More recently, the idea that Sufism is something outside of, or perhaps better, unlimited by a specific religious tradition (i.e. Islam), has been propagated widely in the writings of several popularizers who tend to call every free movement of the soul, every unorthodox attitude 'Sufism', without realizing that a mystical tradition can never be separated from the religion out of which it has grown.[1] As the Sufi masters would say: the *shari*ᶜ*a*, the Divine Law, is the highway, *shar*ᶜ, out of which the *ṭarīqa*, the narrow path, can branch off – but there can be no path when there is no highway.[2]

As Louis Massignon has shown with great lucidity, Islamic mysticism developed out of the meditation of the Koran and the faithful imitation of the actions of the Messenger of God.[3] The early ascetics in Iraq, Syria, and Egypt were well aware of the importance of nightly prayer (recommended but not prescribed in the Koran) which developed in the course of time into one of their most cherished activities – for the night is the time when every lover is alone with his beloved, when man enters the loving dialogue with God in which he glorifies the Lord as does everything created, and in which he finally no longer addresses Him: 'O my Lord!' but: 'O my Beloved!'[4] The constant meditation of the Koran, which was accepted as the uncreated word of God by the faithful, made the early ascetics and mystics discover unending mysteries behind each and every word of the Holy Book; they lived in it, for the Koran was God's only tangible revelation, and to read it meant to meet face to face with the Creator and Judge. To ponder the meaning of each single verse in the Koran could lead the pious to deeper and deeper layers of understanding so that some of them could find 7000 interpretations of a single line – for since God is without beginning and end his word, too, has to be endless, and thus is capable of offering new meanings every time one approaches it. Thus, the words of the Holy Book were the spiritual nourishment on which the pious lived so that Père Nwyia rightly speaks of a 'koranization of the memory', which enabled the Sufis to understand everything in the light of one or another Koranic sentence.[5] The Koranic vocabulary coloured their expressions, and whoever has read Persian or Turkish poetry knows to what extent its imagery and symbolism are influenced by Koranic stories, and how often a seemingly trivial sentence reveals, at closer inspection, an allusion to a Koranic word. Indeed, 'a Sufi who does not know the Koran by heart is like a lemon without scent', as one of the early masters stated.[6]

Besides constantly living with and out of the Koran the mystics turned to the words and actions of the Prophet who very soon assumed a central place in Muslim thought. To obey him meant to obey God, as the Koran (Sura 4/82) says; therefore, to follow his noble example in every detail was incumbent upon the Muslim. But besides this *imitatio Muhammadi* in words and actions, a mystical veneration of the Prophet grew among the pious, and as early as the mid-eighth century, some 150 years after his death (632) the Prophet was transformed into a luminous spiritual power;[7] soon the mystics saw him as light from the uncreated Divine Light, preceding everything created. The tradition makes him say: 'I was a prophet when Adam was still between water and clay', i.e. uncreated. The great hymn in honour of the Prophet, which Ḥallāj sang in the early years of the tenth century in his *Kitāb aṭ-ṭawāsīn*,[8] served as a model for many later Sufis who never ceased expressing their love and veneration for the 'beloved of God'. They praised Muhammad as the Perfect Man (thus in theosophical Sufism); or as the loving intercessor for his community at doomsday; as the final prophet whose finger split the moon (see Sura 54/1); or, again, as the tender-hearted grandfather who played with his ill-starred grandsons Hasan and Ḥusain.

Thus, early Sufism firmly relied upon the two parts of the profession of faith: that 'there is no deity save God' and 'Muhammad is the messenger of God'. However, the first half of the profession of faith was soon to develop into the acknowledgement of God's all-embracing presence; most mystics felt that nothing really exists besides his overwhelming presence. The central duty of a Muslim, *tauḥīd*, the acknowledgement that God is One, was soon extended to mean that 'there is nothing existing save God'.[9] What, then, was the most dangerous sin a Sufi could commit? To recognize himself as a separate entity, for that would make 'a deity besides God'. For this reason the early mystics developed highly refined systems of psychological education in order to 'qualify themselves with the qualities of God', that is, to eliminate the insinuations of the lower soul, *nafs*, or rather: to transform the base instincts into something useful. Just as a restive horse can be broken and finally trained to become a vehicle to carry man into the presence of the king,[10] so the lower faculties have to be educated by constant ascetic measures, by long periods of fasting and sleeplessness, until they are finally transformed into a useful instrument for higher purposes. The constant 'greater holy war' against the lower instincts led in the beginning, to the ideal of conformity of man's will to God's will, to a complete surrender, *islām*, into his hands, and an acceptance – rather, a joyful acceptance – of everything that came from him. While the earliest generations of Sufis performed incredible ascetic feats in the pursuit of this goal through the *via purgativa*, others, headed by the Iraqi woman saint Rābiᶜa, discovered love as the true expression of the relations between man and God.[11] Rābiᶜa (d. 801) understood that Paradise and Hell are only veils which separate man from the Creator, and she introduced – or at least openly expressed for the first time – the idea that God should be worshipped neither out of fear of Hell nor hope for Paradise but only for the sake of his eternal beauty. Rābiᶜa also discovered in her interpretation of the Koranic statement 'He loves them and they love Him' (Sura 5/59) that God's love precedes man's love, which means that man can never begin to love God unless the initiative comes from God – an idea which was later expressed in the Sufis' emphasis on the *oratio infusa*, prayer as inspired by God. For:

> You gave and you hear this prayer –
> Otherwise, how could a rose grow out of the dust?

as Rūmī asks repeatedly in his *Mathnawī*.[12] The alchemy of love made the Path easier, and the generations following Rābiᶜa developed theories of love in ever more refined form. The ascetic preliminaries were maintained, but when fulfilled out of love they were no longer a heavy burden but, despite their extreme difficulties, a work of joy – could there be anything more beautiful than to do everything the Divine Beloved wanted? This approach includes the careful and meticulous following of the Koranic prescriptions and the Prophetic tradition: to love God means to love obedience to him.

At the same time the mystics slowly began to rediscover the world, that world which was called in the idiom of the ascetics, 'a rotten carcass', or was considered to be less important than a gnat's wing. Yet, the loving eye discovered that it carried the traces of God's creative power, and increasingly the mystics understood the deeper meaning of the Koranic word: 'We have put signs in the horizons and into yourselves – do you not see?' (Sura 51/43), and began to highlight the other Koranic saying: 'Whithersoever ye turn, there is the Face of God' (Sura 2/109). They now understood that everything created praises God in its own language, silent or in sounds unknown to man, as the Koran had stressed several times, and in ecstatic states they might be able to listen to the fish in the water and the flowers in the meadows praising the Lord.[13] It is out of this feeling that all nature is filled with praise of the Creator that later Persian mystical poetry developed; but as early as in the tenth century some Baghdadian mystics, particularly Abū'l-Ḥusain an-Nūrī, described the growth of the soul and the cleaning of the heart in images taken from gardens and rainclouds.[14] Already half a century before him Dhū'n-Nūn in Egypt had listened time and again to the unending hymn of the creatures which led him to the adoration of the one, sole Creator.

The experience of Divine Love, basically ineffable, made the Sufis try to express their feelings in a highly charged language, and they often reverted to poetry. The 'sober' mystics, on the other hand, were well aware that the divulgence of the secret of loving union between man and God is dangerous if not fatal for the mystic. That is why the masters of Baghdad around 900, such as Kharrāz and Junaid, developed the art of speaking in *ishārāt*, subtle allusions, which only the initiated would understand[15] – an art which later was almost carried *ad absurdum* in the long lists of mystical meanings given to each and every word, by which the interpreters claimed that even the outwardly most heterodox and hedonistic poem was completely in tune with the requirements of the law if it was only interpreted along the lines developed by the masters. Thus, verses of fragile beauty, which in themselves constituted a crystal-like, perfect expression of mystical experience were fettered by the heavy chains of a 'philosophical' interpretation which completely demolished their artistic beauty. The glosses of ᶜAbdul Ghanī an-Nābulusī to Ibn al-Fāriḍ's tender love poems are an example of this art of interpretation, as is the list of 'deeper' meanings given by the seventeenth-century commentator Muḥsin Faiḍ -i Kāshānī for poetry in the Persian tradition.[16]

Junaid and his contemporaries perceived the dangers that might arise from too open an expression of the mystery of Divine Unity (which meant, for them, the existential experience of man's being carried back into the Divine Unity before its bifurcation into Creator and created). To achieve this experience, long years of asceticism and ardent love were required, a love which burns the heart to ashes before the Divine Majesty; or, to use another image dear to the Sufis, the mirror 'heart' has constantly to be polished by works of piety so that finally nothing but the Divine Light is reflected in it. Junaid wanted to lead man back to the moment in which God addressed the not-yet-created souls in pre-eternity with his word *alastu bi-rabbikum*, 'Am I not your Lord?' (Sura 7/171) to which they replied *balā*, 'Yes, we witness it', thus acknowledging his rule from that moment till doomsday and accepting, at the same time, all the affliction (*balā*) which he would shower upon them to test their love. The Persian poets largely dwelt upon this 'banquet of *alast*', the starting point of creation, which they often call *dūsh*, 'yesterday', while the Day of Judgement is, with a Koranic expression, *fardā*, 'tomorrow'. According to Junaid, man is called to return, at the end of the mystical path, to the state before the *alast*, so that 'he becomes as he was when he was not', i.e. lost in the undivided Divine Unity.[17]

In those days, that is to say in the late ninth century, the theories of mystical love were also tested in daily life. Nūrī offered his life for his Sufi brethren when the government began to persecute them, and Ḥallāj developed his exquisite mysticism of love and suffering, culminating in the statement: 'Happiness comes from Him, while suffering is He Himself'. That means that God's love (which, according to Ḥallāj, is the innermost core of his Essence) shows itself in the afflictions which he sends to those who claim to love him.[18] The lover enjoys these afflictions because they are proof that the Beloved looks at him and makes him feel his hand, even though by afflicting him. This mysticism of extreme, joyful suffering finds its expression in

How could God ce hidden ?

later Persian, Turkish, and Indo-Muslim mystical poetry the imagery of which often shocks western, and even modern oriental, readers in its outright cruelty. Ḥallāj, however, developed his theories out of his feeling that the innermost essence of God is that dynamic love which made God say: 'I was a hidden treasure and wanted to be known, and therefore I created the world' – one of the extra-Koranic Divine words which form the basis of later Sufi theories. Ḥallāj realized that the fulfilment of true love is possible only through death – 'Death is beautiful because it is a bridge that leads the lover to the beloved', as the Sufis in the ninth century said; for in death the veil of corporeal existence is for ever lifted. Ḥallāj himself longed for death and was finally, after nine years of imprisonment, cruelly executed (922) to become *the* martyr of mystical love and a model for all those who walk undeviatingly on the path to God, ready to sacrifice everything for him, including their lives, for they will be recompensed by the beatific vision, or by God himself – for God revealed to them: 'Who has been killed by love for me, I become his bloodmoney'. Ḥallāj, who was not only a wonderful writer and author of exquisite Arabic verse but also a man interested in a more just social order and an implementation of the living faith in the Muslim community, has become, in Islamic tradition, the lover *par excellence*, and his figure looms large in later Persian, Turkish, and Indo-Muslim poetry. Lately his memory has been revived by most of the modernist Arabic writers who see in him not so much the great mystic but the man who aimed at a new social order and was hanged by the establishment, the representatives of religious orthodoxy. His name has been, since long, the symbol for spiritual freedom versus petrified formalistic religion.[19]

During the days of Junaid and Ḥallāj, the theories of the Sufi path were elaborated. Their basis was compliance with all injunctions of the Divine Law; instead of introducing greater freedom, the Sufis would rather add little extras to make their task more difficult. The Sufis of that period usually followed a normal profession, be they artisans, craftsmen, or scholars. Only in the course of the following centuries, when regular orders and brotherhoods were formed and Sufism grew out of an elitist way of life into a mass movement, the Sufi master (*shaikh*, *pīr*) developed into a true institution.

One of the extras that the Sufis added to the prescribed ritual duties was the *dhikr*, the constant remembrance of God, which could mean the repetition of the word *Allah*, or of one of the ninety-nine Most

Beautiful Names by which God calls himself in the Koran, or of a religious formula such as the profession of faith.[20] The Koran had admonished the faithful to think often of God, and soon their leaders developed methods to count the long sequences of names or formulas which were charged with spiritual power, so much so that legends tell of Sufis who, after repeating the word *Allah* hundreds of thousands of times, were so permeated by it that their every drop of blood was inscribed with this word; according to other legends, the limbs of certain Sufis were seen to separate from their bodies and perform the motions of the *dhikr* independently.[21] The institution of *dhikr* 'by which hearts become tranquil' (Sura 13/28) was in the beginning rather spontaneous but was organized later along very strict lines, with every attitude and movement prescribed. It could be loud, as is often the case in the communal meetings of the dervish groups in which the participants gradually get into an ecstatic state, or could be silent, extending through the whole body and mind to set free immense spiritual powers. The Sufis knew exactly which formula should be used at which spiritual stage, and the mystical powers of the names of God had to be applied at the right moment.[22] In fact, it was one of the most important duties of the spiritual guide to see to the correct *dhikr* formula for his disciple at every stage of his spiritual progress.

In connection with the *dhikr*, mystical dance developed: the Sufis, moved by a Koranic word or even some profane poetry, might feel a rapture that made them whirl around themselves. In the beginning a spontaneous movement, this dance, generally accompanied by some music, was to become a distinguishing feature of Sufism although it was always viewed with great distrust by orthodox circles and even by the 'sober' orders, such as the Suhrawardiyya and Naqshbandiyya.[13] The orthodox held that mystical dance, especially with 'unbearded' handsome boys participating in it, could lead to not exactly spiritual joys and therefore prohibited the use of music and dance; other masters saw in it a way of dissipating the novices' lust which otherwise might have found less innocent outlets. Advanced mystics felt that the true lover can be moved by every tune because he is spiritually tuned towards God, and his dance is, in a certain way, the expression of the eternal harmony that permeates the cosmos.[24] But European travellers in the Ottoman Empire who saw the Mevlevis ('Whirling Dervishes')[25] or, in other parts of the Islamic countries, met with the

Rifa'is who on account of their loud rhythmical *dhikr* became known as the 'Howling Dervishes' and performed strange feats such as wounding themselves or eating glass and live snakes, perceived the Sufis as mere jugglers and libertines, given to dance and wild movements not sanctioned by the Islamic law. The more orthodox orders were aware of this danger; the *bī shar*ᶜ dervishes – those who stand 'outside the law' – who roamed through the countries as wandering *faqīrs* or disorderly beggars were always disliked by the more structured orders, and medieval Indian sources report tensions between the Haidaris, Qalandars, and similar deviant sects and the masters of the established orders, particularly the Suhrawardiyya and the Chishtiyya;[25] likewise Maulana Rumi complained, at the same time, of the marauding bands of dervishes like the *abdálán-i Rúm* who caused unrest in the decaying Selijukid kingdom.

Sufism, in its beginning, was an outspoken elitist form of religion that laid particular emphasis on man's religious duties and super-erogatory works of piety, and demanded complete surrender from the disciple. Perfect obedience to a *shaikh* in whose hands the novice should be like a corpse in the hands of the undertaker was necessary to survive the extreme conditions of the Path, particularly the forty days' seclusion in which the disciple's mind was constantly watched by the master who taught him how to respond to the various psychic phenomena that appeared to him during this period: the work of Najmuddīn Kubrā (d. 1220) most eloquently described the possible visions during that crucial period,[26] and a few years before him the mystical poet Farīduddīn 'Aṭṭār had objectivized the mystic's experiences in the forty days' retreat in his wonderful Persian epic *Muṣībat-nāme*.[27] But as essential as the guidance of the *shaikh* or *pīr* was for the disciple, for whom he assumed the role of the spiritual physician, absolute submission to a master could also lead to dangerous consequences; in later times, when the office of *pīr* became hereditary and the master was not always endowed with the highest spiritual qualities, his very presence could impede any major progress among his followers who acted blindly according to his orders and sacrificed everything for him. The inherited *baraka*, the blessing power that surrounded a *shaikh*, made people flock around his *dargāh*; the generally illiterate followers were absolutely devoted to the master who, besides, was surrounded by a hard core of select disciples who would gladly sacrifice even their lives for him.[28] This unhealthy influence of the *shaikh*, who might even become in the course of time a wealthy feudal lord, is one of the reasons for the modernists' intense aversion to 'Pirism' which seemed to them, as to a number of European students of the dervish system, the greatest impediment to true spiritual progress in the Islamic world.[29]

Popular
level

One should not forget, however, that the formation of orders from the mid-twelfth century onwards helped to bring the teachings of Islam to the remotest places,[30] and many of the conversions not only in the Middle Ages but also in modern times were achieved by devoted preachers who brought the simple message of love of God and his messenger not only to the elite but to the masses. Muslim India in the thirteenth century is a fine example of the success of Sufi missionaries. It is due to the Sufi preachers that the various regional languages developed into vehicles of higher literature. In their aim to address themselves to the masses they had to make use of the idioms of the people, for the masses would neither know the Arabic language of the Koran and of Muslim theology nor be acquainted with the Persian that was widely used between Istanbul and Bengal for official and literary purposes. Thus the Sufis sang little poems, memorable and simple, filled with allusions to the daily occupations of women, such as the *chakkīnāme*, 'Millstone poem', or *charkhīnāme*, 'Poem of the spinning wheel', and by means of these poems introduced the basic Islamic faith to all levels of the population, at the same time enriching the various languages with a new, religiously charged vocabulary which then became part and parcel of the newly developing literatures.[31] The heroes and, even more, the heroines of old folk tales were transformed into symbols for the progress of the soul, and flowers and trees were seen as symbols for God – the banyan tree which is one and yet shelters many in its pleasant shade[32], or the jasmine flower which grows in man's heart when it is watered by the water of constant *dhikr*.[33] Love of God and love of his prophet thus percolated down to the level of lullabies and popular conundrums, and although the general knowledge of Islamic theology thus imparted was certainly not very deep, yet the feeling of 'being a Muslim' and belonging to the community of the Prophet who will intercede for his friends at doomsday was more important for the people than theological discussions about the essence and attributes of God, or of complicated ritualistic prescriptions.[34]

To be sure, the Sufis increasingly felt that there was only One Reality behind all the various manifestations in the world. Not only was God, the One, the single cause of everything, but nothing besides him had real existence. Even before the Spanish-born Ibn ᶜArabī (d. 1240) developed his grand theosophical system, Persian poets had already sung, full of enthusiasm, that *hama ūst*, 'Everything is He'. Ibn ᶜArabī systematized the earlier currents in Sufism and from the late thirteenth century onward it was his books that furnished the Sufis with a technical terminology and a well-defined vocabulary.[35] His system has been discussed from various angles by Islamic and western scholars, and it shows the continuing aversion to his so-called 'pantheistic' interpretation of Islam that his main work was recently, in February 1979, banned in Egypt. Later poets and thinkers, who often were unaware of the full implications of Ibn ᶜArabī's thought, accepted his theories of the descent and ascent of the soul, which, based on neo-Platonic and gnostic speculations, had long been in the air, or they subscribed to his theories of the Perfect Man, who is embodied in the Prophet of Islam who thus assumes a far more than human stature, or elaborated his theories of the Divine Names which work, like heavenly archetypes, on each and every thing created. Most poets, however, simply summed up the theories of *waḥdat al-wujūd*, 'Unity of Being', in their jubilant expression, 'He is everything' and sang in never-ending repetitions that He is manifest in Moses as in Pharaoh, in Ḥallaj and in his judge. Or even more daringly they identified themselves with everything created, claiming to have reached a state beyond differentiations so that in one moment they were Noah and in the next one He who sent the flood, or in one moment Moses, in the next Jesus. In this state of cosmic consciousness they might also claim that they were now beyond good and evil, and exempt from the obligations of the law so that Islam and paganism, Ka'ba and idol temple become one. This is the kind of Sufi poetry that spread in the whole Islamic world, particularly in its eastern part and these were the expressions of Sufism with which western scholars were first confronted in the eighteenth century. Small wonder that they decided that even less outspoken poets like Maulānā Rūmī or ᶜAṭṭār must be full fledged pantheists who had nothing to do with Islam anymore . . .[36]

However they overlooked an important fact. That is the deep love of the Prophet that permeates Sufism and thus separates it from every other religion. To be sure, it was easy, particularly in India, for Hindu mystics to join the Sufis in their emphasis on the all-embracing Unity of Being; the Sufis in turn, discovered the *advaita* mysticism of their Hindu neighbours as they were impressed by the psychological treatises of the yoga tradition, by the technicalities of breath control and various ways of attaining to higher levels of spiritual progress. Hindus, on the other hand, admired some of the Sufi masters and even pledged allegiance to them, joining with them in the praise of Muhammad, the Perfect Man, or composed eulogies on the great saints who had reached perfect union with God. Nevertheless, the Islamic background of even the most enthusiastic Sufi poetry is always visible. In many cases, to be sure, even extremely orthodox and conscious Muslim poets would employ the whole vocabulary developed by the intoxicated Sufis, and claim without hesitation that they would prefer a loving *brahmin* to a non-loving Muslim *shaikh*, or that they performed their prayers in the tavern, colouring the prayer mat with red wine. To take these expressions at face value is in fact to read into them a meaning that was not intended, for most of this vocabulary belongs to a long-standing literary tradition. Even mystical reformers who vehemently denied saint-worship and condemned visits to shrines, or gave sober analyses of man's religious duties, might indulge in these inherited formulas and images without leaving the fold of Islam. Shāh Walīullah, Maẓhar Jānjānān and Mīr Dard in eighteenth-century Delhi are excellent examples of strictly *sharīᶜa*-bound Naqshbandi mystics whose poetry is replete with seemingly unorthodox images.[37] The misinterpretation of such poetry is another root of the general misunderstanding by Western readers of the character of Sufism.

To sum up: Sufism grew organically out of the Islamic soil by an interiorization of the basic duties of every Muslim, by a 'koranization' of the memory, an increasing emphasis upon the pre-eternal covenant between God and man, and the introduction of the idea of mutual love between God and man – God's love preceding man's love, for man cannot act unless the Lord has taken the initiative. A deep veneration for the Prophet, who grew into an almost mythical being, is an important part of Sufi life. It goes without saying that the Sufis adopted numerous ideas that were so to speak in the air, and took from the Neoplatonic, Hermetic, Christian, and Zoroastrian heritage whatever was congenial to their own ways of thinking, incorporating it skilfully into the Path. Out of these elements Ibn ᶜArabī developed his towering systems in which, however, the early Sufi emphasis on ᶜ*amal*, religious work, is replaced by ᶜ*irfān*, gnosis: the Sufi's goal is now no longer the voluntaristic one of uniting his will with the will of God to become his instrument in perfect *islām*, 'surrender', but is rather to remove the veils of ignorance that separate him from God until he understands the true significance of God's Unity.

The organization of the Sufi orders that set in around 1150 converted Sufism into a mass movement, for people longed for a more emotional approach to religion than that offered by the traditional orthodox theologians. It seems that the Mongol invasion in the thirteenth century, which swept away many of the old structures in the Islamic lands, including the venerable institution of the Abbasid caliphate, was counterbalanced in the spiritual field by a hitherto unexperienced upsurge of mystical power – from Ibn ᶜArabī to the greatest of all Persian language Sufi poets, Jalāluddīn Rumi (the spiritual father of the Whirling Dervishes); from the intimately tender poetry of the Egyptian mystic Ibn al-Fāriḍ to the active founders of rustic orders (as Aḥmad al-Badawī in Egypt); from the sober, restrained orders like the Shādhiliyya to the powerful works of Najmuddīn Kubrā and his disciples; from the great masters of Sufism in India (Muᶜīn-uddīn Chishtī, Bahā'uddīn Zakariya Multānī Suhrawardī, Niẓāmuddīn Auliyā and many others) to the first and most influential Turkish popular Sufi poet, Yūnus Emre: all the different facets of Sufism seem to reach their climax during the thirteenth century. Then from about 1300 onward Ibn ᶜArabī's theories became the guideline for individual authors and fraternities to the extent that even everything written *before* 1300 was interpreted in the light of his formulations. Although a mystic might disagree to a certain extent with the viewpoint of Ibn ᶜArabī, he could not help using his vocabulary.

There were, of course, always some individuals and orders which worked along the lines of a mystically deepened fundamentalist Islam. Their most important representatives are the Naqshbandis. Coming from Central Asia, they extended their influence particularly over India shortly after 1600 to fight Akbar's 'dangerous' attempt to bridge the gap between Islam and Hinduism on the basis of the unitive

mystical experience.[38] They defended mystical 'sobriety', because the
'intoxicated' approach to religion, as expressed by so many poets as
well as in the conciliatory attempts of Akbar and later his great-
grandson Dara Shikoh (executed 1659),[39] seemed to blur the
boundary between Islam and infidelity. The Naqshbandis succeeded
in creating a highly influential fundamentalist-mystical interpretation
of Islam whose outstanding representatives are Shāh Walīullāh (d.
1762), Maẓhar Jānjānān (d. 1781), and Khwāja Mīr Dard (d. 1785)[40],
who lived in Delhi during the period when the once powerful Moghul
empire was for all practical purposes reduced to ashes.

Even among the most pious Sufis there were always some to
criticize the development of the movement, and to attack Pirism,
saint-worship as it was practised on the lower levels of popular
religion, veneration of tombs, and similar tendencies. This complaint
about the degeneration of Sufism is almost as old as the movement
itself. Hujwīrī, the saint of Lahore, writes in the eleventh century:
'Formerly Sufism was a reality without name, now it is a name
without reality!'[41] This criticism continues through the centuries –
the Delhi reformers, headed by Shah Walīullāh (who had a multiple
initiation into the greatest Indian orders) spoke of 'miracle-selling
shaikhs', and Walīullāh even claimed that 'the books of the Sufis may
be useful for the initiated, but for the common believer they are like
deadly poison'.[42] In our century, Muḥammad Iqbāl has taken up this
criticism once more so intensely that many of his critics consider him
to be absolutely inimical to Sufism as a whole. To be sure, he wrote
against that kind of Sufi poetry which lulls people into sweet dreams
by singing of the Unity of Being and of the lovely manifestations of
God's beauty, without mentioning the need for creative activity. This
kind of Sufi poetry is for him, as it was for Shah Walīullāh, most
dangerous for Muslims. However, Sufism as lived and preached by
Maulānā Rūmī, who advocates the free, powerful religion of love and
sings of the constant, unresting movement of the soul towards God
and of the ecstatic flight of the soul-falcon towards his Lord – this
Sufism seems to him valid because it leads man to grow until he
reaches the utmost limits of his personality and then, as the perfect
'servant of God', is able to speak with God and act together with him,
as did the Prophet during and after his *miᶜraj*, his ascension into the
Divine Presence. Even Ḥallāj, whose utterance *anā'l-ḥaqq*, 'I am the
Absolute Truth' or 'I am God', was believed for centuries to brand

him as a true pantheist, was rediscovered by Iqbal, who saw him as a kind of forerunner of himself: for his mission was to call spiritually dead people to resurrection by teaching them the personal experience of *tauḥīd*, which means to become a living witness to God's dynamic love, which can be discovered everywhere, but best in suffering for his sake. With his revival of the Ḥallājian message for our time, Iqbal shows that he has understood the secret of Islamic Sufism, as it was expressed by his spiritual guide, Maulānā Jalāluddīn Rūmī, who says in the *Mathnawī*:

> What is Sufism? – He said: to feel joy
> in the heart when the time of affliction comes![44]

What can this mean to God?

NOTES

1 Unfortunately, the widely read books of Idries Shah belong to this category; but even the publications of some Europe- and America-based Sufi groups tend to forget the Islamic basis of Sufism.

2 Thus Quṭbuddīn al- 'Ibādī, *At-taṣfiya fī aḥwāl aṣ-ṣūfiya* (*Ṣūfīnāma*) ed. Ghulam Muhammad Yusufi (Tehran 1347 sh/1980), p. 15. For the problem see Annemarie Schimmel, *Mystical Dimensions of Islam* (Chapel Hill, 1975), pp. 98ff.

3 Louis Massignon, *Essai sur les origines du lexique technique de la mystique musulmane* (Paris, 1928).

4 Abū Nuᶜaim al-Isbahānī, *Ḥilyat al-auliyā* (Cairo, 1932 ff.), vol. ix, p. 332; the expression is by the Egyptian mystic Dhū'n-Nūn (d. 859).

5 Paul Nwyia, S. J., *Ibn ᶜAṭṭā' Allāh et la naissance de la confrérie šadilite* (Beirut, 1972), p. 46; for the whole problem see also Nwyia, *Exégèse coranique et langage mystique* (Beirut, 1970), and Louis Massignon, *La Passion d'al Hosayn ibn Mansour al-Hallaj, martyr mystique de l'Islam, exécuté à Bagdad le 26 mars 922*, 2 vols (Paris, 1922), p. 465. (The new edition of Massignon's *opus magnum* appeared in four volumes, Paris, 1977). E. T. by H. Mason (Princeton, 1982).

6 Quoted by Maulānā ᶜAbdar Raḥmān Jāmī, *Nafaḥāt al-uns*, ed. Mahdi Tauhidipur (Tehran, 1336sh/1957), p. 131.

7 See for the whole development: Tor Andrae, *Die person Muhammads in Glaube und Lehre seiner Gemeinde* (Stockholm, 1918); Annemarie Schimmel, 'Der Prophet Muhammad als Zentrum des religiösen Lebens im Islam', in W. Strolz-A. Falaturi (eds), *Glaube an einen Gott* (Freiburg, 1975); id., 'The Veneration of the Prophet, as reflected in Sindhi Poetry',

in: S. G. F. Brandon (ed.), *The Saviour God* (Manchester, 1963); id. *Und Muhammad ist sein Prophet* (Cologne, 1981).

8   al-Hallāj, *Kitab aṭ-ṭawāsīn*, texte arabe avec la version persane d'al-Baqlī, ed. Louis Massignon (Paris, 1913), 'Ṭāsīn as-sirāj'; see also Schimmel, *Mystical Dimensions of Islam*, pp. 214–16, about the 'light of Muhammad'.

9   Richard Gramlich, S. J., 'Der mystische Monotheismus im Islam', in Strolz-Falaturi, *Glaube an einen Gott*; id. *Schiitische Derwischorden* Teil II, 'Glaube und Lehre' (Wiesbaden, 1976).

10   See Annemarie Schimmel, 'Nur ein störrisches Pferd . . .', in *Ex Orbe Religionum*, Festschrift Geo Widengren (Leiden, 1972).

11   Margaret Smith, *Rābiʿa the Mystic and Her Fellow Saints in Islam* (Cambridge, 1928).

12   Jalāluddīn Rūmī, *Mathnawī-yi ma'nawī*, ed. Reynold A. Nicholson, (London–Leiden, 1925–1940), Daftar II, verse 2443; see Annemarie Schimmel, *The Triumphal Sun* (London–The Hague, 1978), pp. 352–65, 'The problem of prayer in Jalaluddin's work'.

13   Schimmel, *Mystical Dimensions*, p. 46; for more examples in Islamic prayers see Annemarie Schimmel, *Denn Dein ist das Reich. Gebete aus dem Islam* (Freiburg, 1978).

14   Nwyia, *Exégèse coranique*, p. 336ff.

15   Schimmel, *Mystical Dimensions*, pp. 55, 59.

16   See Arthur J. Arberry, *Sufism: An account of the Mystics of Islam* (London, 1956), pp. 113ff.

17   A fine analysis of Junaid's position in Robert C. Zaehner, *Hindu and Muslim Mysticism* (London, 1960), pp. 135ff.

18   Louis Massignon, 'Interférences philosophiques et percées métaphysiques dans la mystique Hallajienne: notion de L'Essentiel Désir', in *Mélanges Maréchal*, vol. ii (Paris, 1950); Massignon's *Passion* comes back to this concept time and again.

19   M. Kāmil ash-Shaibī, *al-Ḥallāj mauḍūʿan fi'l adab al-ʿarabī* (Bagdad, 1976); Annemarie Schimmel, *Al-Halladsch, Märtyrer der Gottesliebe* (Cologne, 1968); id. 'The martyr mystic Ḥallāj in Sindhi folk poetry', in *Numen* ix, 3, 1962; id. 'Iqbāl and Ḥallāj', in Hafeez Malik (ed.), *Iqbal – Poet-Philosopher of Pakistan* (New York, 1971); id., 'Zur Verwendung des Ḥallāj-Motivs in der indo-persischen Dichtung', in S. H. Nasr (ed.), *Mélanges offerts à Henry Corbin* (Tehran, 1977).

20   Louis Gardet, 'La mention du nom divin, *dhikr*, dans la mystique musulmane', in *Revue Thomiste*, 1953; see Schimmel, *Mystical Dimensions*, pp. 167ff.

21   Fritz Meier, 'Qušayrī's Tartīb as-sulūk', in *Oriens* xvi, 1963; the separation of limbs during the *dhikr* is mentioned in Dara Shikoh,

Sakīnat al-auliyā, ed. M. Jalālī Nā'inī (Tehran, 1344sh/1965), p. 207; Muḥammad Aᶜẓam-i Tattawī, *Tuḥfat aṭ-ṭāhirīn*, ed. Badr-i ᶜAlam Durrani (Karachi, 1956), p. 159, Nr. 146; Khwāja Mīr Dard, *ᶜIlm ul-kitāb*, (Bhopal, 1309h/1891–2), p. 505; see also Francis Brabazon, *Stay with God* (Woombye, Queensland, 1959).

22 Abū Ḥāmid al-Ghazzāli, *Al-maqṣad al-asnā fī sharḥ asmā' Allāh al-ḥusnā*, ed. Fadlou Shéhadi (Beirut, 1971); Ibn ᶜAṭā Allāh al-Iskandarānī, *Miftāḥ al-falāḥ wa miṣbāḥ al-arwāḥ* (Cairo, 1961); a fine medieval Indian example for the various uses of *dhikr* is Sayyid Bāqir ibn Sayyid 'Uthmān Bukhārī of Ucch, *Jawāhir al-auliyā*, ed. Ghulam Sarwar, 2 vols (Islamabad, 1976).

23 See Schimmel, *Mystical Dimensions* pp. 178–86; a good example of moderately orthodox attitude in: Margaret Smith, *Readings from the Mystics of Islam* (London, 1950), Nr. 100.

24 For the role of dance in religions, see Friedrich Heiler, *Erscheinungsformen und Wesen der Religion* (Stuttgart, 1961); Gerardus van der Leeuw, *En den hemelen is een dans* (Amsterdam, 1932); Marijan Molé, 'La Danse extatique en Islam', in *Sources Orientales*, iv: *La Danse Sacrée* (Paris, 1963); Fritz Meier, 'Der Derwischtanz', in *Asiatische Studien* viii, 1954; Hellmut Ritter, 'Die Mevlânafeier in Konya vom 11.–17. Dezember 1960', in *Oriens* xxv, 1962.

25 Simon Digby, 'Qalandars and related groups: elements of social deviance in the religious life of the Delhi Sultane of the 13th and 14th centuries A.D.' (Paper read to the conference on Islam in Asia (Jerusalem, April 1977).)

26 Fritz Meier, *Die fawā'iḥ al-ǧamāl wa fawātiḥ al-jalāl des Naǧmuddīn al-Kubrā* (Wiesbaden, 1957).

27 For an analysis of this work see Hellmut Ritter, *Das Meer der Seele* (Leiden, 1977, repr. 1979).

28 A modern example of a dervish group completely devoted to their master, the Ḥurr (followers of the Pir Pagaŕo in Pakistan), is given in the fascinating book by H. T. Lambrick, *The Terrorist* (London, 1970).

29 Iqbal has attacked 'Pirism' in many of his poetical and prose writings; see in general Annemarie Schimmel, *Gabriel's Wing. A Study into the Religious Ideas of Sir Muhammad Iqbal* (Leiden, 1963); for the Turkish scene see John K. Birge, *The Bektashi Order of Dervishes* (London, 1937, repr. 1965), p. 202.

30 Sir Thomas Arnold, *The Preaching of Islam* (London, 1896, repr. Lahore, ca. 1950); see also J. Spencer Trimingham, *The Sufi Orders in Islam* (Oxford, 1971).

31 See Richard M. Eaton, *The Sufis of Bijapur* (Princeton, 1977); Annemarie Schimmel, 'Sindhi Literature', in: J. Gonda (ed.), *History of*

Indian Literature (Wiesbaden, 1974); id. *Pain and Grace*, A Study of Two Mystical Writers of Eighteenth Century Muslim India (Leiden, 1976), Part II: Shāh ᶜAbdul Laṭīf of Bhit.

32 *Qāḍī Qādan jō Kalām*, ed. Hiro J. Thakur (Delhi, 1978), Nr. 56. Qāḍī Qādan is the first known Sufi poet in Sindhi; he died in 1551and was the maternal grandfather of Miān Mīr (d. 1635), the spiritual guide of the Moghul heir apparent Prince Dārā Shikōh. Until recently only seven of his verses were known; about a hundred more verses (*dōha* and *bherva*) were discovered in 1977.

33 Thus Sulṭān Bāhū, *Abyāt*, ed. and tr. Maqbool Elahi (Lahore, 1967), first poem. A similar image is already found in the Persian poetry of Masᶜūd Bakk, the enthusiastic Chishti mystic of fourteenth century Delhi; see S. M. Ikram, *Armaghān-i Pāk*, p. 110.

34 For a survey of popular Sindhi poetry see Annemarie Schimmel, 'Neue Veröffentlichungen zur Volkskunde von Sind', *Die Welt des Islam*, NS ix 1–4, 1964; id., 'Hochzeitslieder der Frauen im Industal', in *Zeitschrift für Volkskunde*, 1961.

35 H. S. Nyberg, *Kleinere Schriften des Ibn ᶜArabī* (Leiden, 1919) (the first thorough interpretation of his work in a western language); A. A. Affifi, *The Mystical Philosophy of Muḥyīd'Dīn Ibnul'Arabī* (Cambridge, 1963); Seyyid Hoseyn Nasr, *Three Muslim Sages* (Cambridge, Mass., 1963); Henry Corbin, *Creative Imagination in the Sufism of Ibn Arabi*, tr. Ralph Manheim (Princeton, 1969).

36 For a typical interpretation in the first generation of European scholars see F. A. D. Tholuck, *Ssufismus sive theosophia persarum pantheistica* (Berlin, 1821).

37 For Dard see A. Schimmel, *Pain and Grace*, Part I.

38 A good analysis in Yohanan Friedmann, *Shaykh Aḥmad Sirhindī, An Outline of His Thought and a Study of His Image in the Eyes of Posterity* (Montreal, 1971).

39 K. R. Qanungo, *Dara Shikoh* (Calcutta, 1935); B. J. Hasrat, *Dara Shikuh: Life and Works* (Shantiniketam, 1953).

40 See Annemarie Schimmel, 'The Golden Chain of Sincere Muhammadans', in Bruce B. Lawrence (ed.), *The Rock and the Rose* (Durham, 1979).

41 ᶜAlī ibn ᶜUthmān al Jullabī al-Hujwīrī, *The Kashf al-maḥjūb, the Oldest Persian Treatise on Sufism*, tr. Reynold A. Nicholson (London–Leiden, 1911, repr. 1955 and later), p. 44.

42 Shāh Walīullāh, *At-tafhīmāt al-ilāhiyya*, ed. Ghulām Muṣṭafā al-Qāsimī, (Hyderabad Sind, 1967), vol. ii, p. 246.

43 Rūmī, *Mathnawī* Daftar III, verse 3261.

ANNEMARIE SCHIMMEL received her Ph.D in Islamic Studies at the University of Berlin, and her doctorate in the History of Religions at the University of Marburg. She has taught at Marburg and the University of Ankara and is now Professor of Indo-Muslim Culture at the University of Bonn and Harvard University. Professor Schimmel holds three honorary degrees from Pakistani universities and has received several awards in Germany and Austria for her translations of Oriental poetry. She is a foreign member of the Royal Dutch Academy. Among her publications are: *Islamic Calligraphy* (1970); and *Mystical Dimensions of Islam* (1975).

Experience and Dogma
in the English Mystics

H. P. OWEN

Mysticism is a many-sided word. It can indicate various forms of religious experience. No definition of it is satisfactory. Yet some experiences are, by widespread agreement, called mystical. These are regarded by the experient as special means of obtaining contact with absolute reality. A question that then arises is how mystical experiences are related to beliefs concerning God or the Absolute. There are two possible answers: first, that mystical experiences generate beliefs and, secondly, that antecedently held beliefs shape the character of mystical experiences. My contention in this essay is that with regard to Christian mysticism the second answer is the right one. Christian forms of mystical experience are shaped by antecedently held beliefs.

This essay has a significance for the study of mysticism as a whole. It has often been maintained that all mystical experiences are identical and that the differences between them are due to doctrinal additions that do not affect them *per se*. My thesis is that in the case of Christian mysticism the very nature of these experiences is determined by dogmas to which the mystic has already given assent on non-mystical grounds. Therefore the experiences of Christian mystics differ from those of non-Christian mystics in proportion to the differences between Christian and non-Christian views of God and his relation to the world.

I certainly do not want to deny either (what is manifestly the case) that there are similarities as well as differences between Christian and non-Christian forms of mysticism or (what is also manifestly the case) that the similarities are significant from various points of view. Obviously to the extent that non-Christian mystics hold theistic beliefs and permit these beliefs to determine their experiences the more closely the latter will resemble the experiences that Christian mystics claim to have obtained. Yet the resemblances will never be complete; for Christian forms of mystical experience are determined,

148

not only by undifferentiated theism, but also by distinctively Christian doctrines (chiefly those of the Trinity, the Incarnation, and the Atonement).

My particular conclusions (drawn from an analysis of Christian texts) fully support the thesis argued by Steven Katz in an essay he contributed to a recent symposium on mysticism.[1] Having affirmed that 'there are no pure (i.e. unmediated) experiences' he claims that therefore 'in order to understand mysticism it is *not* just a question of studying the reports of the mystic after the experiential event but of acknowledging that the experience itself as well as the form in which it is reported is shaped by concepts which the mystic brings to, and which shape, his experience.' He makes this fundamental point with regard to Christian mysticism thus. 'The Christian mystic does not experience some unidentified reality, which he then conveniently labels God, but rather has the at least partially prefigured Christian experiences of God, or Jesus, or the like.' He then adds this on the following page. 'The nature of the Christian mystic's pre-mystical consciousness informs the mystical consciousness such that he experiences the mystic reality in terms of Jesus, the Trinity, or a personal God, etc., rather than in terms of the non-personal, non-everything, to be precise, Buddhist doctrine of nirvāṇa.'

Obviously I cannot examine the writings of every Christian mystic. Rather, I have chosen as my examples the four great English mystics. The reasons for my choice are two. First, these mystics exhibit both homogeneity and variety within a manageable scope. Secondly, they are the mystics with whose writings I am most familiar. They all wrote in the fourteenth century and their names, in chronological order, are Richard Rolle, the unknown author of *The Cloud of Unknowing*, Walter Hilton, and Julian of Norwich. I shall treat them in this order and select those elements in each writer that are doctrinally most important.

Little is known biographically of these mystics. Rolle was a hermit who, after studying in Oxford and Paris, lived in various places until he finally settled in Hampole, near Doncaster. The authorship of the *Cloud* is still debated. It may have been written by Hilton or by an unknown person who was a secular priest. Hilton himself was an Augustinian canon who was at one time head of the Augustinian Priory at Thurgarton in Nottinghamshire. Julian was an anchoress who lived in a cell attached to the church of St. Julian at Norwich.

Rolle's main work is the *Fire of Love*.[2] Although he is the least
theologically significant of the four his testimony is impressive. Early
on he gives a sophisticated account of the Trinity. The God whom he
seeks to know is not a nameless Absolute but the triune God defined
by the Church's theologians. God, he affirms, is one Essence in the
three Persons of Father, Son, and Holy Spirit. 'They are also three
Persons and one God; one Essence; one Substance; one Godhead:
and, though ilk Person betokens the Essence, although there be three
Persons yet three Essences shall not therefore be understood. And as
our God, the Father the Son and the Holy Ghost we call one Essence
and not three, so we shall say the High Trinity to be three Persons, not
one alone.' (pp. 35–36) Rolle then affirms the distinctiveness of the
Persons in terms that reflect the concept of 'subsistent relations'–that
is, the view (first stated by Augustine and developed by Aquinas) that
the Persons differ only in their relation to each other. 'The Father is so
called, because of Himself He gat a Son; the Son is so called, because
of the Father He is gotten; the Holy Ghost, because of both the Holy
Father and the Holy Son He is inspired.' (p. 36) The aim of every
Christian is to love Christ as the incarnation of the Son (loc. cit). In
his *The Mending of Life* Rolle again makes it clear that his aim is to
seek his joy in Jesus as his God. (p. 229) Towards the end of this book
he affirms his union with Christ thus in terms that express his
identification with all his fellow-Christians. 'Charity truly is the
noblest of virtues, the most excellent and sweetest, that joins the
Beloved to the lover, and everlastingly couples Christ with the chosen
soul. It re-forms in us the image of the high Trinity, and makes the
creature most like to the Maker.' (p. 233).

Secondly, there is *The Cloud of Unknowing*.[3] As the title of this
work implies the author was deeply influenced by Denis the
Areopagite whose *Mystical Theology* he translated. Hence he is
anxious to emphasize God's transcendence and incomprehensibility.
However, although the human soul cannot pierce God's mystery by
rational understanding it can become united with him by love. 'For
why, he may well be loved, but not thought. By love may he be gotten
and holden; but by thought neither.' (p. 14) Moreover, it is Jesus as
God incarnate who is the object of the mystic's love. (p. 11) In other
words the God who is unknowable in his essence becomes known in
the revelation he gave of himself in Christ. Consequently the mystic
does not have a privileged acess to God. The God whom he seeks to

know and love is the God to whom all Christians have access through their membership of the Church. (pp. 41–42).

Furthermore the author sets union with God firmly in the context of the two following Christian beliefs. First the ontological difference between the Creator and all his creatures makes it impossible for any human soul to become actually divine. The closest possible degree of union is one whereby a human will, though wholly possessed by God through love, remains distinct from him. Secondly this union is due solely to God's grace. The author expresses both beliefs thus:

> Above thyself thou art: because thou attainest to come thither by grace, whither thou mayest not come by nature. That is to say, to be oned to God, in spirit and in love and in accordance of will. Beneath thy God thou art: for although it may be said in a manner that in this time God and thou be not two but one in spirit – insomuch that thou or another that feeleth the perfection of this work may, by reason of that onehead, truly be called a god, as Scripture witnesseth – nevertheless thou art beneath him. For he is God by nature without beginning; and thou sometimes wert nought in substance; and afterwards, when thou wert by his might and his love made aught, thou wilfully with sin madest thyself worse than nought. And only by his mercy without thy desert art thou made a god in grace, oned with him in spirit without separation, both here and in the bliss of heaven without any end. So that, although thou be all one with him in grace, yet thou art full far beneath him in nature. (pp. 89–90)

The extent of the author's familiarity with the Christian doctrine of grace was well brought out by Dom David Knowles in his book on these mystics.[4] The author distinguishes, Knowles writes, 'with great care between the different species of grace, between operating and co-operating grace (*gratia operans, co-operans*), between grace that stirs and grace that assists (*gratia excitans, adjuvans*) and between graces external to the will itself, whether creatures used by God as instruments, or illuminations and persuasions given to the mind by God, and the actual movement of the will by grace that later Thomism knew by the name of "physical premotion".' Obviously only a skilled theologian could have made these distinctions, which place him firmly in the Dominican tradition.

The same author wrote another work entitled *The Epistle of Privy Counsel*.[5] From the latter I shall select two interconnected themes. First, there is an insistence on the indispensability of Christ's saving work and so on the doctrine of the Atonement. As 'all men were lost in Adam' so all shall be saved 'by the virtue of the passion of only Christ' (p. 109). Secondly, Christ is the only way to spiritual perfection. The author cites John 10 where Jesus compares himself to a 'door' through which all those 'sheep' who wish to be saved must enter. He then comments:

> They enter by the door, that in beholding of the passion of Christ sorrow their wickedness, the which be cause of that passion, with bitter reproving of themselves that have deserved and not suffered, and with pity and compassion of that worthy Lord that so vilely suffered and nothing deserved; and then lift up their hearts to the love and goodness of his Godhead, in the which he vouchsafed to meek himself so low in our deadly manhood. All these enter by the door, and they shall be safe. And whether they go in, in the beholding of the love and the goodness of his Godhead, or go out, in beholding of the pains of his Manhood, they shall find ghostly food of devotion, enough, sufficient, and abounding to the health and saving of their souls, although they come never further inwards in this life.
>
> And whoso entereth not by this door, but climbeth otherwise to perfection, by the subtle seeking and the curious fantastic working in his wild, wanton, wits, leaving this common plain entry touched before and the true counsel of ghostly fathers: he, whatsoever he be, is not only a night thief, but a day skulker. A night thief he is, for he goeth in the darkness of sin, more leaning in his presumption to the singularity of his own wit and his will, than to any true counsel or to this common plain way touched before. (pp. 124–5)

Doctrinal presuppositions continue to operate in the writings of the next mystic whom I shall consider: Walter Hilton whose *The Ladder of Perfection* charts the whole of the spiritual life with unsurpassed fullness and clarity.[6] In describing the highest (the third) degree of contemplation Hilton affirms, first, that this degree consists in being restored by grace in the image of the Trinity, and, secondly, that the union of the soul with God is one of 'spirit', not 'nature'.

> The third degree of contemplation, which is the highest attainable in this life, consists of both knowledge and love; that is, in knowing God and loving Him perfectly. This is achieved when the soul is restored to the likeness of Jesus and filled with all virtues. It is then endowed with grace, detached from all earthly and carnal affections, and from all unprofitable thoughts and considerations of created things, and is caught up out of its bodily senses. The grace of God then illumines the mind to see all truth – that is, God – and spiritual things in Him with a soft, sweet, burning love. So perfectly is this effected that for a while the soul becomes united to God

in an ecstasy of love, and is conformed to the likeness of the Trinity. The beginnings of this contemplation may be experienced in this life, but its consummation is reserved for the bliss of heaven. Saint Paul says of this union and conformation to our Lord: *Qui adhaeret Deo, unus spiritus est cum illo* (1 Cor. 6. 17). That is, whenever a soul is united to God in this ecstasy of love, then God and the soul are no longer two, but one: not, indeed, in nature, but in spirit. In this union a true marriage is made between God and the soul which shall never be broken. (pp. 7–8)

Hilton states the ecclesiological and doctrinal setting of mysticism generally thus: anyone who wishes to make spiritual progress must hold 'a firm belief in all the articles of faith and in the sacraments of the Church'. (p. 23) Again: 'test all your feelings by the truth of Holy Church, and submit yourself humbly to it'. (p. 27) Hilton affirms the importance of assent to dogma, in the crucial case of belief in Christ's deity, thus: 'For it is the truth that from the beginning of the world to the end, no one was ever saved – nor will be saved – except through a belief in Jesus Christ and his coming, whether this belief be general or explicit.' (p. 117) A dispassionate reading of *The Ladder of Perfection* can leave one in no doubt that its author's spiritual aim is wholly christocentric and that he regarded mystical experience, in its highest and distinctive form, as being simply the consummation of the experience obtainable, in less intense forms, by all Christians who attempt to appropriate, with what Newman would call 'real assent' and in submission to divine grace, the Church's authoritative exposition of Revelation. And so I fully endorse Knowles's following verdict on Hilton: 'he is clear that contemplation is a development, in higher degree and in fuller measure, of the sanctifying grace common to all baptized Christians'.[7]

Let us now consider the work of Julian of Norwich. To begin we recall the strongly doctrinal elements in the topics of her *Revelations*.[8] These elements include the Trinity, the fall and redemption, the Passion of Christ, and the problem constituted by the presence of evil in a world created by an almighty and loving God. The first Revelation begins with an affirmation of God's triunity. 'And in the same Shewing suddenly the Trinity fulfilled my heart most of joy. And so, I understood, it shall be in heaven without end to all that shall come there. For the Trinity is God: God is the Trinity; the Trinity is our Maker and Keeper, the Trinity is our everlasting lover, everlasting joy and bliss, by our Lord Jesus Christ. And this was shewed in the

First [Shewing] and in all: for where Jesus appeareth, the blessed Trinity is understood, as to my sight.' (p. 7) Julian then proceeds to meditate on God's creative power exemplified in a hazel-nut. 'In this Little Thing I saw three properties. The first is that God made it: the second is that God loveth it: the third, that God keepth it.' (p. 9) Within the same Revelation Julian declares that the thought of God's condescension in becoming man is the chief cause of joy. (p. 14) She concludes by affirming, first, her sense of unity with all her fellow-Christians and, secondly, her conviction that her Revelation was wholly congruous with the teaching of the Church. (pp. 17 and 18)

The subsequent Revelations continue to exhibit an acceptance of orthodox beliefs concerning God and Christ. Thus the second Revelation contains the following admirably succinct summary of the Atonement. 'We know in our Faith, and believe by the teaching and preaching of Holy Church, that the blessed Trinity made Mankind to his image and to his likeness. In the same manner-wise we know that, when man fell so deep and so wretchedly by sin, there was none other help to restore man but through him that made man. And he that made man for love, by the same love he would restore man to the same bliss, and overpassing. And like as we were like-made to the Trinity in our first making, our Maker would that we should be like Jesus Christ, our Saviour, in heaven without end, by the virtue of our again-making.' (p. 20)

The thirteenth Revelation contains a remarkable instance of Julian's readiness to accept the Church's teaching. It was revealed to her that at the end 'all thing shall be well'. Her problem was how to reconcile this promise with the commonly taught view that some men will ultimately be damned. Even though she is unable to see how this reconciliation can be effected she does not reject the Church's teaching and sums up her position thus. 'For though the Revelation was shewed of goodness in which was made little mention of evil, yet I was not drawn thereby from any point of the Faith that Holy Church teacheth me to believe. For I had sight of the Passion of Christ in diverse Shewings, – the First, the Second, the Fifth, and the Eighth, as is said afore – wherein I had in part a feeling that saw him in pain; but I saw not so properly specified the Jews that did him to death. Notwithstanding I knew in my Faith that they were accursed and damned without end, saving those that [were] converted by grace. And I was strengthened and taught generally to keep me in the Faith in every point, and in all as I had before understood: hoping that I was therein with the mercy and the grace of God; desiring and praying in my meaning that I might continue therein unto my life's end.' (pp. 58–59)

Like the author of *The Cloud* and Walter Hilton Julian refuses to interpret the union of her soul with God in terms of substantial identity. Although God and the soul indwell each other by grace the difference between the Creator and his human creatures prevents them from becoming identical. At one time Julian *felt* that she had become ontologically one with God; but on reflection she realized that this could not be the case. This is how she puts it in her account of her fourteenth Revelation. 'And I saw no difference betwixt God and our Substance: but as it were all God; and yet mine understanding took that our Substance is in God: that is to say, that God is God, and our Substance is a creature in God.' (p. 110)

This passage may seem to lend support to the view that all mystical experiences consist in the feeling of identity between the soul and the Absolute, and that differences between theistic and non-theistic forms of mysticism arise from secondary interpretations of the experience. Yet it would be invalid to quote the passage in support of this view. It is enough to note the following points: (*a*) Julian says 'took', not 'take'. Her interpretative correction took place at the moment of the experience itself. (*b*) It is understandable that a person overwhelmed by the feeling of God's presence – and especially a woman (for sexual differences operate here as in every other sphere) – should feel at some time that in being possessed by a loving God he or she is actually identified with him. (*c*) Instantaneous correction of one's first interpretation of experiences occurs in many non-religious acts of cognition that exhibit an incalculably lower degree of intensity than the degree expressed in mystical contemplation. (*d*) Julian's admission at this point must be seen in the context of her otherwise complete identification of her experiences with the content of the Church's teaching. Ordinary fairness, combined with an objective reading of the text, compels one to applaud her intellectual honesty rather than to twist one sentence to support a view of 'mystical identity' that she would probably not have understood or, if she had understood, would certainly have disowned.

In the eightieth chapter Julian sums up the whole of Christian salvation thus in words that decisively show how she regarded her Revelations as constituting further experiential confirmation of truths available to all Christians:

> By three things man standeth in this life; by which three God is worshipped, and we be speeded, kept, and saved.
>
> The first is, use of man's Reason natural; the second is, common teaching of Holy Church; the third is, inward gracious working of the Holy Ghost. And these three be all of one God: God is the ground of our natural reason; and God, the teaching of Holy Church; and God is the Holy Ghost. And all be sundry gifts to which he willeth that we have great regard, and attend us thereto. For these work in us continually all to God; and these be great things. Of which great things he willeth that we have knowing here as it were in an A B C, that is to say, that we have a little knowing; whereof we shall have fullness in heaven. And that is for to speed us. (p. 161)

To summarize, the relation between experience and dogma in the English mystics takes six forms.

1. These mystics constantly appeal to the Church's authority in the realm of religious belief. They accept unconditionally those dogmas that the Church teaches and in which all Christians believe. Moreover in varying degrees they show a detailed knowledge of the ways in which dogmas have been formulated. Assent to dogma affects their experiences in the following ways.

2. The doctrine of creation. Because they assume that the Creator is ontologically distinct from all his creatures they refuse to interpret their felt union with God in terms of identity. Mystical union is one of will and love, not substance. The soul never becomes to any extent divine. The more the mystic is aware of God's immanence the more he is also aware of God's transcendence.

3. The doctrine of the Trinity. The God whom these mystics worship and with whom they claim to be united is not a nameless Absolute; he is the God who has revealed himself in the three persons of Father, Son, and Holy Spirit. In these writings there is no suggestion of belief in a supra-personal Godhead that lies behind this triune form. The Trinity (it is assumed) expresses the whole of God's nature.

4. The Incarnation and the Atonement. The thought and experience of these mystics is radically christocentric. Their whole aim is to know and love Jesus, not merely as a man, but as God incarnate.

Christ, for them, is the only mediator between God and man and the only means by which union with God is possible. Spiritual perfection consists in the imitation of Christ through the power of the Holy Spirit so that the soul is remade in the image of the Trinity. Moreover, union with God in Christ presupposes a recognition of the Atonement. No spiritual progress can be made until the Christian has accepted the saving efficacy of the cross.

5. Grace. Because union with God depends wholly on God's supernatural revelation in Christ it is wholly unmerited. Mystical union, like the Christian life as a whole, is due, not to human effort, but to divine grace. And at least one of these mystics was familiar with medieval distinctions between the various forms that grace assumes.

6. The Church. I have already referred – under 1 – to these writers' unconditional acceptance of ecclesiastical authority in the sphere of dogma. They accepted the same authority with reference to the sacraments. Their aim is to appropriate experientially those truths enshrined both in the Church's teaching and in its liturgy. Moreover, they all show a sense of solidarity with their fellow-Christians and of the equality that exists between all Christians as members of Christ's mystical Body.

I have examined only one group of Christian mystics. However, the relation between dogma and experience that is exhibited by this group is exhibited by all Christian mystics who stand in the orthodox tradition of Christianity. I cannot even begin to discuss other mystics here; but I shall quote two contemporary scholars whose work supports the view that the experiences of Christian mystics are shaped by their prior acceptance of Christian doctrines.

First, there is David Knowles's *What Is Mysticism?*[9] Knowles begins his chapter entitled 'Mysticism and Dogma' thus:

The mystic's vision and the normal Christian adherence to precise dogma have often been contrasted or declared incompatible. The latter opinion is demonstrably false. The mystics belonging to denominations of dogmatic Christianity, and above all those of the Roman Catholic and Orthodox Churches, have been distinguished, almost without exception, by a lifelong adherence to the doctrines received in childhood. Moreover, of the few apparent exceptions who departed from common beliefs some, such as Eckhardt, held their unorthodox opinions (if indeed they had them) as philosophers or speculative theologians rather than as mystics.[10]

Knowles especially emphasizes the christocentric character of Christian mysticism. 'The great army of Christian mystics', he suggests,[11] 'are unanimous in their assertion that it is through and in Christ that they attain to union with God and a knowledge of divine things.' After quoting a passage in *The Cloud of Unknowing* that I have already mentioned he cites the following words written by St John of the Cross:

> He that would now inquire of God, or seek any vision or revelation, would not only be acting foolishly, but would be committing an offence against God, by not setting his eyes altogether upon Christ, and seeking no new thing or aught beside. And God might answer him after this manner, saying: If I have spoken all things to thee in my Word, which is my Son, and I have no other word, what answer can I now make to thee, or what can I reveal to thee which is greater than this? Set thine eyes on Him alone, for in Him I have spoken and revealed to thee all things, and in Him thou shalt find yet more than that which thou askest and desirest . . . He is my complete locution and answer and He is all my vision and all my revelation.[12]

My second corroborating authority is a collection of essays entitled *Mystery and Mysticism*.[13] Among the contributions to this symposium is an essay by A. Leonard in which he affirms that mystical theology 'has no other function than that of linking personal experience with revealed truth'.[14] The God whom Christian mystics experience is the personal God of biblical revelation. 'To interpret the "cloud" of the Areopagite, the "darkness" of Angela of Foligno, the "eternal non-being" of Henry Suso by the notion of a "modeless God" of some sort of metaphysical conception, without recognizing here the God of Jesus Christ is to make an enormous blunder.'[15] Like Knowles, Léonard stresses the christocentric nature of Christian mysticism which rests on the contemplation of the incarnate Son and has as its aim, not the acquisition of esoteric *gnosis*, but participation in the divine charity that Christ embodied. Léonard writes thus of St Teresa:

> St Teresa insisted most emphatically that at no moment of the mystical life, not even after having received the loftiest divine communications of the sixth Mansion, can one abandon the consideration of the mysteries of the incarnate Christ. At one epoch of her life, however, she did fall into this illusion, but only to repent of it soon after. 'I cannot endure to abandon

entirely the consideration of Chirst, and the association of his divine body with our own wretchedness.' To consider the humanity of Christ as an obstacle to contemplation would imply a conscious and deliberate pursuit of mystical knowledge, which is in direct contrast to the general attitude of Catholic mystics. Mystical experience is not the fruit of a direct and systematic effort, but a free gift from God. The end in view is the perfection of charity and not, as is the case with other mystics, a mysterious means of acquiring transcendental knowledge. (p. 99)

The relation between dogma and experience that we find in the English mystics can, therefore, be said not to be confined to them alone. It is found in all the great mystics of the Church. Obviously some Christian mystics have sometimes made statements that are incompatible with what they held to be the authoritative teaching of the Church. Yet such statements are exceptions that prove the rule. When one recollects the immensely private nature of mystical contemplation and the immense spiritual energy it releases – an energy that the vast majority of Christians are incapable of understanding – the striking thing is, not that unorthodox statements occur, but that they are so few.

What finally impresses one about the English mystics is their catholicity. By 'catholicity' I mean, in the first place, sheer universality. What they say of their experiences is essentially the same as what is said by St Teresa and St John of the Cross. And it is the same because they all conceived themselves to be experiencing, not something that they had found for themselves, but the revelation that God had given of himself in Christ, that was normatively recorded in the Scriptures and that was authoritatively expounded in the dogmas enunciated by the 'catholic' (universal) Church. Of course all the mystics I have named wrote before the division in the Western Church caused by the Reformation. Fortunately I am writing at a time when that division is increasingly being overcome.

Furthermore, there is one doctrine stressed by the English mystics that is held by all theists and that distinguishes all theistic from all non-theistic forms of religious experience. This is the doctrine of creation according to which the Creator and the creature are substantially distinct so that although mystics can enjoy an inconceivably close and intense union with God they can never be merged into or become identical with him. The experiential implication of the doctrine is incisively made by Geoffrey Parrinder in his *Mysticism in the World's Religions.*[16] Parrinder quotes the following summary of Jewish mysticism given by G. G. Scholem.

> It is only in extremely rare cases that ecstasy signifies actual union with God, in which the human individuality abandons itself to the rapture of complete submersion in the divine stream. Even in this ecstatic frame of mind, the Jewish mystic almost invariably retains a sense of the distance between the Creator and His creature. The latter is joined to the former, and the point where the two meet is of the greatest interest to the mystic, but he does not regard it as constituting anything so extravagant as identity of Creator and creature.[17]

Parrinder then draws the following general conclusion:

> Here is the true distinction, between communion and union on the one hand, and identity on the other. Identification with God in the sense of 'Thou art That', or 'I am God', is rejected not only by Jewish mystics but by nearly all Christian mystics, by orthodox Sufis, and by monotheistic Hindus going back to Ramanuja and the *Bhagavad Gita*. This is the watershed in mysticism, not between prophecy and wisdom, or Semitic and Indian, but between theism and monism, between communion and identity.[18]

The following points must be noted concerning Jewish and Christian mystics' adherence to the doctrine of creation. First, they adhered to it because it was axiomatic in the religious tradition that they inherited and in which they had been instructed from their earliest days. Therefore it shaped their whole understanding of God and of those religious experiences that are humanly obtainable. Moreover it determined the meaning that the Church gave to further, distinctively Christian, doctrines. That is why it is stated at the beginning of both the Apostles' and the Nicene creeds. Hence it also determined Christian expectations of the kind of union that is possible with God in Christ.

I shall conclude with three comments on the relation between experience and dogma in the writings of the English mystics.

1. These mystics do not enunciate new dogmas concerning God and Christ on the basis of their experiences. Their aim is not to discover theological truths of which non-mystics are ignorant, but to experience the truth of those dogmas to which all Christians give assent. Therefore they do not regard themselves as constituting an intellectual élite possessing an esoteric *gnosis* concealed from ordinary believers.

2. These mystics never give their own experiences as a ground for establishing or even confirming the truth of Christian dogmas. They assume that this truth is established by the teaching of the Scriptures and the Church. This, of course, is a large assumption that they do not examine. They are not to be blamed for not examining it; for the truth of dogmas was, in the light of their experience, self-evident; and in any case their aim was to engage in spiritual contemplation, not philosophical reflection.

3. The relation between dogma and experience that is found in these mystics can be summed up in terms of love. They wrote to affirm their knowledge of the divine love indicated by the doctrines of the Trinity, the Incarnation and the Atonement. Their spiritual life was actuated by the belief that out of pure love God, in the person of the Son, had become man for their salvation. God's love (they further believed) required a response of love on their part. And this response determined the nature of the union with God that they claimed to experience.

NOTES

1   *Mysticism and Philosophical Analysis* (London and New York, 1978), p. 26. In the same volume similar assertions concerning the relation between mystical experiences and antecedently held beliefs are made by Peter Moore (pp. 109–12) and Robert M. Gimello (pp. 192–93).

2   My references both to this and to his *The Mending of Life* will be to F. M. Comper's edition (London, 1914). This edition contains an introduction by Evelyn Underhill.

3   My references are to Abbot Justin McCann's edition (London, 1952). McCann's introduction contains a succinct account of *The Cloud*'s theological background. The edition also contains a commentary on *The Cloud* by the seventeenth-century Benedictine writer Augustine Baker. For a detailed modern discussion of this work – a discussion that fully supports my thesis – see William Johnston's *The Mysticism of the Cloud of Unknowing* (New York, 1967).

4   *The English Mystical Tradition* (London, 1961), p. 94. This excellent book (written by a highly distinguished medieval scholar) contains separate chapters on each of the mystics I have chosen as well as chapters on Margery Kempe and Augustine Baker. It also contains introductory chapters on the historical and theological background.

5   I shall quote from McCann's edition contained in the volume I have already mentioned.

6 My references will be to Leo Sherley-Price's edition (Harmondsworth, 1957). I have examined Hilton's teaching at length in *Religious Studies*, vol. vii, no. 1 (March 1971). There is an abridged version of *The Ladder* with a helpful introduction by Illtyd Trethowan (London, 1975).

7 Op. cit., p. 113.

8 All my references are to her *Revelations of Divine Love*, ed. Roger Hudleston (London, 1952). Hudleston's introduction contains a useful analysis of the Revelations.

9 London, 1967.

10 Ibid., p. 73.

11 Ibid., p. 75.

12 Ibid., p. 76.

13 London, 1956.

14 Ibid., p. 92.

15 Ibid., p. 94.

16 London, 1976.

17 Ibid., p. 119. S. Katz makes the same point with regard to Jewish mysticism in the essay to which I have already referred (op. cit., pp. 33–36).

18 Ibid., pp. 119–20.

H. P. OWEN, M.A. (Oxon.), is the author of *Revelation and Existence* (1957); *The Moral Argument for Christian Theism* (1965); *The Christian Knowledge of God* (1969); *Concepts of Deity* (1971); and *W. R. Matthews: Philosopher and Theologian* (1976). He has also contributed a variety of articles to philosophical and theological journals. After teaching for twelve years in the University of Wales he joined the staff of King's College in the University of London where he has been Lecturer, then Reader, in the Philosophy of Religion (1962–69) and (since 1970) Professor of Christian Doctrine.

Francis of Assisi:
Christian Mysticism at the Crossroads

EWERT H. COUSINS

In the history of Christianity, Francis of Assisi played the role of a radical innovator. Against the background of Benedictine monasticism, he launched, along with his contemporary Dominic, a new religious lifestyle: that of the mendicant, or wandering beggar and preacher. In the history of world spirituality, mendicancy is the oldest recorded form of monasticism, emerging among the Jains and Buddhists from the *śramaṇa* movement as early as the sixth century B.C., before the stable monasteries of Buddhism and Hinduism.[1] The pattern is reversed in Christianity, where stable cenobitic monasticism emerged early in the East as the classical form, with Benedictine monasticism and its various reforms dominating in the West. The monks were attached to specific monasteries, where they lived in permanently established communities. Often owning vast tracts of land, these monasteries supported themselves on agriculture with such skill and industry that they tended to become wealthy, even in spite of themselves.

As an alternative to this monastic establishment Francis proposed his new mendicant lifestyle, with its radical poverty. While Dominic stressed preaching, Francis emphasized poverty as the basis of his mendicant way of life. Drawing his guidelines from the most radical New Testament statements on poverty, Francis presented his form of mendicancy as a return to the Gospel ideal, to an imitation of Christ in utter simplicity and humility. His friars were not to own anything, not even as communities. They were not to build large convents nor amass books.

At the very outset and throughout the following century, Francis's proposal struck many as too radical and evoked the opposition of Church authorities, the secular clergy and members of his own Order. When he first presented his plan to Pope Innocent III and the cardinals in Rome in 1209, they hesitated to approve since it seemed, as a medieval biographer states, 'to be something novel and difficult

beyond human powers'.[2] On the advice of a certain Cardinal John of
St. Paul, they approved, fearing that otherwise they might implicitly
claim that the Gospel ideal could not be lived. Although Francis's
ideal was in principle accepted, it needed the political acumen of his
Cardinal Protector, Hugolino, later Pope Gregory IX, for it to be
realized concretely within the Church structure.

In the mid-thirteenth century, his Order was attacked by the
secular masters of the University of Paris, who wrote treatises
claiming that Franciscan and Dominican poverty was actually
contrary to the Gospel.[3] Even within the Franciscan Order tensions
arose early between those who espoused the original life of simplicity,
with its ideal of radical poverty, and those who wished to accept more
institutionalization.[4] The Order had grown rapidly, establishing
itself at the University of Paris and eventually at other centres of
learning. In the midst of this growth, there was a constant trend to
institutionalize and clericalize the Order. This trend was crystallized
in the administration of Bonaventure, who held the office of Minister
General from 1257 to 1274. A philosopher – theologian as well as
a saint, he represented the intellectual wing of the Order. Through
his administrative talents and the respect won by his holiness, he
was able to give shape to an institutionalized version of the Franciscan ideal. Eventually, in the late thirteenth and early fourteenth
century, the contrary trend reached its peak in the Franciscan
Spirituals, who were in the end suppressed by the official
Church.

Innovation in Mysticism

In the sphere of mysticism, Francis was also an innovator; his
religious experience dramatically shaped the future of western
Christianity. He was the recipient of the most celebrated mystical
experience of the Middle Ages: the ecstatic vision on Mount La Verna
in 1224 of the Six-winged Seraph in the form of the Crucified, during
which he received the stigmata. Yet this vision and his other mystical
experiences were not characteristic of the mainstream Christian
mystical tradition that preceded him both in the Greek East and the
Latin West. For centuries the patristic and medieval periods were
dominated by the speculative mysticism of the Neoplatonists, which
had been given a Christian form by the Alexandrians in the East and
Augustine in the West. The writings of the pseudo-Dionysius became

the handbook for this speculative mysticism, which reached its climax in the *via negativa*, negating all images in order to plunge into the divine darkness. Even in its *via affirmativa*, it did not cultivate visionary mysticism, but rather a metaphysical ascent of the Neoplatonic ladder of creatures.

It is true that the monastic tradition cultivated the contemplation of biblical symbols, which the Victorines of the twelfth century developed extensively through the allegorical interpretation of Scripture. Yet Francis's symbolic mysticism represents a different current; for his form of visionary mysticism is prophetic in character, drawing much of its content as well as its prophetic role in society from the tradition of the Hebrew prophets. In Francis the prophetic visionary mysticism reaches a peak in the Middle Ages. It is not surprising, then, that many of his followers saw him as the culmination of the apocalyptic visions of the twelfth-century prophet Joachim of Fiore.

While Francis brings to fruition a resurgence of prophetic visionary mysticism in the Middle Ages, what is most innovative is the content of his visionary material. Francis's vision at La Verna of the Six-winged Seraph was derived from Isaiah's vision in the temple, when the latter received his mission as prophet (Isa. 6.1–13); but it contained also the figure of Christ crucified. This figure ushered in a major trend in the history of Western Christianity: devotion to the humanity of Christ, especially in his suffering and death. The very stigmata imprinted on Francis's flesh – the first recorded case in history – graphically displays his innovative Christ mysticism. In contrast to earlier mysticism which saw Christ as the eternal Logos and resurrected Lord, Francis focused on the incarnate Christ: on his birth at Bethlehem, his preaching and public life and especially his passion and death. For Augustine, Christ was primarily the Logos as interior Teacher of wisdom; for Bernard of Clairvaux he was the interior Lover, the Bridegroom of the soul; for Francis he was his crucified Redeemer. Francis represents a watershed in the history of Western Christianity. After him Western religious experience flows in two currents: speculative Neoplatonic mysticism gains vigour, reaching a culmination in the Rhineland mystics. But the devotional current flowing from Francis – with its focus on the humanity and passion of Christ – spreads throughout the people at large and becomes the characteristic form of Western religious sensibility for centuries to come.

Mysticism of the Historical Event

This devotion to the humanity of Christ issues in a form of mysticism which I will call 'the mysticism of the historical event'. In this type of consciousness, one recalls a significant event in the past, enters into its drama and draws from it spiritual energy, eventually moving beyond the event towards union with God. Of course, for Christians the significant events were those of the life of the historical Jesus, especially his birth at Bethlehem and his death and resurrection at Jerusalem. Although this type of consciousness was present in Christianity from the beginning, especially in the liturgy, it emerged in the thirteenth century in a new form and with new vigour. Under the impetus of Francis, it developed a specific form of meditation which became the characteristic form of Christian meditative prayer for centuries. In this form of prayer, one imagines the physical setting of the event – the place, the persons, the circumstances, for example the birth of Jesus in the stable at Bethlehem, with Mary and Joseph, an ox and an ass. However one does not remain a detached spectator, but enters into the event as an actor in the drama, singing with the angels and worshipping the infant with the shepherds. This immersion in the event opens its spiritual meaning – for example its message of poverty and humility – draws us into its deeper archetypal significance and leads ultimately to union with God. Cultivated in the Franciscan milieu, this form of prayer reached its culmination in *The Spiritual Exercises* of Ignatius of Loyola, where it was developed into one of the most systematic techniques of prayer in the history of Christian spirituality.

It is important to recognize 'the mysticism of the historical event' as a distinctive form of mystical consciousness. Without it a typology of Christian mysticism would be incomplete, and yet it has not been adequately isolated or identified. If this is lacking in one's typology, it would be impossible to study accurately the history of Christian mysticism from the thirteenth century to the present, especially its development from Francis to Ignatius of Loyola. Furthermore, its inclusion in one's typology throws light upon the wide variety and inner tensions in the forms of Christian mysticism – from the a-historical, world-transcending forms of speculative Neoplatonic mysticism to the focus on the concrete, human, dimensions of the mysticism of the historical event. Once these poles are isolated and identified, then it is possible to study the attempts and techniques employed throughout history to integrate them, whether successfully or not.

In proposing this category, I must clarify what I mean by 'the mysticism of the historical event'. In a generic sense, it belongs to that form of consciousness whereby we remember a past event, of our own lives or of our collective history. But it is more than merely recalling, for it makes us present to the event and the event present to us. This consciousness has a secular and a religious form. For example, when we visit a place where a great event occurred, especially a battlefield like Waterloo or Gettysburg, we can feel the power of the event – as a moment when thousands clashed and died and where the flow of history itself was altered. This experience of presence may be so strong that we feel ourselves swept up into the action of the event as if we ourselves were fighting in the battle. In and through our immersion in the event, we can discern its meaning as it reveals mankind's struggle for justice and power. If the event is religious, then its revelatory power is greater; for it manifests God's plan of salvation history and through salvation history God himself. For this reason medieval Christians flocked to shrines, where saints were martyred or buried. They especially wished to make a pilgrimage to the Holy Land, to walk the streets that Jesus walked and to visit the site of his birth, his crucifixion, and resurrection. If they could not make the physical journey, they could at least imagine they were in the Holy Land, present to the great religious events that happened there.

Some might argue whether this type of consciousness should be called mystical. I believe it is legitimate to designate it as such for two reasons. First, it is different from our everyday forms of consciousness, even different from our ordinary modes of recalling the past. In it we transcend the present moment and are transported into the past, entering into a unity with a past event that manifests its meaning. Such consciousness is analogous to nature mysticism, where we have a similar experience with regard to space. There is another reason to consider it mystical, because in its religious form it provides a path to another form of transcendence, namely, contact with God. The great religious events are seen as modes of God's manifestation to us and of our union with God. Again this is analogous to nature mysticism. In its religious form, our union with nature becomes a mode of God's communication of himself to us through his creation and of our union with him by perceiving his presence in the physical world.

If Francis was innovative in evoking the mysticism of the historical event, it should not be surprising that he is equally innovative in nature mysticism. Considered the prime example of a nature mystic in the history of Christianity, he took spontaneous joy in the material world, singing its praises like a troubadour poet in his 'Canticle of Brother Sun'. With a disarming sense of immediacy, he felt himself part of the family of creation, rejoicing in the least significant creature – in an earthworm or a cricket – and seeing God's reflection everywhere. As is the case with the mysticism of the historical event, this is a far cry from Neoplatonic speculative mysticism, which focuses on an abstract cosmological structure and which turns quickly from the material world and its individual creatures to scale the metaphysical ladder to the spiritual and divine realms by means of universal concepts.

If we were to search for a position within the Middle Ages itself to view Francis as innovator, we could find no better ground than Bonaventure's mystical writings. Minister General of the Franciscan Order at a crucial point in its history, he gained the title of its Second Founder. Along with Thomas Aquinas, he is considered one of the two major philospher–theologians of the thirteenth century. His mystical treatises are among the classics of the genre. Writing several decades after Francis's death, Bonaventure attempted a double task: (1) to situate Francis's experience within the mainstream speculative, metaphysical, cosmological Neoplatonic tradition; and (2) at the same time to extend this tradition to encompass the devotional, Christ-centred focus of Francis, with its mysticism of the historical event. In his masterpiece, *The Soul's Journey into God*, he has written the *summa* of medieval Christian mysticism, for he attempts to give a typology of the major strands of medieval mystical consciousness that preceded Francis and at the same time to integrate the new Franciscan sensibility into this framework. His achievement here is not unlike that of Thomas Aquinas in theology. What Thomas achieved for Aristotle in theology, Bonaventure did for Francis in mysticism.

The remainder of our investigation will be a case study of transition in medieval mysticism. We shall begin with an exploration of Francis's mystical experience, drawn from historical documents and analysed phenomenologically. We shall then see how Bonaventure integrated Francis's experience into the mainstream, speculative, Neoplatonic tradition in his treatise *The Soul's Journey into God*. Already in this work the image of Christ is central, though not explored in detail or treated devotionally. Bonaventure's later work, *The Tree of Life*, comprises a classical expression of the mysticism of the historical event in the form of an extended meditation on events in the life of Jesus. His treatment of Christ the Centre in his *Collations on the Hexaemeron* constitutes the final stage of his integrative process: it deals with Christ speculatively, situating him within the Neoplatonic metaphysical and cosmological scheme. In this way Bonaventure draws the innovations of Francis's experience into the established tradition, and at the same time transforms the tradition by these very innovations.

Francis's Visionary Mysticism

From the beginning to the end of his religious life, as the early biographers witness, Francis was guided by dreams and visions and was himself the catalyst for dreams and visions among his immediate companions. As a young man, while considering embarking on a military career, he had a dream in which, as his biographer Bonaventure describes, 'God in his goodness showed him a large and splendid palace full of military weapons emblazoned with the insignia of Christ's cross'.[5] At first Francis misinterpreted the dream, thinking it directed him to military service. He set out for Apulia to cast in his lot with a certain count, hoping to win the glory of knighthood for himself. But during the night he received from God instructions that the dream had a spiritual meaning and was not to be taken literally. So he abandoned his military plans and returned to Assisi.

Not long afterwards, his religious journey was given decisive direction by an experience which Evelyn Underhill uses to illustrate her first stage of the mystic way: the awakening of the self.[6] This occurred at the church of San Damiano, a short distance from the city of Assisi, in 1225 when Francis was twenty-five years old and at a transition period in his life. Having wandered into the church, which was threatening to collapse, he began to pray before a crucifix. 'While his tear-filled eyes were gazing at the Lord's cross,' Bonaventure writes, 'he heard with his bodily ears a voice coming from the cross, telling him three times: "Francis, go and repair my house which, as you see, is falling completely into ruin."' The account continues: 'Trembling with fear, Francis was amazed at the sound of this astonishing voice, since he was alone in the church; and as he received in his heart the power of the divine words, he fell into a state of ecstasy.'[7] Although this would be categorized technically as an 'audition', since it is the hearing of a voice, it falls into the general class of extraordinary sense impressions, of which visions form a part; furthermore, it contains the visual content of the crucifix, which 'his eyes were gazing at'. As in the case of the dream above, Francis at first took the instructions literally and began physically to repair church buildings around Assisi. As his life unfolded, it became apparent – and as Bonaventure tells us, the Spirit taught him – that 'the principal intention of the words referred to that Church which *Christ purchased with his own blood* [Acts 20.28].'[8]

The intense visionary life of Francis was communicated to the circle of his early companions. Visions and dreams, especially involving the cross, were common in this milieu. For example, a composer of popular songs, known in his day as the King of Verses and later called Brother Pacificus after becoming a friar, had two visions of Francis involving the cross. On his first meeting with Francis, Pacificus saw him 'signed with a cross, in the form of two flashing swords, one of which stretched from his head to his feet, the other crossed his chest from one hand to the other.'[9] In a second vision, he saw 'a great Tau on Francis's forehead, which shone in a variety of colours and caused his face to glow with wonderful beauty.'[10] Another early friar, Silvester, had a recurrent dream which led to his following Francis. According to Bonaventure's account, Silvester 'saw in a dream the whole town of Assisi encircled by a *huge dragon* [Dan. 14.22] which threatened to destroy the entire area by its enormous size. Then he saw coming from Francis's mouth a golden cross whose top touched heaven and whose arms stretched far and wide and seemed to extend to the ends of the world. At the sight of its shining splendour, the foul and hideous dragon was put to flight.'[11]

The visionary mysticism of the early Franciscan milieu reached its climax in Francis's vision of the Six-winged Seraph in the form of the Crucified. This occurred on Mount La Verna in Tuscany around the feast of the Exaltation of the Cross, 14 September 1224, two years before Francis's death. Towards the end of the summer, Francis retired with several of his close companions to the mountain of La Verna, which previously had been given to him by Count Orlando of Chiusi. At the time the vision occurred, Francis had been observing a Lenten fast for about a month and devoting himself to prayer. Because of the importance of the details of this vision, we present a full account from early biographical sources. The version below is taken from Bonaventure, who draws heavily and often verbatim from the earlier accounts of Thomas of Celano:

> On a certain morning about the feast of the Exaltation of the Cross, while Francis was praying on the mountainside, he saw a Seraph with six fiery and shining wings descend from the height of heaven. And when in swift flight the Seraph had reached a spot in the air near the man of God, there appeared between the wings the figure of a man crucified, with his hands and feet extended in the form of a cross and fastened to a cross. Two of the wings were lifted above his head, two were extended for flight and two covered his whole body. When Francis saw this, he was overwhelmed and his heart was flooded with a mixture of joy and sorrow. He rejoiced because of the gracious way Christ looked upon him under the appearance of the Seraph, but the fact that he was fastened to a cross *pierced his soul with a sword* of compassionate sorrow. [Luke 2.35]
>
> He wondered exceedingly at the sight of so unfathomable a vision, realizing that the weakness of Christ's passion was in no way compatible with the immortality of the Seraph's spiritual nature. Eventually he understood by a revelation from the Lord that divine providence had shown him this vision so that, as Christ's lover, he might learn in advance that he was to be totally transformed into the likeness of Christ crucified, not by the martyrdom of his flesh, but by the fire of his love consuming his soul.[12]

After describing the vision, Bonaventure gives a detailed account of Francis's reception of the stigmata:

> As the vision disappeared, it left in his heart a marvellous ardour and imprinted on his body markings that were no less marvellous. Immediately the marks of nails began to appear in his hands and feet just as he had seen a little before in the figure of the man crucified. His hands and feet seemed to be pierced through the centre by nails, with the heads of the nails appearing on the inner side of the hands and the upper side of the feet and their points on the opposite sides. The heads of the nails in his hands and his feet were round and black; their points were oblong and bent as if driven back with a hammer, and they emerged from the flesh and stuck out

beyond it. Also his right side, as if pierced with a lance, was marked with a red wound from which his sacred blood often flowed, moistening his tunic and underwear.[13]

Francis in the Prophetic Tradition

From the standpoint of our study, we must analyse the content of this vision and situate it within its typological and historical setting. There is abundant evidence for seeing this vision in continuity with the visionary experience of the Hebrew prophets. In the early Franciscan milieu there was a resurgence of precisely this kind of visionary material, which was drawn explicitly from the Old Testament prophets, but which was transformed and reinterpreted to fit the thirteenth-century cultural context. Among the Franciscans, this visionary imagery, drawn from the classical Hebrew prophets, became embedded within another stratum of prophetic visionary material, namely apocalyptic imagery, derived ultimately from the Jewish and Christian apocalyptic consciousness of the intertestamental period and revived in the Middle Ages, chiefly through the twelfth-century monk Joachim of Fiore. The precise relation between Francis's visionary experience and the apocalyptic stratum of medieval consciousness is a complex question, and one that was hotly debated in the thirteenth century itself. We simply wish to call attention to the relation here, without attempting to explore the issue in depth.

The content of Francis's vision at La Verna is directly connected with the vision of Isaiah in which the latter received his call as a prophet: 'In the year of King Uzziah's death I saw the Lord Yahweh seated on a high throne; his train filled the sanctuary; above him stood seraphs, each one with six wings: two to cover its face, two to cover its feet and two for flying' (Isa. 6.1–2).[14] When he is overwhelmed by his unworthiness, a seraph purifies him by touching his lips with a burning coal. He then receives his commission as a prophet from the Lord, who commands him: 'Go, and say to this people, "Hear and hear again, but do not understand; see and see again, but do not perceive"' (Isa. 6.9). The seraphim here are heavenly beings which Isaiah is the first to associate with Yahweh. The name itself means 'burning one' and is probably related to the 'burning' serpents of Numbers 21.6f. and Deuteronomy 8.15, and the flying dragons of Isaiah 14.29; 30.6. These seraphim are perhaps the same as the cherubs on the ark of the covenant, Exodus 25.18.[15] By Francis's time, however, the seraphim had lost their dragon ancestry while retaining their fiery ardour. Through medieval angelology, especially *The Celestial Hierarchy* of the Pseudo-Dionysius, they were securely established as the loftiest of the nine choirs of angels, who worshipped God in a pure fire or ardent love.

The connection between the two visions is strikingly apparent. Although Francis does not see the throne of God, he does feel heavenly joy at the sight of the Seraph, which descends from heaven with fiery wings. As in the case of Isaiah, the Seraph approaches him; but instead of the purification by the burning coal, he receives the imprint of the wounds of Christ. Although he is given no formal prophetic commission, his call is implicit in the experience, for he bears the marks of Christ himself in his body as a prophetic witness to the mystery of Christ's passion and as the divine seal on his own holiness. The visions function differently in the lives of the two prophetic figures, for Isaiah receives the vision at the beginning of his career and Francis at the climax, near the end of his life. For Isaiah it is a commission, for Francis a seal; but as a seal of divine approval it lifts his prophetic mission to a new level and directs it to the people at large.

The visionary mysticism which flourished among the Hebrew prophets was cultivated by the *Merkabah* tradition, a major current of Jewish mysticism which continued from the first century B.C. until the tenth century.[16] Deriving its name from the Hebrew word for chariot (*merkava*), it drew heavily from Ezekiel's vision of the chariot of Yahweh (Ezek. 1.4–28). It cultivated the image of the throne, like that in Isaiah's vision, and sought to ascend from this world to a vision of the heavenly realm, where images of light and fire predominated. In the early period of this tradition's development, the classical prophetic imagery was brought in touch with apocalyptic visionary consciousness which flourished in that era. Although there are probably no discernible historical influences on Francis, there is a typological similarity between his imagery and that cultivated by the *Merkabah* tradition, due at least in part to the fact that they both drew from the same source of prophetic imagery.

Within the larger context of prophetic imagery, it is not surprising to see how Bonaventure interprets Francis as a prophet in the prologue to his biography. Drawing from biblical sources, Bonaventure sees Francis as a prophet, associating him with John the Baptist, Elijah lifted up in a fiery chariot, and the angel of the sixth seal of the Apocalypse.[17] That Bonaventure should so interpret Francis shows how deeply the prophetic–apocalyptic imagery had permeated the Franciscan milieu. In his political role as Minister General, Bonaventure stood far from the camp of the Franciscan Spirituals and from their radical Joachimite apocalypticism. In the prologue to his biography, Bonaventure depicts Francis as the prophet who has been lifted up *in these last days* (Acts 2.17; Heb. 1.2). 'Like John the Baptist he was appointed by God *to prepare in the desert a way* [Isa. 40.3] of the highest poverty and to *preach repentance* by word and example' (Luke 24.47). Bonaventure describes Francis as '*filled with the spirit* of prophecy', and 'totally aflame with a Seraphic fire'. Like the prophet Elijah, 'he was lifted up in *a fiery* chariot' (2 Kings 2.11). Drawing from apocalyptic imagery, Bonaventure sees Francis 'symbolized by the image of the Angel' of the sixth seal (Rev. 6.12), a crucial image in the apocalyptic traditions of the thirteenth century.[18]

Bonaventure's reference to the fiery chariot is related to a specific incident in Francis's life, which he recounts later in the biography: 'At about midnight while some of the friars were resting and others continued to pray, behold, a fiery chariot of wonderful brilliance entered through the door of the house and turned here and there three times through the house. A globe of light rested above it which shone like the sun and lit up the night.' The apparition, the friars realized, was actually Francis: 'They realized that by supernatural power the Lord had shown him to them in this glowing *chariot of fire* [2 Kings 2.11], radiant with heavenly splendour and inflamed with burning ardour . . . Like a second Elijah, God had made him *a chariot and charioteer* for spiritual men' (2 Kings 2.12).[19] Thus Francis himself is identified with the image of the chariot (which is central in *Merkabah* mysticism) although he is associated here with Elijah's chariot rather than that of Ezekiel's vision.

As the climax of a life of prophetic visionary mystical experience, Francis's vision of the Six-winged Seraph heralds a new age – not the age of the Spirit predicted by the Joachimites, but ironically, the age of devotion to the humanity of Christ. In the prophetic visions of the Bible and in *Merkabah* and apocalyptic visions, the mystic is lifted up from the earth to receive a glimpse of heaven. In Francis's vision, heaven descends to earth, for the Seraph comes down to manifest the union of the divine and the human in the crucified humanity of Christ. Bonaventure describes Francis's psychological state during the vision as follows: 'When Francis saw this, he was overwhelmed and his heart was flooded with a mixture of joy and sorrow. He rejoiced because of the gracious way Christ looked upon him under the appearance of the Seraph, but the fact that he was fastened to a cross *pierced his soul with a sword* of compassionate sorrow' (Luke 2.35).[20]

Francis's reaction to the vision is paradigmatic of the religious sensibility of the West for centuries after. It heralds one of the great shifts of consciousness in the history of Christianity; for in an unprecedented way, through the cultivation of the mysticism of the historical event, the West began to concentrate more and more on the humanity of Christ, especially upon his Passion. In the thirteenth century there emerged widespread compassion for the suffering Saviour, which became the hallmark of late medieval piety and a permanent stratum of the religious consciousness of Western Christianity. Although this had been germinating for centuries in the Western psyche – in pilgrimages to the Holy Land, the crusades, Bernard of Clairvaux's notion of the 'carnal love' of Christ – compassion for the suffering Saviour was given an archetypal expression in Francis and through him was channelled into Western devotion, art, and culture as a whole. It blossomed in meditations on the life of Christ, in the Stations of the Cross, in hymns like the 'Stabat Mater' and 'O Sacred Head Surrounded by Crown of Piercing Thorn,' in realistic depictions of the passion of Christ, in Michelangelo's Pietà, in the graphic mystical vision of the dying Christ of Julian of Norwich, and in widespread popular piety.

Bonaventure and Neoplatonism

As a philosopher–theologian and mystical writer, Bonaventure attempted to integrate Francis's innovative, visionary, Christ-centred mysticism into the classical Christian speculative mysticism derived from Neoplatonism. Different in personality and education from Francis, Bonaventure was heir to a different mystical tradition. As a youth he travelled from his birthplace, Bagnoregio, in central

Italy near Orvieto, to the University of Paris, where he studied in the faculty of arts and entered the Franciscan Order. A disciple of the first eminent Franciscan intellectual, Alexander of Hales, Bonaventure emerged as the leading Franciscan theologian of his day. Instead of pursuing an academic career, however, he was elected Minister General of the Franciscan Order in 1257, a post which he held for seventeen years. During his years as an administrator he continued to write, especially spiritual and mystical treatises, as well as series of lectures in the heated controversies over Aristotelianism at the University of Paris.

At the university under Alexander of Hales, Bonaventure was trained in the Christian Neoplatonic tradition which provided him with a speculative framework for all of his subsequent work. This Christian Neoplatonism had come from two main sources: Augustine and the Pseudo-Dionysius. Flowing through Anselm and the twelfth-century Victorines, it was transmitted to the University of Paris in the thirteenth century. This Christian Neoplatonism was very self-consciously Trinitarian, with a Christology that was focused on the Logos rather than the humanity of Christ. It was cosmological, emphasizing the emanation of all things from the Trinity and their subsequent return through the stages of a hierarchical ascent. It was very metaphysical in its delineation of the grades of being; it was also very analytic – and with the Victorines very psychological – in its examination of the spiritual journey.

In Bonaventure this speculative Neoplatonism is dominant, in sharp contrast with the prophetic visionary mysticism of Francis. We have no evidence that Bonaventure had visionary mystical experiences. There is, however, a rich stratum of mystical symbols throughout his writings, especially in the later period: for example, the mountain, the temple, the cross, light and darkness. Although some of these overlap with the prophetic material, they are drawn chiefly from the great cosmic transformation symbols rather than from the distinctive prophetic visionary symbols. Bonaventure takes the prophetic visionary symbol of the Six-winged Seraph and deals with it as a symbolic representation of the Neoplatonic cosmic structure and the Neoplatonic spiritual ascent, all the while supporting this interpretation by cosmic symbols of transformation.

Bonaventure's interpretation in Neoplatonic terms of Francis's vision appears in his *Soul's Journey into God*. In the prologue he describes the circumstances of its composition. Two years before, he had been elected Minister General and had to deal with growing tensions within the Order. In 1259 he retired to Mount La Verna, where Francis's vision had occurred, 'seeking a place of quiet,' as he tells us, 'desiring to find there peace of spirit'. He goes on to say: 'While I was there reflecting on various ways by which the soul ascends into God, there came to mind, among other things, the miracle which had occurred to blessed Francis in this very place: the vision of a winged Seraph in the form of the Crucified.' Suddenly he sees the connection between this vision and the Neoplatonic spiritual ascent: 'While reflecting on this, I saw at once that this vision represented our father's rapture in contemplation and the road by which this rapture is reached.' More specifically he sees that 'the six wings of the Seraph can rightly be taken to symbolize the six levels of illumination by which, as if by steps or stages, the soul can pass over to peace through ecstatic elevations of Christian wisdom.'[21] As we shall see, these stages are precisely the steps, drawn from Augustine, by which the soul moves through the Neoplatonic cosmos from the outside to the inside to the above.

The three pairs of wings, according to Bonaventure, symbolize the ascent of the soul through the three levels of the Neoplatonic cosmos: the material realm, which is perceived as outside us; the realm of the soul, which is within; and the realm of God, which is above. Yet these three levels, which also represent stages of the journey, can be multiplied into six, each pair taken as two stages, thus giving a symbolic meaning to each of the six wings. 'Any one of these ways can be doubled,' he says, ' . . . therefore it is necessary that these three principal stages be multiplied to a total of six.'[22] In each of the chapters of the *Soul's Journey*, Bonaventure explores one of these stages: in Chapter 1, he contemplates God reflected through the external material world; in Chapter 2, he discovers God reflected in our act of sensation, by which the material world enters our consciousness through our five senses; in Chapter 3, he sees God reflected in the depths of our spirit: in our memory, understanding and will; in Chapter 4, he contemplates God in these same faculties as they are reformed by grace; in Chapter 5, he turns above to contemplate God as Being; and in Chapter 6 he contemplates the Trinity as the mystery of the self-diffusive Good; finally, in Chapter 7, he leaves behind the *via affirmativa* to penetrate the divine darkness through the unknowing of the *via negativa*. Through the Neoplatonic ascent, the soul reaches in the seventh chapter the same level that Francis reached when he was lifted up in ecstasy in his prophetic vision on La Verna.

The Neoplatonic Soul's Journey

Bonaventure begins the ascent up the Neoplatonic ladder with the reflection of God in the material world. 'Since we must ascend Jacob's ladder before we descend it, let us place our first step in the ascent at the bottom, presenting to ourselves the whole material world as a mirror through which we may pass over to God, the supreme Craftsman.'[23] In this chapter he contemplates God as reflected in his 'vestiges' in the material world, seeing in the power, wisdom, and goodness of the universe a manifestation of God's power, wisdom, and goodness, and ultimately of the Father, as power, the Son, as wisdom, and the Spirit, as goodness. The Latin term *vestigium* means literally footprint and it was used by Augustine to express the reflection of the Trinity in power, wisdom, and goodness perceived in creation. Although placed on the first rung of the ladder, the contemplation of vestiges presupposes the entire Christian Neoplatonic theological-philosophical structure, which Bonaventure will describe only gradually through his treatise. It presupposes the doctrine of the Trinity, in which the Father expresses his own Image in his Son and in so doing produces the ideas or *rationes* of all he can create. These *rationes* are the Platonic ideas, which Augustine situated in the divine mind, specifically within the Logos or Son in the Trinity. When God freely decides to create a material universe, he images himself in the world through the principle of Platonic exemplarism. The world manifests its creative source, both by reflecting the 'eternal reasons' or ideas in the Son and by manifesting the Trinitarian process out of which creation has sprung. In this way creation is a vestige of the Trinity. Thus the ascent of the soul upon which Bonaventure has embarked presupposes the descent of creatures from God. This descent of creatures from the Trinity is a Christian version of Neoplatonic emanation, a term which Bonaventure uses (*emanatio* in Latin) to describe his entire vision. In his final series of lectures he says: 'This is our entire metaphysics: emanation, exemplarity, and consummation, to be illumined by spiritual rays and to be led back to the height.'[24] Thus in the *Soul's Journey* Bonaventure begins the ascent at the point of farthest emanation from the source, in the material world, which nevertheless bears the imprint of the Trinity.

Although Bonaventure derives his Christian Neoplatonism in this case from Augustine, he cultivates the contemplation of God in the material world to a much greater extent than Augustine. In this he is more the follower of the nature mystic Francis, than of the converted Manichee Augustine, who throughout his life remained ambivalent towards matter. Granted his Franciscan love of nature, Bonaventure's contemplation within the speculative cosmology of Neoplatonism has a very different quality from Francis's nature mysticism. If one compares Bonaventure's contemplation of the sevenfold properties of creatures in *The Soul's Journey* with Francis's 'Canticle of Brother Sun', one will perceive strikingly different modes of consciousness. In Francis's canticle, the reader can see, hear, taste, smell, and touch nature; and Francis responds to the heat of Brother Sun and the coolness of Sister Water with immediate joy and poetic spontaneity. In contrast, Bonaventure takes the abstract path of the Neoplatonic dialectic. Although their paths converge at a point of deep religious experience, they represent two different forms of nature mysticism: the sense-laden nature mysticism of the poet Francis and the speculative cosmological mysticism of the Neoplatonists, who do not linger on sense impressions, but quickly move through abstraction to the world of ideas.

In the second stage of the ascent, Bonaventure contemplates the reflection of God in the very act of sensation. 'Man, who is called the smaller world, has five senses like five doors through which knowledge of all things which are in the sense world enters his soul.'[25] He proceeds to give a psychological-epistemological analysis of the act of sensation, focusing on the experience of beauty. He derives both his epistemology and his aesthetics from Augustine, referring explicitly to the latter's *De musica* and its theory of harmony. In our perception of beautiful objects, we grasp the eternal laws, 'existing eternally in the Eternal Art, by which, through which and according to which all beautiful things are formed.'[26] Although Bonaventure does not explicitly mention Francis here, in his biography he describes Francis's sense of beauty in terms which echo Plato and Plotinus: 'In beautiful things he saw Beauty itself and through his *vestiges* imprinted on creation *he followed his Beloved* everywhere [Job 23.11; Song of Sol. 5. 17] making from all things a ladder by which he could climb up and embrace him who is *utterly desirable*' (Song of Sol. 5.16).[27]

In Chapter 3 Bonaventure moves from the material world and sensation to the inner world of the spirit, where he contemplates God reflected in our faculties of memory, understanding, and will. This is the realm symbolized by the second pair of the wings of the Seraph. Once again he draws from Augustine, echoing Book VII of *The Confessions* and drawing explicitly from the *De Trinitate*. In continuity with his treatment of beauty in the previous chapter, he sees God reflected in the soul as eternity in the memory, truth in the intellect, and goodness in the will: 'See, therefore, how close the soul is to God, and how, in their operations, the memory leads to eternity, the understanding to truth, and the power of choice to the highest good.'[28]

In the next chapter he asks why is it, if 'God is so close to our souls, that so few should be aware of the First Principle within themselves.'[29] He gives a classic Neoplatonic answer: Our intelligence is clouded by sense images and our will trapped by desire. 'Thus lying totally in these things of sense, it cannot re-enter into itself as into the image of God.' We need someone to lift us up from our fallen state, and this one is Christ as Eternal Truth itself. 'So our soul could not rise completely from these things of sense to see itself and the Eternal Truth in itself unless Truth, assuming human nature in Christ, had become a ladder, restoring the first ladder that had been broken in Adam.'[30] Bonaventure proceeds to describe the restored image of God in the soul in terms drawn from Bernard of Clairvaux's *Sermons on the Song of Songs* and from the Pseudo-Dionysius, who was the chief transmitter of the Neoplatonic hierarchical structure to Christianity. In the tradition of the Pseudo-Dionysius, Bonaventure sees the soul purified, illumined, and perfected through an ordering of the soul which resembles the hierarchical ordering of the nine choirs of angels. 'We are led through the hierarchies and hierarchical orders which are to be arranged in our soul as in the heavenly Jerusalem.'[31]

In Chapters 5 and 6 Bonaventure turns above the soul to contemplate God, as is symbolized in the third pair of the Seraph's wings. First he contemplates God as Being, reflecting the treatment of God as Being in *The Divine Names* of the Pseudo-Dionysius and in the thought of Bonaventure's contemporary, Thomas Aquinas. Having eliminated all nonbeing from the contemplation of God, Bonaventure concludes: 'Therefore that being which is pure being and simple being and absolute being is Primary Being, eternal, utterly simple, most actual, most perfect and supremely one.'[32] In Chapter 6 Bonaventure contemplates God as Trinity under the aspect of the Good. It is here that Bonaventure deals with Neoplatonic emanation; however, instead of proposing a subordinationist emanation of Nous and Soul from the One as in the original tradition of Plotinus and his non-Christian followers, the Christians linked emanation to the processions of the Trinity, seeing the Father, Son, and Spirit as equally divine. Under the influence of the Pseudo-Dionysius, Bonaventure sees the Good as self-diffusive: 'For good is said to be self-diffusive; therefore the highest good must be most self-diffusive.' This principle Bonaventure sees realized only in the Trinity since creation is too limited to actualize fully the divine self-diffusive goodness: 'For the diffusion in time in creation is no more than a centre or point in relation to the immensity of the divine goodness.'[33]

In Chapter 7 Bonaventure reaches the climax of *The Soul's Journey*. Here he moves from the *via affirmativa*, which he had been pursuing in the previous chapters, to the *via negativa*. As he drew previously from the Pseudo-Dionysius's *Divine Names*, here he quotes extensively the latter's *Mystical Theology*: 'Leave behind your senses and intellectual activities, sensible and invisible things, all nonbeing and being; and in this state of unknowing be restored insofar as is possible to unity with him who is above all essence and knowledge.'[34] It is here that Bonaventure reaches the height of his presentation of Neoplatonic mysticism by, like the Pseudo-Dionysius, placing the highest rung of the ladder in the darkness of knowing. It is here, too, that we encounter a great irony in his treatment of Francis; for he links Francis's vision of the Seraph with the imageless final stage of Neoplatonic mysticism. It is here, then, that his integration of the Neoplatonic speculative mysticism reaches its final integration with Francis's visionary experience, but this is achieved not by correlating the prophetic visionary experience itself with that of Neoplatonism, but by seeing the vision as a symbol of the Neoplatonic cosmology and the spiritual ascent. In so doing, Bonaventure has drawn upon the major sources of the Christian Neoplatonic tradition as symbolically represented in Francis's vision:

chiefly Augustine and the Pseudo-Dionysius. Because of its grounding in the tradition, and because of its presentation of a comprehensive typology of states of mystical consciousness, *The Soul's Journey*
takes on the character of a *summa* of medieval Christian mysticism.

Christ Mysticism

Bonaventure's attempt to situate Francis's mysticism within the
main-stream of Christian mystical tradition had an effect on the
tradition itself. Bonaventure progressively integrated into the tradition Francis's focus on the humanity and passion of Christ and the
emerging mysticism of the historical event. He wrote *The Soul's
Journey* at a transitional period in his life, when his Christian
Neoplatonism was beginning to assimilate Francis's innovative
Christ-centred religious experience. As a result, the work manifests
the Neoplatonic speculative mysticism more than the new Franciscan
Christocentricity. The humanity of Christ does not play a central role
in *The Soul's Journey*, but it does feature graphically in the prologue
and serves a decisive function at the climax. When Bonaventure
describes Francis's vision in the prologue, after interpreting the wings
of the Seraph symbolically he focuses on the figure of Christ crucified.
This symbolizes that 'there is no other path but through the burning
love of the Crucified.' The six wings of the Seraph, he repeats,
'symbolize the six steps of illumination that begin from creatures and
lead up to God, whom no one rightly enters except through the
Crucified.'[35] Later at the climax of the *via affirmativa*, at the end of
Chapter 6, Bonaventure contemplates the humanity of Christ,
symbolized by the Mercy Seat above the Ark in the Holy of Holies.
After contemplating both the divine nature and the Trinity as a
coincidentia oppositorum, Bonaventure turns his gaze upon Christ,
who is even a greater coincidence of opposites.[36] The soul is rapt in
wonder when it contemplates Christ as 'the first and the last, the
highest and the lowest, the circumference and the centre, *the Alpha
and the Omega* [Rev. 1.8], the caused and the cause, the Creator and
the creature. . . .'[37] This contemplation of Christ causes the soul to
abandon the *via affirmativa* and pass over to the negations of the
darkness of unknowing in the seventh and final level of the ascent into
God. The soul can 'transcend and pass over not only this sense world
but even itself. In this passing over, Christ is the *way and the door* [cf.

John 14.6; 10.7]; Christ is the ladder and the vehicle, like the Mercy Seat placed above the ark of God and the *mystery hidden from eternity*' (Eph. 3.9).

In *The Soul's Journey*, the humanity of Christ functions as a vehicle of transformation in the journey towards mystical consciousness. In the prologue, the image of Christ crucified symbolizes the death of 'ego', the superficial or false self, so that true mystical consciousness can emerge at the centre of the true self. In the climax, the juxtaposition of opposites contemplated in the humanity of Christ functions like a Zen Koan, shattering the limits of finite consciousness and opening the soul to union with the infinite, eternal divinity.

In contrast with this mystical role of the humanity of Christ, Bonaventure composed shortly after *The Soul's Journey* a series of meditations on scenes from the life of Christ under the title *The Tree of Life*. In these meditations the mysticism of the historical event emerges with remarkable fullness. The impetus that Francis had given to the imitation of Christ is here translated into a method of meditation and applied to forty-eight events in Christ's life, from his birth to his ascension into heaven. I will cite two examples from these meditations which best illustrate the essence of Franciscan devotion to the humanity of Christ. Francis himself most directly evoked these, and they became the most dramatic scenes in the development of the mysticism of the historical event in the subsequent centuries: the birth of Jesus at Bethlehem and his physical suffering on the cross.

At Christmas in 1223, Francis produced a crib at Greccio, near Rieti. Although this is not the first crib in Christian history, it had a profound influence on Franciscan spirituality – focusing as it did on the realistic dramatization and the stark simplicity which revealed Jesus' poverty and humility.[39] Drawing heavily from the *Vita prima* of Thomas of Celano, Bonaventure describes the scene as follows: 'He [Francis] had a crib prepared, hay carried in and an ox and an ass led to the place. The friars are summoned, the people come, the forest resounds with their voices and that venerable night is rendered brilliant and solemn by a multitude of bright lights and by resonant and harmonious hymns of praise.'[40] Note the realistic scene, with live animals and hay, with no mention of statues and with no specific mention of a bambino. Then Francis injects his own sensitivity into the scene: 'The man of God stands before the crib, filled with affection, bathed in tears, and overflowing with joy. A solemn Mass is celebrated over the crib, with Francis as deacon chanting the holy Gospel.' As deacon, Francis preached, emphasizing the poverty and tenderness that were subsequently cultivated in the Franciscan devotion to the infant Saviour: 'Then he preaches to the people standing about concerning the birth of the poor King, whom, when he wished to name him, he called in his tender love, the Child of Bethlehem.'[41]

By reproducing the setting of Bethlehem, Francis led the people into the historical event and drew from it the meaning which he himself had perceived. As Thomas of Celano says: 'There simplicity was honoured, poverty was exhalted, humility was commended, and Greccio was made, as it were, a new Bethlehem.'[42] In *The Tree of Life*, Bonaventure provides a technique of meditation for entering into the event in a way comparable to Francis's dramatization. He first summarizes the Gospel account from Luke 2. 1–18, emphasizing Francis's perception of poverty and humility: 'He chose to be born away from a home in a stable to be wrapped in swaddling clothes, to be nourished by virginal milk and to lie in a manger between an ox and an ass.'[43] With the scene vividly set and the message revealed, he bids the reader enter into the event as an actor in the drama: 'Now, then, my soul, embrace that divine manger; press your lips upon and kiss the boy's feet.' The reader is to join in with the other actors in the drama and respond as they responded: 'Then in your mind keep the shepherds' watch, marvel at the assembling host of angels, join in the heavenly melody, singing with your voice and heart: "Glory to God in the highest and on earth peace to men of good will."'[44]

Bonaventure takes the same approach in dealing with Christ's suffering and death. As his model, he has an even more dramatic incident than Francis creating the crib at Greccio; for at La Verna in 1226 Francis received the marks of Christ's crucifixion imprinted on his flesh. This miraculous occurrence made graphically concrete – for Bonaventure and the Franciscan milieu – the event of Christ's crucifixion. It is not surprising, then, that Bonaventure should devote one third of *The Tree of Life* or a total of sixteen meditations to Christ's passion. He draws the reader into the event by having him identify with Mary, sharing her feelings of compassion for the suffering Saviour.

In these meditations, there is a heightened concentration on the physical details of Christ's suffering, with a subsequent evoking of compassion. Addressing himself to Mary, Bonaventure says:

This blessed and most holy flesh – which you so chastely conceived, so sweetly nourished and fed with your milk, which you so often held on your lap, and kissed with your lips – you actually gazed upon with your bodily eyes now torn by the blows of the scourges, now pierced by the points of the thorns, now struck by the reed, now beaten by hands and fists, now pierced by nails and fixed to the wood of the cross, and torn by its own weight as it hung there.[45]

By thus identifying with Mary, we can share Christ's suffering and penetrate the meaning of his redemptive death.

For Bonaventure and the subsequent tradition, this mysticism of the historical event focused primarily on the moral values revealed in the scene. This is made abundantly clear in *The Tree of Life*, for Bonaventure identifies by name the moral virtues which are manifested in the scenes of Christ's life. On the popular level, this form of mystical consciousness can issue in a superficial sentimentalism, divorced from any deeper levels of the spirit. If it penetrates beyond mere emotion to the level of moral value, it can remain superficial even here. To realize its ultimate religious possibility, it must open itself to the deeper archetypal realities concretized in these events: for example, the archetype of transformation – both spiritual and cosmic – embodied in the Christian understanding of Christ's death and resurrection. And even beyond this, it must penetrate to that deeper level of mystical awareness where it experiences God himself as he is manifested in the events. In the medieval categories of scripture interpretation it must ultimately move through four senses of scripture. Beginning on the literal level, this mysticism must draw out from the event its moral meaning, as is explicitly done by Bonaventure in *The Tree of Life*. The moral meaning is closely linked to the allegorical, which deals with Christ's work in salvation history, specifically with the transformation involved in his death and resurrection. The fourth sense is the anagogic, which reveals the ultimate mystical meaning: the union of the soul with God after death or the foretaste of that union in this life through mystical experience.

The medieval mind was sensitized to respond to an event on all four levels, even though this might not be spelled out in a specific work. For example, Bonaventure's *The Tree of Life* deals explicitly with the literal and moral senses, and implicitly with the allegorical. *The Soul's Journey into God* deals with the allegorical and the anagogic. Although the medieval reader of each treatise would be inclined spontaneously to read each on all four levels, the modern reader can read the two treatises together, seeing the explicit connection between the literal-moral meaning of *The Tree of Life* and the allegorical-anagogic meaning of *The Soul's Journey*. The crucified Christ perceived by the mysticism of the historic event in *The Tree of Life* becomes in *The Soul's Journey* the figure of the Crucified in Francis's vision of the six-winged Seraph, leading the mystic through the death of his ego to the union with God that Francis experienced ecstatically on Mount La Verna.

Christ the Centre of Metaphysics

The historical-moral Christ of *The Tree of Life* and the allegorical-anagogic Christ of *The Soul's Journey* lead eventually, in Bonaventure's thought, to the metaphysical Christ of the *Collations on the Hexaemeron*. A series of twenty-three lectures given at the University of Paris in 1273, these *Collations* were introduced by a programmatic discussion of the topic: Christ the Centre of All the Sciences. It is in this piece that Bonaventure's speculative Neoplatonism becomes completely focused on Christ as its centre. Francis's vision at La Verna, which Bonaventure had integrated into the Christian Neoplatonic mystical tradition, now transforms that tradition by centring all of its principles on Christ. In this way the dynamics of innovation–tradition–transformation-of-tradition reaches its completion. Although Christian Neoplatonic mysticism emphasized the Trinity and Christ as eternal Logos, it did not focus on the incarnate Logos through the mysticism of the historical event. This is true both in Augustine, for whom Christ is the eternal Truth, the Art of the Father, the internal teacher of wisdom, and in the Pseudo-Dionysius, for whom Christ plays no major role. After Bonaventure has assimilated Francis's focus on the humanity of Christ, he translates this into the metaphysical principle of Christ the centre.

In the first collation on the Hexaemeron, he links Christ with metaphysics, seeing him as the centre of the seven sciences: metaphysics, physics, mathematics, logic, ethics, politics, and theology. This means that Christ is the centre of all the areas studied by these sciences, including the realms that constitute the Neoplatonic universe. For Bonaventure, Christ is the metaphysical centre in his generation from the Father in the Trinity; he is the middle person of the Trinity and the link between God and creation since he contains within himself, as Exemplar, the eternal reasons or ideas of all possible creatures. If you consider Christ in this way, Bonaventure says, 'you will be a true metaphysician'.[46] That Christ is the metaphysical centre is the basis for his being the centre of the other sciences. He is the physical centre in his incarnation, since he joins in himself all the dimensions of reality, from matter to divinity; and from him as centre all spiritual energies flow throughout the universe. In his crucifixion, he is the mathematical centre, since he has measured out in his Passion the extremes of divinity and the humility of the cross. In his resurrection he is the logical centre, since he enters into a cosmic debate with Satan, whose logic leads to death and destruction. Although Christ subsumes the destructive logic of Satan to the point of death, he overcomes the destruction of evil by transforming death into life in his resurrection. In his ascension he is ethical centre, for he leads his followers back to the Father along the path of the virtues. In his final judgement of the world, he is the political or juridical centre, for he will issue judgement upon the deeds of all men. Finally, in eternal beatitude, Christ is the theological centre, who draws all things back to union with the Father.

Thus Bonaventure places Christ at the centre of the Neoplatonic universe and the Neoplatonic ascent of the soul. He is the centre of the eternal emanations of the Trinity and the centre of the emanation of all creation in its hierarchical structure reaching from the spiritual realm to that of matter. He is also the centre of history: of the return of all things to the Father, first by effecting redemption through his suffering, death, and resurrection, then by leading men through an ascent of virtue, through judgement to ultimate union with the divinity. The Neoplatonic universe has been Franciscanized, by placing the incarnate Christ at the centre of the cosmos, of history, of the soul, and of the spiritual journey.

The prophecy implicit in Francis's vision at La Verna has been fulfilled in Bonaventure's Neoplatonism. The crucified Christ has assumed a new position within religious devotion of the culture at large, mystical consciousness, and metaphysics. Although Bonaventure's notion of Christ as metaphysical centre did not provide the main thrust of theology in the centuries to come, the popular devotion to the humanity of Christ did. While Bonaventure has integrated Francis's visionary, Christ-centred mysticism into the

188   *Mysticism and Religious Traditions*

Neoplatonic structure, this structure itself has been Franciscanized
by the metaphysical concept of Christ the centre.

NOTES

1   Cf. N. Shanta, 'Perpetual Pilgrimage: The Doctrine and Life of the Jaina
    Nuns', *Cistercian Studies*, ix (1974), 243–52; Sukumar Dutt, *Buddhist
    Monks and Monasteries of India: Their History and Their Contribution to
    Indian Culture* (London, 1962); Patrick Olivelle, *The Origins and
    the Early Development of Buddhist Monachism* (Colombo, 1974);
    G. S. Ghurye, *Indian Sadhus* (Bombay, 1964).

2   Bonaventure, *Legenda maior S. Francisci*, III, 9; English translation by
    Ewert Cousins in *Bonaventure: The Soul's Journey into God, The Tree of
    Life, The Life of St. Francis* (New York, 1978), p. 205. On the
    approbation of the rule, cf. the following early biographies: Thomas of
    Celano, *Vita prima S. Francisci*, 32–33, and *Legenda trium sociorum*,
    46–53. For the critical text of Bonaventure, cf. *Doctoris Seraphici S.
    Bonaventurae opera omnia* (Quaracchi, Collegium S. Bonaventurae,
    1882–1902) x volumina, and *Legenda maior* in *Analecta Franciscana*,
    vol. x, pp. 555–652.

3   Cf. Decima Douie, *The Conflict between the Seculars and the Mendicants
    at the University of Paris in the 13th Century* (London, 1954).

4   Cf. J. R. H. Moorman, *A History of the Franciscan Order: From its
    Origins to the Year 1517* (Oxford, 1968); Rosalind Brooke, *Early
    Franciscan Government: Elias to Bonaventure* (Cambridge, 1959);
    Marjorie Reeves, *The Influence of Prophecy in the Later Middle Ages: A
    Study of Joachimism* (Oxford, 1969).

5   Bonaventure, *Legenda maior*, I, 3; English translations of Bonaventure's
    biography of Francis are taken from my translation cited in n. 2, above;
    for the present passage, cf. trans., p. 187; on this incident, cf. Thomas of
    Celano, *Vita prima S. Francisci*, 5 (hereafter cited as *I Celano*) and *Vita
    secunda S. Francisci*, 6 (hereafter cited as *II Celano*); also *Legenda trium
    sociorum*, 5 (hereafter cited as *Soc.*). In the body of my text, I have
    quoted only from the biography of Bonaventure, but I cite additional
    sources in the notes. Although Bonaventure's biography is later than
    some of the others, it draws from earlier sources; and since it is written
    by one of the greatest writers on mysticism in the Middle Ages, it
    contains details relevant to mysticism which others do not include.

6   Cf. Evelyn Underhill, *Mysticism: A Study in the Nature and Development
    of Man's Spiritual Consciousness* (New York, 1961), pp. 180–81.

7   Bonaventure, *Legenda maior*, II, 1; trans., p. 191; on this incident, cf. *II Celano*, 10, and *Soc.*, 13. Celano's account describes it in part as a miraculous vision, since he states that 'the painted image of Christ crucified moved its lips and spoke'.

8   Bonaventure, *Legenda maior*, II, 1; trans., p. 191.

9   Ibid., IV, 9; trans., p. 214; cf. *II Celano*, p. 106.

10 Ibid. Tau is a letter of the Hebrew and Greek alphabets; its Greek form, which corresponds to the English capital T, was employed as a variant form of the cross. Francis used the Tau as his mark or signature.

11 Ibid., III, 5; trans., pp. 201–02. Cf. *II Celano*, 109; *Soc.* 30; *Fioretti*, 2.

12 Bonaventure, *Legenda maior*, XIII, 3; trans., pp. 305–6. Cf. *I Celano*, 94; *Soc.* 69.

13 Ibid.

14 The translation is from *The Jerusalem Bible* (Garden City, N.Y., 1966).

15 Ibid., n. 6.

16 On *Merkabah* mysticism, cf. Gershom Scholem, *Major Trends in Jewish Mysticism*, 3rd rev. edn (New York, 1954), pp. 41–79; also David Blumenthal, ed., *Understanding Jewish Mysticism, A Source Reader: The Merkabah Tradition and the Zoharic Tradition* (New York, 1978), pp. 3–97.

17 Bonaventure, *Legenda maior*, prol., 1.

18 Ibid., trans., pp. 180–81.

19 Ibid., IV, 4; trans., p. 209.

20 Ibid., XIII, 3; trans., p. 305.

21 Bonaventure, *Itinerarium mentis in Deum*, prol., 203; English translations of Bonaventure's *Itinerarium* are taken from my translation cited in n. 2 above; for the present passages, cf. trans., p. 54.

22 Ibid., I, 5; trans., p. 61.

23 Ibid., I, 9; trans., p. 63.

24 Bonaventure, *Collationes in Hexaemeron*, I, 17.

25 Bonaventure, *Itinerarium*, II, 3; trans., p. 70.

26 Ibid., 9; trans., p. 74.

27 Bonaventure, *Legenda maior*, IX, i; trans., p. 263.

28 Bonaventure, *Itinerarium*, III, 4' trans., p. 84.

29 Ibid., IV, 1; trans., p. 87.

30 Ibid., IV, 1–2; trans., pp. 87–88.

31 Ibid., 7; trans., p. 93.

32 Ibid., V, 5; trans., p. 97.

33 Ibid., VI, 2; trans., p. 103.

34 Ibid., VII, 5; trans., pp. 114; the quotation is from the pseudo-Dionysius's *De mystica theologia*, I, 1.

35 Ibid., prol., 3; trans., pp. 54–55.

36   On the coincidence of opposites, cf. my study of this theme: *Bonaventure and the Coincidence of Opposites* (Chicago, 1978), especially pp. 69–95, 131–97.

37   Bonaventure, *Itinerarium*, VI, 7; trans., pp. 108–9.

38   Ibid., VII, 1; trans. p. 111.

39   Cf. the note on this history of the crib in Omer Englebert, *Saint Francis of Assisi: A Biography*, a new translation by Eve Marie Cooper, second English edition revised and augmented by Ignatius Brady, O. F. M., and Raphael Brown (Chicago, 1965), p. 488.

40   Bonaventure, *Legenda maior*, X, 7; trans., p. 278; cf. *I Celano*, 84–87.

41   Ibid.

42   *I Celano*, 85; English translation by Placid Hermann, O. F. M., in Thomas of Celano, *St Francis of Assisi: First and Second Life of St Francis, with Selections from Treatise on the Miracles of Blessed Francis* (Chicago, 1962), p. 76.

43   Bonaventure, *Lignum vitae*, 4; English translations of the *Lignum vitae* are taken from my translation cited in n. 2, above; for the present passage, cf. trans., p. 128.

44   Ibid.; trans., p. 129.

45   Ibid., 28; trans., p. 152.

46   Bonaventure, *Collationes in Hexaemeron*, I, 17.

EWERT H. COUSINS, Ph.D. (Fordham), a specialist in early Franciscan mysticism and theology, has written *Bonaventure and the Coincidence of Opposites* (1978). He is chief editorial consultant for the 60-volume series The Classics of Western Spirituality and translator and editor of the Bonaventure volume in the series: *Bonaventure: The Soul's Journey into God, The Tree of Life, The Life of St. Francis* (1978). Involved in the dialogue of world religions, he is a consultant to the Vatican Secretariat for Non-Christians. In contemporary religious thought, he has specialized in Teilhard de Chardin and process theology, editing *Process Theology* and *Hope and the Future of Man*. He is director of the Graduate Program in Spirituality at Fordham University and visiting professor at Columbia University.

Conceiving Hindu 'Bhakti' as Theistic Mysticism

JOHN B. CARMAN

I. *Questions of Definition*

This essay is an attempt to relate two broad religious categories in different cultural contexts. Of the two, mysticism is considerably more ambiguous; it is in fact understood in quite different ways by different people, both in common speech and in scholarly analysis. It might therefore seem futile to use it in gaining a Western understanding of Hindu *bhakti*, but it has in fact been so utilized, both positively and negatively. *Bhakti* has been conceived as mysticism *par excellence*, as a secondary or hybrid type of mysticism, or as a religious category quite distinct from mysticism.

'Theistic mysticism' is a more restricted term, which some students of mysticism would consider a contradiction in terms, since for them theism implies a fundamental distinction between creator and creature which mysticism denies or overcomes. At most they would view theistic mysticism as a mixed type or impure variety of mysticism, a practical compromise concealing a metaphysical contradiction. A quite different view of mysticism sees theistic mysticism as a fully legitimate type, possibly even the most legitimate type of mysticism, exemplified repeatedly in the tradition from which the concept derives, the mystical theology or *via contemplativa* of Christian tradition, both Eastern and Western.

Mysticism is not only variously defined; it is also quite diversely evaluated. It may be understood either as the essence of all true religion or as a form of human expression and experience distinct from religion. It may be conceived either as the intense personal experiencing of the realities of faith, whether Christian or other, or as a dangerous alternative to Christian or Islamic faith. Mysticism may be regarded as essentially alien to the monotheistic traditions of the West but at the very heart of Indian religious traditions. On the other hand, it may be considered as one of many strands both in Indian religion and in Western religion. Mysticism may be thought to provide empirical evidence of truth or it may be considered as the clearest expression of the absurdity of all religious truth claims. Mysticism may be thought to exhibit a common character in all cultures, or it may be treated as an abstraction from the quite different mystical dimensions of each distinct religious system.

For those who stress the ineffability of mystical experience, these diverse understandings may appear inevitable. Any attempt at defining what transcends our words and concepts might seem self-defeating. The diversity, however, can be otherwise explained, for the different definitions do not go in every conceivable direction, but fall into certain categories. There is a division according to the prototype that consciously or unconsciously is being followed, and there are differences in emphasis depending on which one of the three features of both major prototypes is considered primary.

On the level of metaphysics, at least, there are two prototypes rather than one, for this contemplative life was expressed by some in orthodox Christian categories, maintaining a fundamental distinction between Creator and creature, and by others in terms considered heretical by Church authorities, terms that continued the Neoplatonic tradition of Plotinus with a goal of total unity transcending the Creator–creature distinction. Since the Renaissance those outside the Christian establishment have frequently regarded this latter monistic tradition as the true or pure form of mysticism. That interpretation, but with an opposite, negative evaluation, not only has become firmly entrenched in German Protestant theology, but also has influenced more recent understandings by European historians of religion.

Definitions of mysticism tend to stress one or more of the following features:

(*a*) a particular ontology, in accord with the mystic's insight, usually either monistic or theistic;
(*b*) an immediacy or intensity of experience not present in other forms of religion;
(*c*) a separation from the physical, or from ordinary social life, or from ordinary forms of consciousness.

Unless mysticism is restricted to religious practice assuming a simple monistic ontology, it is possible to find a place for theistic mysticism under all these definitions, and indeed many of the major interpreters of western mysticism give an integral rather than a secondary place to theistic or personalistic mysticism. Rufus Jones and Evelyn Underhill do so because they are trying to deal comprehensively with the whole range of Christian religious phenomena. Moreover, their own religious predilections are theistic. The comprehensiveness of Gershom Scholem's and Annemarie Schimmel's surveys of the Jewish and Islamic mystical traditions, respectively, lead them to a similar balance. William James is equally emphatic in insisting on a broad definition of mysticism that includes its theistic varieties. His reason, however, is rather different: the relative lack of correlation between typical states of mystical feeling and any specific metaphysical position.[1]

Modern definitions of mysticism rarely acknowledge that they are extending the range of mysticism on the basis of an ancient or medieval prototype. Instead they seize upon that characteristic or those characteristics that they consider most essential to 'mysticism', which they usually assume to be potentially or actually present in all human cultures. Each of the many definitions emphasizes certain features present in Christian mysticism, both orthodox and heterodox.

When the category of mysticism is applied to Islamic or Jewish phenomena, the particular definition is not so crucial, for these are whole movements clearly analogous to Christian mysticism, both in themselves and in their relation to other aspects of their religious tradition. Even so, it has been questioned whether 'Jewish mysticism' is 'truly' mysticism, since it stops short of total identification between creature and Creator. On the other side, it has been questioned by some modern historians of religion as well as by some conservative Muslim scholars and some modern Muslim reformers whether Sufism is truly Islamic. In all three of these interrelated monotheistic religions important mystical movements have developed and been of great historical significance, yet many of them have been in an ambivalent relation, sometimes of open conflict, with other institutions in their respective communities. Those forms of mysticism most harmoniously present in these western religious traditions, on the other hand, do not fit some modern definitions of mysticism because of their theistic rather than monistic emphasis. In short, 'mysticism' seems to be neither fully 'at home' nor quite 'purely' manifest in what would seem to be the religious worlds where we know it best.

This curious situation is apparently reversed in the great religions of the East, especially those originating in India. India is seen by many as the original home of mysticism and the place where it flowers in its purest form. This judgement of some nineteenth-century romantics and indologists became a part of the neo-Hindu ideologies that have developed during the last century. To some extent this attribution of mysticism has extended to Buddhism, but with more reservations and scholarly puzzlement. Likewise Jainism is something of a puzzle for students of comparative mysticism: its ascetic disciplines seem so clearly analogous to a large number of mystical practices, but its ontology is both dualistic and pluralistic. But if, with some, we take the systematic disentangling of the soul from the body as the hallmark of mysticism, then Jain mysticism must be one of the purest varieties.

So widely is the term mysticism applied to Hindu religion that S. N. Dasgupta treats many major strands of Hindu tradition in his little book entitled *Hindu Mysticism*, and even includes a chapter on 'Buddhist Mysticism'.[2] The closer we come to including all Indian religion under mysticism, however, the more difficult it is to give that concept any specific meaning.

II. *Rudolf Otto's Comparative Approach*

Many scholars have found it quite natural to extend the Western concept of mysticism to apply to many Indian religious phenomena. Both Indian and western scholars have often treated mysticism as a universal or near-universal human phenomenon. India, moreover, is regarded as the home of mysticism, *par excellence*. Such Indian mysticism is epitomized for some in the monistic position of Śankara or of some of the Mahāyāna Buddhist schools. For them theistic mysticism is either a variety of popular religion or an antechamber to the true mysticism of identity.

The applicability of the western category of 'mysticism' to Indian religious phenomena seems to me by no means so self-evident. What is to be described as 'mysticism' depends on the particular definition, but if the Western category is to be used at all, the devotional movements should qualify as mysticism, since they are at least as analogous to Western mysticism as is the supposedly more typically Indian mysticism of identity. Two modern Hindu scholars belonging to one of the devotional communities go still further: it is only the mysticism of union with the personal Lord that is true mysticism.[3]

There is one important interpretation, however, that seems to oppose or at least heavily qualify this way of proceeding, that of Rudolf Otto. Otto's general study of religion owes much to a theistic model, and many of Otto's writings on Hindu religion show that his personal sympathy lies more with the devotional movements related to a personal Lord than with the monistic philosophy of Śankara. Yet Otto takes Śankara and Eckhart as the two great mystics worth comparing in *Mysticism East and West*. Though his actual definition is not in terms of identity or of union, his understanding of higher mysticism is based primarily on a Neoplatonic model.

> It is the wholly non-rational character of this conception of God with its divergence from the intimate, personal, modified God of simple theism, which make the mystic. Mysticism is not first of all an act of union, but predominantly the life lived in the 'knowledge' [*das Leben in dem Wunder*] of this 'wholly other' God . . . Mysticism enters into religious experience in the measure that religious feeling surpasses its rational context . . . To the extent to which its hidden, non-rational, numinous elements predominate and determine the emotional life . . . This definition of the concept of mysticism is supported by the etymology of the words 'mystical' and 'mystic' . . .
>
> 'Mystica' was originally an adjective qualifying the substantive 'theologia'. The essence of the mystica theologia in distinction from the usual theologia lay in the fact that it claimed to teach a deeper 'mystery', and to impart secrets and reveal depths which were otherwise unknown. In this the Scholastic usage was following a still older trail. For long before men spoke of mystical theology they spoke of a mystical *sense*, and of a mystical interpretation of the Scriptures. Such an interpretation was mystical not because it was concerned with a 'unio mystica' but because it unfolded a threefold or sevenfold hidden meaning of the scriptural text, and revealed mysteries which only the eye of the enlightened could perceive.[4] [*sondern dass man hinter, in und unter dem gewöhnlichen Sinne der Schrift geheimen Sinn, Tiefen-sinn suchte und fand.*]

Otto regards it as an advantage of his definition that by adopting it we can understand how mysticism can exist 'where there is no conception of God at all, or where for the final experience itself his existence is a matter of indifference', as in classical Hindu yoga and 'original

Buddhism'.[5] Both are entirely soul-mysticism, whereas both Śankara and Eckhart combine soul-mysticism with God-mysticism.[6] This distinctive combination both incorporates theism and transcends theism. It is also distinct from theistic mysticism. Thus the 'lower knowledge' recognized by Śankara is very close to Rāmānuja's interpretation of Vedānta, which insists on 'the personal conception of Brahman'. This lower knowledge, even though it is surpassed [aufgehobene] 'is nevertheless lower *knowledge* . . . to be clearly distinguished from error in the ordinary sense of the word!'[7] So high an estimate does Śankara have of this lower knowledge of the personal Brahman that the borderline between the higher and lower knowledge often entirely disappears.[8] But while there is 'a shifting and interpenetrating relationship' between the impersonal Brahman and the personal Lord, there is a characteristic notion of *jñāna* that is clearly distinct from the different Advaita of the great bhakti texts. When a Śankara advaitin returns to ordinary consciousness after the realization of identity with Brahman in the state of samādhi, 'the knowledge remains with him that Brahman alone is, and that he is himself Brahman, but it is then only knowledge and not knowledge in experience'.[9] He does not return to *bhakti*, the worship of the personal Lord. For a real disciple of Śankara, '*bhakti* or states of emotion are not a step on the ladder to Samādhi'.

Bhakti, however, *is* such a means to monistic realization for the *bhakti* hero of the *Vishnu Purāṇa*, Prahlāda, who,

cast into the depths of the ocean by his unbelieving father on account of his belief in Vishnu, remains firmly true to his faith, directs his thoughts unperturbed to Vishnu in prayer, and brings Him daily his offerings of praise. This elevation of his spirit to the Lord, this *upāsanā*, passes gradually into mystical experience . . . In this instance we see that the mystical experience arises from a determined act of *Bhakti* (State 1). In State 2, the personal, beloved, trusted Lord of ordinary theistic religion expands into the mystical All-Being, which is the One. After He has been 'seen' in such a form, the state of union results; the objects seen consumes the seer. He is Me and so I am He. Object and subject glide into one another and he who experiences is himself the Lord of all being. In the reverse order, this mystical experience afterwards slips back into simple *Bhakti* worship . . . this personal intercourse is here not something lower or of less value . . . but is equal in value to the mystical experience . . . The characteristic of this God is that he can be interchangeably present with the soul, either as blessed all-absorbing All, *or* as personal lover and friend of the soul. We have here what we must call a 'mysticism of poise' . . . The religious experience of Śankara is not more 'consistent' . . . Prahlāda's religion is thoroughly consistent. It is by its nature 'polar', but that is not inconsistent. Such a nature is rather consistent in itself when it acts in a twofold way.[10]

Otto goes on to observe that there are differentiations within *bhakti* mysticism itself. The type of Prahlāda 'stands nearer to the quiet, collected Rāmānuja', whereas in Chaitanya's type

Bhakti becomes 'Prema', a fevered, glowing, Krishna-eroticism, coloured throughout by love passion; and intoxication enters into the experience. In the heat of love's emotion, which breaks through the limitations of the individual in ecstasy, and seeks union with the beloved, the state of unity is striven after. With Prahlāda it is clearly different. On the contrary for him *Bhakti* is the stilling of the soul before God, a trustful, believing devotion . . . Neither fiery Eros nor sentimental Caritas, but complete Faith as Fiducia, a trustful, concentrated believing contemplation leads here to the loss of self, and to becoming one with Him.[11]

Rudolf Otto attempted a nuanced interpretation of mysticism that would give due weight to both similarities and differences.[12] The different types transcend cultural differences; Śankara and Eckhart are similar not only in the types of mysticism that they reject (illuminism, emotional experimentalism, and nature mysticism)[13] but also in the two types of mysticism they both combine: introspection and unifying vision.

The first involves 'withdrawal from all outward things, retreat into the ground of one's own soul, knowledge of a secret depth and of the possibility of turning in upon one's self'.[14] The second 'knows nothing of "inwardness"', and has no need of a doctrine of the soul.[15] The 'unifying vision' or vision of 'Being in Unity', is 'filled with value and awe' and brings a great 'liberation and blessedness'.[16] It 'shows stages of ascension': first, 'the many is seen as one'; second, the One 'takes precedence over the many . . . [and] itself becomes the object of intuition as that which is superior and prior to the many'.[17] Here the contrast with theism is clear, Otto holds.

. . . it attracts or originates an ontology . . . the One is the only true and complete Being behind the many; the many sinks down into the half-being of changing, becoming, perishing, and of fleeting modes . . . In theism the conditioning relation is that of the rational category of cause and effect. But it is not so with the mystical One. It has the power of conditioning but not in the category of causation . . . Where mystical intuition is grafted upon Theism . . . this non-rational One lying at the basis of all things is called God . . . The personal form of address applies without further ado to the mystic One, and mystical and personal attitudes slip into one another.[18]

In the third stage the One 'can no longer be many' and stands alone.

. . . out of the united [*Einigen*] comes the One only [*Einzige*], out of the All-One [*All-einigen*] the Alone [*Allein-ige*] . . . the relationship of original immanence . . . passes, and is transformed into complete transcendence. The realm of the many is now the wholly evil in contrast to the realm of the One.[19]

Śankara and Eckhart are also similar in their close linking of their mysticism to 'a certain type of theism' needed both 'for the sake of its own inward tension and aspiration' and because any mysticism 'always bears within it some faint scent of the soil from which it rises, and from which it draws the sap of life'.[20]

The final part of Otto's comparison, however, is about the decisive difference between these two great mystics of East and West. 'Christian mysticism is not Indian mysticism, but maintains its distinctive character, already explicable by the ground from which it rises.'[21] Eckhart's 'mysticism is quiveringly *alive* . . . very far from Śankara and Indian mysticism . . . ' 'In spite of great formal similarities, the inner core of Eckhart is as different from that of Śankara as the soil of Palestine and of Christian Gothic Germany in the thirteenth century is from that of India . . . '[22]

Otto's work is subject to various criticisms, not least the apparent identification, only partly metaphorical, between religious distinctions, national genius, and geographic 'atmosphere'. It is also clear that the evaluative comparisons between European Christian and Asian Hindu religion, in the areas both of theistic devotion and of supratheistic mysticism, come out markedly in favour of the former. The lack of a phenomenological *epoché* is particularly noticeable in the 'differences' side of his comparisons. With respect to the similarities, however, he may be criticized for imposing Western categories on Indian religion, most fundamentally through assuming the universality of the categories of the holy and the numinous. All these criticisms have some force, but Otto's comparisons, despite their defects, remain more subtle and suggestive than those of many of his critics.

The particular problem that concerns Otto's treatment of theistic mysticism seems to me to have received little attention: the legitimacy of treating 'theism' and 'mysticism' as types of religion that may under special circumstances be united in the hybrid category of 'theistic mysticism'. Theism and mysticism are abstract nouns related to the adjectives 'theistic' and 'mystical'. Whether the nouns designate significant realities in religious life remains to be demonstrated. The Catholic faith of western Europe before the Protestant Reformation included a *via contemplativa*, which can reasonably be translated in modern parlance as mysticism, but only rarely did those on this *way* see their mystical knowledge or contemplative practice as separated from the 'simple theism' of most Christians. Certainly there were accusations of heresy, notably in the case of Eckhart, and there were individual and group schisms, but the self-understanding of most Catholic Christians, both simple and sophisticated, saw the various dimensions of Christian life as fitting together within the life of the universal Church, which in some mysterious fashion kept a fallen world related to the Triune God. The various Protestant reactions against monastic practice and mystical theology led post-Enlightenment Protestant scholars to see a contrast or even a conflict between 'mysticism' and faith that would have surprised medieval theologians. At the same time the natural theology of the scholastics was transformed into the *theism* of liberal Protestant philosophers of religion.

Faith in that Christ who is so closely linked to his Body the Church implies connection as well as distinction between Christ and the faithful. Likewise a faith that is possible only in and through the Holy Spirit implies more than simply the distinction between Creator and creature. The importance of the communion of saints and the angelic hosts in the medieval universe, not to speak of various kinds of spirits and demonic powers, raises additional questions about understanding a medieval Christian's faith as 'simple theism'. Perhaps this faith could be described as a spectrum with 'mystical theism' on one end and 'theistic mysticism' on the other. I would suggest, in any case, that that complex religious reality is remarkably analogous to many of the theistic movements in medieval and modern India.

Otto's interpretation of the profoundest dimensions of the religious life of such movements, which he as well as many other Western scholars have called 'theistic mysticism', is illuminating at many points and represented in his own generation a considerable advance in Western scholarship. Yet it seems to me insufficiently precise and far from comprehensive. He considers a simple devotion (comparable to Lutheran faith?) that maintains a clear distinction between the Lord and the devotee not to be mysticism at all, while he describes in pejorative terms the kind of emotional devotion that seeks to overcome the separation – and sometimes even the distinction – between the Lord and the devotee. Moreover, he says little about the major distinctive forms of devotion to Vishnu and His consorts, to Śiva, and the various expressions of the Great Goddess, and apart from some negative comments about the ethical content of such devotion, does little to place it in a socio-religious context.

III. *Various Approaches to Theistic Mysticism in Hindu Contexts*

Hindu *bhakti* is also a concept with some problems of definition, which is only to be expected, since this has been such a major strand in the total complex of Hindu life for at least the last two thousand years. The word is adequately translated as devotion, as long as we remember that the word *bhakti* itself suggests participation, and that the close personal relation between devotee and Lord is both an external relation between a finite being and the Supreme Person and an internal relation of belonging, of being an infinitesimal part within an Infinite Whole. For many Hindus *bhakti* is one of many strands in their religious life, but for Hindus participating in any of the organized devotional movements, *bhakti* is the central and organiz- ing strand of both their individual and communal existence, and however fragmented the present reality, the ideal is one of single- minded or 'one-pointed' (*ekāntika*) relation with a divine figure who is not one of many lesser deities but the more or less direct expression of supreme Godhead.

When we try to relate Hindu *bhakti* to the Western concept of mysticism, the diverse understandings of mysticism open up a number of possibilities.

S. N. Dasgupta understands mysticism as including the various Hindu paths to *moksha*, release from this transitory existence and entrance into eternal bliss. Dasgupta understands 'mysticism in Europe . . . to refer to the belief that God is reached through ecstatic communion with Him', and Indian mystics or *bhaktas* share with Islamic and Christian mystics 'the vision of God and His grace . . . attained through devotional communion or . . . rapture'. However, in India 'there are types of religious and mystical experience other than that of an intimate communion with God. I have therefore made my definition of mysticism wider'.[23] Dasgupta regards the *bhakti* type as one of the four chief types of Indian mysticism, the others being the Upanishadic, the Yogic, and the Buddhistic.[24]

Dasgupta sees devotional mysticism developing from the self-abnegation and self-surrender to God taught in the *Gītā* through the story of the faithful devotee Prahlāda in the *Vishṇu Purāṇa* and the elevation of devotion to the supreme plane in the *Bhāgavata Purāṇa*, a devotion realized and illustrated in the life of Chaitanya of Bengal (1486–1534 A.D.). The movement away from yogic supression of the senses to the later *bhakta* inclusion and redirection of sensible feelings in religious experience is indicated already in the quest of Prahlāda.

. . . This inmost and most deepseated love for God . . . stirred him to withdraw his mind from all other things and to enter into such a contemplation of God that he became absorbed in Him, his whole personality lost in an ecstatic trance unity with God. But this did not satisfy Prahlāda. He desired such a devotion to God that the very thought of Him would bring the same sort of satisfaction that persons ordinarily have in thinking of sense-objects. He desired not only contemplative union but longed also to taste God's love as one tastes the pleasures of the senses.[25]

The *Bhāgavata Purāṇa*, Dasgupta continues, develops still further this emotion-laden devotion. Those following the path of devotion

come to experience such intense happiness that all their limbs and senses become saturated therewith and their minds swim as it were, in a lake of such supreme bliss that even the bliss of ultimate liberation loses its charm . . . The *bhakta* who is filled with such a passion does not experience it merely as an undercurrent of joy which waters the depths of his own heart in his own privacy, but as a torrent that overflows the caverns of his senses. Through all his senses he realizes it as if it were a sensuous delight; with his heart and soul he feels it as a spiritual intoxication of joy. Such a person is beside himself with this love of God. He sings, laughs, dances and weeps. He is no longer a person of this world.[26]

Dasgupta considers *bhakti* as one of the several equally valid types of Hindu mysticism, in contrast to the view that many in India and the West have come to take for granted: that Śankara's monistic interpretation of the Upanishads is the primary type of Hindu mysticism.[27] This widespread view includes a number of more specific interpretations of the relation of *bhakti* to the 'pure mysticism' of *Advaita*. Rudolf Otto has touched upon four of them. One is to see *bhakti* as the passionate protest of simple faith or theistic piety against the impersonal mysticism of Śankara's *Advaita*: 'a struggle for . . . a real and living God'.[28] A second is to see *bhakti* as the theistic foundation for the lofty flights of Śankara's higher mysticism, a foundation of crucial importance yet finally a detachable stage in the stratosphere of spiritual experience. A third is to see the higher *bhakti* exemplified by Prahlāda as a fluid transition moving back and forth easily between dualistic theism and monistic mysticism. A fourth is to see *bhakti* as a distinct but lower type of mysticism, but one whose emotional extravagance and erotic symbolism make it suspect both to theism and to higher mysticism.[29]

Still another approach is taken in general books on mysticism written by two scholars from within the *bhakti* tradition, specifically the Śrī Vaishnava community of South India, which follows the teachings of Rāmānuja. Both consider the fusion of wisdom, devotion, and service in the theistic interpretation of the Upanishads to constitute the central strand of mysticism. A. Govindacharya of Mysore holds that the quest of mystics is to discover God dwelling in the heart ('the Heart of all hearts')[30] and believes that 'the Vedic notion of the Husband or Bridegroom furnishes the key-note to the Indian mystic'.[31] Krishna reveals God as the supremely Beautiful one, and 'mystic experience everywhere points to the realization of the Beautiful, and the summit of Vedāntic thought proclaims this by the term *Ānanda* [joy].'[32]

P. N. Srinivasachari of Madras, in striking contrast to S. N. Dasgupta, begins by excluding many religious phenomena and even whole religious systems that have sometimes been referred to as mystical. Mysticism is *Brahmananubhava*, the experience of Brahman. It is not limited to Hindus, but it is restricted by its definition to the soul's quest for union with God.

> It is not a special mystic faculty . . . everyone can directly realize God or Brahman as the Inner Self of all beings . . . Mysticism is a body of eternal, spiritual or religious truths which were verified by the ancient Indian *ṛṣis*, Christian mystics and Sufis[33] . . . The Divine Spirit which shines within

man is made manifest and the soul sees the light realizable beyond sight.[34] . . . Mystic feeling is not an explosion from the subliminal state, as James says, but the overflow of superconscious love into the heart of man. In moments of spiritual crisis and conversion, pangs of remorse are followed by feelings of redemptive assurance. The emotional centre shifts from the mood of tranquil-mindedness or equanimity or *śāntabhāva* to that of God-intoxication or divine drunkenness (*madhurabhāva*) . . . *Bhakti* breaks into the spirit, melts it down and becomes an infinite longing for the Infinite. God is infinite and human love expands into the infinite love of God.[35]

For both Govindacharya and Srinivasachari, as well as for Dasgupta, it is the theistic mysticism of both Christian and Islamic traditions that comes closest to Hindu devotional mysticism. All three of these Hindu interpreters would insist on the unity of the two forms of Hindu devotional mysticism that Rudolf Otto so sharply separates: the devotion of balance and peaceful repose (*śānta*) and the devotion of intense emotion and transmuted erotic feeling (*mādhurya bhāva* and *śṛngāra rasa*). The two Śrī Vaishnava scholars would go a step further, however, in identifying this life of devotion with the correct interpretation of the Upanishads, and Srinivasachari would proceed still further in identifying Śankara's 'practical Advaita' with Rāmānuja's devotion-filled understanding of the Vedānta.[36]

We should note the implications of one other set of alternatives in conceiving mysticism. Mysticism may be defined in terms of the path or in terms of the goal. If mysticism is defined as a path leading away from ordinary life and common experience to a higher reality and a transformed 'vision', then the various paths or *mārgas* listed in every introductory account of Hinduism all qualify as forms of mysticism. Most are linked to some form of renunciation (*sannyāsa* or *tyāga*) and some very specifically to a full-fledged ascetic life. If, on the other hand, mysticism is defined according to a common goal, not all these well known paths to *moksha* can qualify, since they explicitly offer quite different goals. It is true that the Hindu and Jain paths do share the notion of the *ātman* as a permanent centre of consciousness distinct from the psychic and physical body that it indwells, but this self can be diversely understood as at the finite or Infinite level, with a consequent difference in the meaning of the goal.

Moreover, the apparently common Indian notion of the self is explicitly denied in all Buddhist schools, along with the rejection of all permanent substantial reality. If the realization of the identity of one's inmost self with the Supreme Self is taken to be the goal, the idealistic schools of Mahāyāna Buddhism might seem to qualify as mysticism, along with Advaita Vedānta, but all other paths, in varying degrees, would have to be regarded as non-mystical. I do not accept this premise, but it is certainly true that Advaita has been immensely influential in Hindu religion and has had a prestige in Indian culture going far beyond the small circles of Advaitin ascetics. This form of Hindu mysticism might seem to be most distinct from Hindu religion in general. In one sense the Advaitic system of thought makes this true by definition. The realization of one's identity with the Absolute is such that, by contrast, all else seems false. Nevertheless, this supreme moment of realization is linked to conventional reality – including the gods, the scriptures, and the socio-religious system – both metaphysically and practically. Brahman is the basis of all apparent reality, in so far as it is the reality beneath the appearance, as well as the radical negation of such apparent reality perceived as things with distinct shapes and qualities. Moreover, Brahman itself appears within the unreal world as the personal Lord endowed with all auspicious qualities, and the devoted worship of the Brahman with personal qualities (*saguṇa*) is itself the most favoured and widespread means among practitioners of Advaita of preparing for the ultimate insight of identity with the Absolute beyond all name and form (*nirguṇa* Brahman).

IV. *Mystical Knowledge in Bhakti: The Dialectic of God's Presence and Absence*

Some mystics are so unconventional, either in their teaching or in their behaviour, or in both, that they stand out clearly in contrast to other members of their respective religious communities. In some cases this distinctiveness may increase the esteem in which they are held, giving evidence that they have attained a higher level of spiritual attainment. In other cases such distinctiveness may lead to disapproval on the part of religious leaders or ordinary adherents, or even to persecution. Even when a mystic stands out in some ways, it is debatable whether the most distinctive aspects of his religious life are the most important, especially most important for defining the quality of that person's mysticism. It is difficult for the later student as well as for contemporary disciples and opponents rightly to assess the more radical and the more conservative elements in the religious life of a mystic, and this difficulty is compounded by the hidden character of much of the mystic's life, especially when there is pressure upon the mystic to conform to the accepted norms of belief and action. Even so we should not too quickly conclude that the 'real' Eckhart or Śankara, or even al-Hallāj, should be interpreted on the basis of his most radical or unconventional expressions. All of these thinkers were sufficiently bold that they need to be taken seriously in their more conservative as well as in their innovative or 'heretical' utterances.

With respect to some of the theistic mystics, our problem in understanding may be the reverse. Some of them seem to affirm the common tradition so completely that we may wonder in what sense they are mystics. Many mystics in such theistic traditions would insist that they are affirming the common truth of the tradition, but attempting to realize it for themselves more intensely and personally. For Hindu *bhaktas* the goal is clearly a vision of God. Within this life such a vision is necessarily incomplete, but there are differing degrees possible.

Three years ago when I was visiting the great temple of Śrī Venkateśvara near Tirupati in South India, two boys called out to me, 'Have you seen God?' I was startled because the Telugu word they used, derived from the Sanskrit *deva*, is the same word I had known from childhood, the word that Telugu Christians use for God. The end of the prologue to the Gospel of John, 'No one has ever seen God', (1.18a) seemed to clash sharply with the Hindu boys' confidence that God was incarnate in the temple and could be seen by every pilgrim. Hindu theistic mysticism might thus seem to be only the intensification of a commonplace truth for every Hindu, whereas Christian theistic mysticism appears to be the mysterious approach to that which is beyond the reach, or even the comprehension, of the ordinary believer in Christ. The second half of the sentence in John both diminishes and clarifies the difference: 'the only Son, who is in the bosom of the Father, he has made him known'. (1.18b) What follows in the Gospel of John further narrows the gap between seeing and the acceptance of revelation, yet the theme returns near the end of this Gospel. After the doubting Thomas has been told to touch the resurrected Jesus and has exclaimed, 'My Lord and my God!' Jesus responds, 'Have you believed because you have seen me? Blessed are those who have not seen and yet believe.' (20. 28–29)

There is certainly an important difference. The Christian believes without seeing his absent Lord while the Hindu can see the Lord incarnate in the image, both in the temple and in the home shrine. Yet both the Christian and the Hindu place great emphasis on remembering the visible presence of the Lord in the past and on anticipating a spiritual seeing beyond the temporal plane. Moreover, for the Hindu devotee, the physical vision of the image, though a real *darśana*, a seeing of God, is incomplete. Remembrance is necessary to deepen physical sight into spiritual insight, and the deeper the insight, the keener the awareness of the absence of the Lord and the more vivid the anticipation of more complete union. The relation of distinction and unity is an epistemological as well as an ontological problem for the *bhakta*. Indeed, if the devotee sees the Lord, the theoretical question of their metaphysical relation is eclipsed by the joy of the Divine presence. The devotees' problem is that the omnipresent Lord of the universe, who has graciously entrusted himself to his worshippers in his countless image incarnations, is nevertheless painfully absent from his devotees' longing sight. During this earthly existence, with only tantalizing glimpses of the Lord's presence, they must persist in their remembering and believe in the goal of their yearning.

The paradoxical dialectic of presence and absence is present in many forms of *bhakti*, but nowhere is it so elaborated as in the dramatic representations of the cowherd Krishna. At one extreme anyone present at the drama enjoys the 'real presence' of Lord Krishna; at the other extreme the divine Rādhā herself experiences the excruciating absence of Lord Krishna. Even when the lovers are united there is the remembrance and anticipation of their separation, while, conversely, the remembrance and anticipation of their union makes bearable the time of separation. In some incomprehensible fashion the extremes meet in the drama – for the players and for the audience. The sharing in the drama brings the Divine presence into ordinary human lives; memory and anticipation are nearly fused in the dramatic vision in spite of (or is it because of?) the absence of the Lord so keenly felt by His most intimate companions.[37]

V. *Distinction and Unity in Mystical Union: The Teachings of Rāmānuja*

The different Vaishṇava theologians were all steeped in the cycle of stories of Krishna, as well as of the other divine incarnations, not only in reading or recitation, but also in sculpture, drama, and temple liturgy. Given the combination of – or alternation between – the presence and absence of God for his devotees, it is not surprising that these theologians approached both the epistemological and the ontological questions for such devotion in somewhat different ways. The Gosvāmins adapted the older theory of aesthetic categories (*rasas*) to provide a finely nuanced analysis of the range of devotional states but referred to their philosophical position as *acintyabhedābheda* – the relation of God and cosmos understood as an unthinkable combination of distinction and unity. Vallabha, while heir to a similar tradition of Krishna–Rādhā devotion, emphasized a pure metaphysical unity (*śuddhādvaita*) devoid of any doctrine of illusion but held up an experiential dualism as its goal: the vivid anguish of the Lord's remembrance in separation is preferable to the loss of devotional consciousness in complete union.[38] Madhva and his school are the most emphatic in their affirmation of eternal distinctions between the Lord and all finite beings, as well as among those finite beings.

The community of Rāmānuja was nurtured, not only on the hymns, meditations, and stories in the Sanskrit scriptures, but also on the hymns of the Tamil post-saints, known as the Āḻvārs. The most philosophically inclined of these, Nammāḻvar, wrote a great theological poem of more than a thousand verses, the Tiruvāymoḻi, which the later Śrī Vaishṇava tradition calls the 'Tamil Veda'. The complexity of the poet's vision of God is set out in some of the opening verses:

He is not: He is. Thus it is impossible to speak of Him, Who has pierced the earth and the sky and become the inner ruler in all. He is unaffected by defects. He is in all without intermission. He is the abode of bliss. Such a person have I attained. (I.1.3)

All is He – that which is called that, this, and that between (mid-thing). That man, this man, mid-man, that woman, this woman, mid-woman, what is that, what is this, and what is in between, those, these and things in between, good and bad, past things, present things and future – all is He. (I.1.4.)

He is the material cause of all ākāśa (ether), air, fire, water and earth, pervading all this like the soul its body. He is the Shining One in all. The scriptures intimate Him to be the end of Śrī [the Goddess Lakshmī], and as having contained all these elements in Himself during the period of deluge [cosmic dissolution]. (I.1.7)

He is the Inner Lord of all; whether said to be existent or non-existent, He is. Possessing both the existent and the non-existent within Him, He pervading all as self is the Total Being. Pervading all He is yet their destroyer and as such He is the eternally permanent Being. (I.1.8)[39]

These verses display a monistic version of reality that at times seems close to pantheism and at times seems deliberately paradoxical. It is clearly different from the Advaita of Śankara, yet it includes familiar themes from the Upanishads as well as other Sanskrit scriptures. Several centuries later Rāmānuja attempted to spell out a rational synthesis between the Sanskrit and Tamil 'Vedas', between the wisdom of ascetic meditation and wisdom of fervent devotion. His theory was named by his followers *Viśishṭādvaita*: the non-duality of the Reality that is internally differentiated. In this view the finite centres of consciousness (selves) form the body or the mode of the Supreme Self just as the physical form provides the body for each finite self. This teaching is synthetic but intentionally non para-doxical, and the emphasis on the devotee's servant-relationship to the Lord gives the impression of much greater sobriety than that of the Bengali and North Indian theologians of Krishna-*bhakti*. The impression of rational balance accords with the community's own self-understanding, but neither paradox nor passion is altogether lacking in Rāmānuja's theistic mysticism.

The first apparent paradox to be resolved is the combination of supremacy and accessibility in the Divine nature. The access to God's presence which neither lesser gods nor great yogins can gain by their own powers is freely granted to those who humbly resort to the Lord and seek refuge with Him. The righteous king Rāma seems to provide the model for God's action in the universe: his voluntary exile for kingly rule, his heroic conquest and destruction of Rāvaṇa, the demon king who abducted his faithful wife Sītā, and above all Rāma's generous forgiveness of all those enemies who surrender and appeal for his grace. The devotion of faithful attendants and forgiven enemies to the exemplary monarch provides a model that may seem to approximate the piety Otto calls simple faith and to differentiate it from mysticism of any variety. Such trusting faith, however, proves later on in Rāmānuja's tradition to contain its own complexities and perplexities.⁴⁰ There are indeed followers who take the Divine incarnation in Rāma as the major model for their devotion, and there are some other Vaishṇava groups in India organized more exclusively around devotion to Rāma. The community of Rāmānuja, however, has a much broader heritage and a more complex system of devotion, one that includes all the divine descents (*avatāras*) of Vishṇu and that is grounded on a theistic interpretation of the Brahman of the Upanishads as the personal overlord of all lesser cosmic lords, the inner controller of each finite being and the Supreme Self ensouling the entire cosmos.⁴¹

The most famous metaphysical doctrine of Rāmānuja is deservedly that of *śarīraśarīribhāva*: the self-body relationship that characterizes both the unity of finite reality with the Infinite Lord and the real distinction between them. With some important qualifications, the relation of the Supreme Self to finite selves is like that of the finite selves to their material bodies, and this relation has three characteristics: the indwelling self – whether Divine or finite – is the body's ontological support (*ādhāra*); its controller (*niyantā*), and its owner (*śeshī*).⁴²

What has not been so widely recognized outside of the Śrī Vaishṇava tradition is that for Rāmānuja the goal of *bhakti* is the realization in intense feeling of what is metaphysically always true in the Divine-human relationship. Each of the three characteristics of this fundamental fact needs to be personally experienced by the serious devotee. First, all finite beings are sustained by the Divine Support, but the *bhakta* desperately yearns for the felt presence of the Lord in order to maintain his very existence, or more paradigmatically, *her* very existence, for the soul is more 'she' than 'he' in relation to the Supreme Lord. Second, all creatures are under the Divine control, but the devotee seeks to remain perpetually conscious that his (her) action are not his (her) own doing: 'they are not mine but Thine.' It is the Lord Himself, as the Inner Controller (*Antaryāmī*), who is the active agent in the life of the devotee. Third, it is true that the whole world is the Lord's property and every creature is totally at his disposal, but the devotee is not satisfied with that metaphysical fact, and he (she) yearns to perform some service for the Lord, not as a means of attaining the goal of *moksha*, release from the imperfections of physical existence conditioned by inherited *karma*, but as the highest privilege to which finite beings can aspire: eternal service to the Lord and the Lord's servants. This service is personal service, at times conceived in the most personal and intimate terms as the wife's service to her husband. At the point of the devotee's union with the Lord, such intimate belonging is transmuted into the ultimate mystery, but this most intimate belonging to the Lord is metaphysically continuous with that most basic and commonplace belonging to the Lord shared in by every blade of grass.

The doctrine of grace is closely linked to the royal metaphor, but that very social metaphor itself seems to me in the traditional Indian context to contain a significant ambiguity. In much of his writing Rāmānuja follows a strong Hindu tradition for which the law of *karma* is basic; *bhakti* then becomes a higher *karma*, and the 'good deed' of devotion, the humble service done to please the Divine Lord, is suitably rewarded by the Lord's grace or favour. Even more fundamental to Rāmānuja's own thought, however, is the concept of belonging noted above. The love of the universal Owner and Master for his creatures both precedes and stretches far beyond the insignificant service rendered by his subjects. Service is now seen as the consequence of Grace instead of its cause. Both groups of Rāmānuja's followers stress the theme of Divine grace, but the ambiguity in his teaching may have contributed to a widening gap in interpretation that helped split the community, the southern school stressing 'grace without cause'; the northern, 'grace with a pretext': i.e. a modicum of human effort to satisfy the requirements of Divine justice.

VI. *The Paradox of Grace and Devotion:*
The Ignoring or Reversing of Cosmic Hierarchy

Such ambiguity in the fusing of two previous traditions linking Divine grace and human effort does not seem to me paradoxical. There is a point in Rāmānuja's interpretation of the Divine-human relation, however, where this generally balanced and rational teaching does approach paradox. It is alluded to at several points in his commentary on the *Bhagavadgītā*, where it is not difficult to see behind the friend-to-friend and teacher-to-disciple relationship of two warriors, the mischievous and amorous play of a much younger

Krishna the fields and forests surrounding a cowherd village.

This theme is first touched on in a phrase at the end of Rāmānuja's Introduction: *āśrita-vātsalya-vivaśaḥ*: overwhelmed with protecting and forgiving love (the eager and urgent affection that impels a cow to lick clean its new-born calf) for his dependents, i.e. those who have come for refuge. The supreme personal spirit, overlord of all lesser lords, who has become mortal for the world's sake, who here on a world stage is about to teach the yoga of devotion to Arjuna, is said to be 'overwhelmed with love for his dependents'. Rāmānuja understands the Krishna teaching in the *Gītā* to be the Supreme Lord, who presides over the exchange of gifts between men and lesser gods and who recommends that his followers also participate in such exchange, not for personal gain, but for the holding together of the world (*lokasaṃgraha*). This God is entirely self-sufficient. He does not need the sacrificial offerings, for his every wish is satisfied and his will is ever accomplished. And yet this majestic Krishna, speaking as Divine teacher, when referring to those few who cannot sustain their souls without constant remembrance and extreme affection for him, goes on to speak of his answering response: 'unable to bear the separation'.

The mutual dependence between God and His favourite devotee is put quite emphatically in the comment on *Gītā* 7.18. This immediately follows verse 17, which expresses the mutual affection between God and the single-minded devotee. In his commentary Rāmānuja refers to Prahlāda, 'pre-eminent among the wise' and roughly quotes a verse about him from the *Vishṇu Purāṇa* (I.17.39):

'But he with his mind absorbed in Krishna, while being bitten by great serpents, did not know his body, feeling only the rapture of remembering Him.' – in the same way he too is dear to Me.

The comment on verse 18 includes the following:

'I consider that the wise person [*jñānī*] is My very self [*ātmā*].' This means that the support for My existence is under his control. Why so? Because the wise person finds it impossible without Me to sustain His self. He take Me alone as his superlative goal. Therefore without him, I cannot sustain My self. Thus he is indeed My self.

Rāmānuja affirms the monistic thrust of this verse, but he interprets it in a somewhat surprising way, considering the *Gītā*'s emphasis on God's independence or aseity, and the necessity for finite beings to acknowledge their total dependence on him. For here Krishna, clearly speaking as God, declares his need for the love of his cherished devotees, a need so great that he cannot live without it. Rāmānuja stands in a tradition of wise saints who know their total dependence on God, yet who precisely in their own moments of greatest need for God's presence know the corresponding need of God for their support and affirm this paradoxical mutuality between creator and creature, king and subject, a mutuality so complete that the Lord can say, 'He is My self.'

In his comment on *Gītā* 9.29, which affirms God's equal regard for all beings but special relation to his devotees, Rāmānuja seems to take a step beyond the mutual indwelling affirmed by the text. He paraphrases Lord Krishna:

> But those who worship Me with such worship as their sole aim, with intense love because they cannot sustain themselves (their souls) without worshipping Me, whether they are born in high caste or low, dwell within My very self in unembarrassed content as if [*iva*] their qualities were equal to Mine. 'I, too am in them' means: I treat them as if [*iva*] they were my superiors.

Here Rāmānuja asserts not only that God treats his devotees of different castes quite equally – denying the worldly hierarchy – but that he treats them all as superior to himself, thus shockingly reversing the cosmic or ontological hierarchy. It is true that, as a rational theologian, he must add the qualifying 'as if' (*iva*), but more than a hint of paradox and mystery remains.[43]

In terms of Indian culture this paradoxical reversal may be understood as the hyperbole of the generous host, but the social analogues for such temporary reversal of values between high and low can only partially help to make intelligible the incomprehensible fact of this mystical experience: the union of Infinite and finite. For Rāmānuja this union never means an identity beyond all distinction, but it does mean an incredible mutuality, with some hints of mysterious intimacy.

In the Tamil devotional poetry of the Ālvārs centuries before, the whole range of devotional relationships to Vishnu in his various incarnations is sensitively explored, sometimes with great philosophical subtlety but without the rational theologian's need to avoid inconsistency or seeming contradiction. The daring of the human partner in the Divine-human encounter is perhaps at its greatest in the lover's quarrel, a motif of still earlier Tamil literature that enlivens the erotic mode in this devotional mediation.

Some centuries after Rāmānuja the love of Krishna and Rādhā is masterfully expressed by Jayadeva in the *Gītagovinda*.[44] The final triumph of Rādhā over Krishna in this context of love again expresses the paradoxical reversal of values in this kind of devotion. What is unthinkable is experienced as a reality of devotional experience. It is true that there are Divine and human analogues that make this relationship more intelligible within Hindu culture. In the tantric tradition the goddess may stand alone without need of male consort or may provide the vital energy to an otherwise lifeless male deity. By a few, Rādhā has been regarded as such a feminine and finally triumphant Divine power (śakti). On the other hand Rādhā may well be understood as the paradigmatic human devotee, vastly inferior to her Divine love in ontological status, but holding her own finally triumphing over him within their mutual love. The human analogue is not confined to India (*She Stoops To Conquer*)[45] yet the expression of womanly triumph may seem even more surprising in a culture that so systematically appears to denigrate women in the social hierarchy. I would suggest that the 'triumph' of Rādhā has various levels of meaning, of which the female enthralment of the physically stronger male may be one, but certainly not the most important one. It is the fervent love of Rādhā and the tireless devotion of Āndāl (in her own Tamil poem as well as in the stories about her in the Ālvārs' hagiography) that win Krishna's heart, not simply or mainly their feminine beauty. There is an evident power in such love that is linked at a deep level of feeling with the power to bear and nurture children and, more broadly, to fill a home with well-being. All this is summed up in the crucial concept of the auspicious, of which married women are not only the sign but the clearly experienced embodiment. At least in South India, it is not simply sexual union but marriage, the ceremony establishing which is the epitome of auspiciousness, that stands for the most intimate relation between God and the devotional soul, as well as often expressing the central relation between the masculine and feminine persons in Divinity. The Hindu wife is expected to be the devotee as well as the servant of her husband, whom she is to treat as a god, but at the same time she is completely necessary to her husband's ritual as well as physical fulfilment. It is woman with such ambivalent roles and with such ambiguous sacred and even ontological status who is considered in Hindu theistic mysticism to be the most appropriate human partner of the Supreme Lord, conceived as the highest male person (*purushottama* or *paramapurusha*). Both the humblest and the most exhalted role of the devotee can thus reflect the same human reality in Hindu society and culture, whether the emphasis is on 'beloved mistress' or 'faithful wife'.

It is true that Hindu devotional poetry sometimes moves back and forth between a state of relationship and a state of distinctionless identity, but except where there is strong influence from Śankara's *advaita* or some comparably monistic position, the state of identity is not conceived as 'higher', and often the state of relationship is explicitly preferred, sometimes in conscious opposition to the Brahmanical establishment. Yet the problem of the *bhakti* poet or theologian only begins with the affirmation of fundamental Divine-human relationship. How can the union of the Infinite with the finite even be conceived? In personal terms, how can my relationship, as insignificant and sin-enmeshed creature, with the source and ruler of all being even be imagined, let alone intensely experienced? To describe this as the problem, however, is to adopt too modern and too academic a perspective. For the Hindu theist the relationship is a fact, or at least a potential fact. The problem, if we may call it that, is what it is for all mystics, how the believed truth may be personally experienced or realized.

The previous sketch has dealt with a few of the Vaishnava devotional movements. The same general points could be illustrated from Śaiva devotion, with some shift in the emphasis. Śaivites have generally been much more tolerant of paradox; some have found in the unpredictable playfulness of Lord Śiva or the rule-shattering intervention of the Goddess the most intense experience of transcendence. It is also true that much Śaiva *bhakti*, like some North Indian Vaishnava *bhakti* and the *nirguṇa bhakti* of the Sants, tends to a goal that appears more advaitin: a distinctionless unity in which the finite self disappears. Yet the concern with the Divine-human relationships along the way are common to most forms of *bhakti*, as well as the wonder that such an impossible link between Infinite and finite, universe and single individuals, auspicious God and powerless man can indeed be a personally experienced reality. For most Hindu *bhaktas* it is axiomatic that the Supreme Lord in some sense includes all, even is all, but there is also the fervent aspiration that the Lord who is even more than the all and the devotee who is so much less than the all may find union in love.

VII. *The Open Secret*

'So you've studied Rāmānuja. Very good. He is the teacher who democratized Hinduism. Do you know the story of how he shouted out the secret of salvation from the temple tower . . . ' – Such was approximately the response of the first two educated Hindu laymen I encountered on my first visit back to India after completing my dissertation. Indeed, I did know the story, one of the most striking of many stories about this great teacher–saint in the traditional biographies. The story has grown even more democratic in its modern version, to be sure, since those familiar with South Indian temples would assume that the tower in question was a *gopuram*, the tall tower over the gate. If the great teacher climbed such a tower to broadcast his words, he must have intended them to reach the populace outside the temple on the main street of the town, people of every caste, many of them perhaps not even lay devotees of Lord Vishnu. It happens that the particular temple about which this story is told is different, however. The tower is in the middle of the temple enclosure and contains shrines on three floors, each housing an image of Vishnu, one standing, one sitting, and one reclining. Outside the upper shrines are balconies, and to one of those did Rāmānuja climb to 'shout the secret'. The hearers were therefore not the unbelieving public, the worshippers approaching or leaving this temple shrine. That detail, however, modifies only slightly the point of the story, which has but an indirect connection with modern democracy, but reveals much of the spirit of the *bhakti* movement.

Rāmānuja's great predecessor Yāmuna had died before the new leader of the community had not more than once received the piercing glance of the old teacher across a temple courtyard. Since Yāmuna had entrusted the various secrets of the tradition to five different disciples, who had scattered to various towns in the central Tamil country after their master's death, the young Rāmānuja, though already chosen to head the community, had to travel from town to town humbly requesting instruction from these chief disciples of Yāmuna and meeting whatever conditions each set for divulging his special knowledge. The fifth of these disciples had to be visited eighteen times before he consented to share his secret with Rāmānuja and two inseparable disciples, and then only on condition that Rāmānuja keep the teaching secret. The very next day, however, Rāmānuja, went up to the second-floor balcony in the temple and revealed this teaching to a number of Śrī Vaishnavas below; i.e. to some who were already initiated members of the community of Vishnu and his Divine Consorts. Of course Rāmānuja was summoned back to explain his misconduct. He acknowledged that he would go to hell for breaking a promise to his teacher, but he alone would suffer, while all those who had thus shared the teacher's secret would be saved. The teacher was so impressed by Rāmānuja's concern for the welfare of others that he embraced him and gave him a new and divine title, 'Our Lord'.[46]

Both the story itself and the frequency of its retelling testify to a central feature of this *bhakti* tradition: the individual relationship of a single teacher to a single chosen disciple is greatly broadened into a community of many teachers and even more disciples. The community has its entrance requirements, but in principle they are those of single-minded devotion, not of caste, and the secret transmission of arcane interpretations has been broadened to pass on the benefit of such secret knowledge to a larger community.

In some of the other *bhakti* movements even sharper contrasts are drawn between the secretive tradition of a few elite masters of yoga or Vedānta and the much more broadly based communities of devotees, sustained by the freely offered grace of God. Many of the *bhakti* movements seem to stand with one foot in the sphere of renunciation and contemplative discipline but the other foot in the relatively popular and this-worldly sphere of temple worship. There seems often only a limited place for the hidden wisdom of yoga, which sometimes is disavowed altogether, as impossibly difficult for the very limited powers of beings in this degenerate age, too much relying on the powers of spiritual virtues and too little on the gracious love of God.

Since one important dimension of mystical theology or the contemplative way in medieval Christianity was that of secret or hidden knowledge, a problem of definition again arises. Even if Hindu *bhakti* can qualify as mysticism in terms of its goal of Divine-human union, does its very openness not remove it from the mystical sphere?

In the community of Rāmānuja, the term *rahasya* (secret) is still very much in use, referring to the interpretation of the three most significant ritual formulas invoked by members of the group. In the generations after Rāmānuja more and more of these interpretations were written down. A new genre developed: commentaries on the *rahasyas*.[47] What is striking about these 'secrets', however, is that they are primarily concerned with the doctrine of grace. It was such a secret of grace that Rāmānuja is said to have disclosed. One import of these 'secrets' is that God is the means (*upāya*) as well as the goal (*upeya*) of the devotional life. With reference to mysticism as the pursuing of a disciplined meditation through a series of stages, this doctrine might be considered anti-mystical, a rejection of the ideology and in part also of the practice of ascetic piety. In another sense, however, this doctrine of God's all-sufficiency at the heart of more popular and communitarian *bhakti* is profoundly mystical. The all-supporting, all-controlling, all-enveloping God is present in one's religious path at the beginning and the middle as well as at the end.

Different devotional movements made different uses and different reinterpretations of the symbolism of yoga and of ascetic renunciation, as well as of the temple ritual, in some cases making sharp criticism of mystical as well as popular piety, most notably the Vīra Śaivas in South India and the Sants in the North. The community of Rāmānuja did not become to such a degree a popular or socially radical movement, and has appeared in recent times to many outsiders a bastion of religious and social conservatism, dominated by rank-conscious Brahmins.

It is true that the import of the 'secrets' is primarily a reinterpretation of the motivation for engaging in both ascetic and popular religious practice, rather than the establishment of a new ritual or a new social order, but in this respect the theistic mysticism of Śrī Vaishṇavas resembles large parts of western mystical movements. Yet the radical impulse is there, and the modern democratic interpretation of Rāmānuja contains an important truth. Every so often the secret passed on by Brahmins and ascetics is proclaimed from the temple gate to the main street of Indian society outside. But those who know the secret best know that it remains concealed. This is true liturgically: one's personal guru must whisper the sacred words into one's ear in the moment of solemn initiation. It is also true theologically: only God can disclose and make real the Divine presence in both shrine and market-place, make real a sustaining power that enables one to stop clinging to all other supports, both 'religious' and 'secular', enables one to pray for well-being for the world but nothing for oneself, except the privilege of eternal service to the One of incomparable power and matchless beauty.

VIII. *Conclusion*

This effort to conceive Hindu *bhakti* as some form of a general cross-cultural category of mysticism has led to a brief survey of some of the characteristic features of Hindu *bhakti*, each of which seems similar to an important element in western mystical traditions, especially to the more theistic traditions in which the concern for union with God is linked with a firm sense of God's immeasurable superiority to his creation. This complexity is expressed in a number of dialectical combinations that may be conceived by some as paradoxes. These include God's presence with and absence from the devotee, God's distinction from and union with the devotee, and the obscuring, ignoring, or even reversing of God's infinite superiority to the devotee.

The final dialectic I have noted in the *bhakti* tradition also is present in the western monotheistic religions as a whole, but might seem to differentiate *bhakti* from a narrower definition of western mysticism, just as it clearly does differentiate *bhakti* from many classical and more recent traditions of Hindu yoga. This is the matter of secrecy. The concern for gaining a hidden knowledge is not only important in the etymology of the word mystical, but has, as Otto pointed out, been important for mystical movements with diametrically opposed metaphysics. The *bhakti* tradition has both preserved and challenged and thus to some extent transformed the secret knowledge of yoga and tantra. While this could be regarded as a further indication of the hybrid character of *bhakti* (an 'impure' form of mysticism), there is sufficient evidence of a similar dialectic in many western movements that we call mystical to make it preferable to indicate 'the open secret' as a frequent feature in the group of cross-cultural phenomena that may be designated as 'mysticism'.

The modern western penchant for investing adjectival qualities with substantial reality through shifting from adjective to noun has been criticized by Wilfred Cantwell Smith, with special reference to the shift from 'religious' to 'religion'.[48] A similar development might be shown from 'mystical' to 'mysticism', but whether or not that development should be deplored seems to me to require a religious or philosophical judgement.

In historical and phenomenological understanding some use of '-isms' can be quite helpful, provided we are clear as to what kind of reality is implied by various interpreters, many of whom make a positive or negative evaluation of the substantive in question, in this case 'mysticism'. Thus mysticism may be taken as a universal religion or super-religion more or less closely attached to or concealed beneath the various historical religious complexes. This is probably the strongest use of the substantive, mysticism with a capital M. The term may be used as a scholarly abstraction to refer to similar features of religious life in various cultures, in some cases organized into distinct master–disciple chains of tradition and different circles, brotherhoods, or ascetic communities. A third use is to designate as mysticism the total religious life of a particular community in which some mystical element predominates. It is this third use that I have in mind in considering the various Hindu devotional movements as examples of theistic mysticism.

If we take this approach, however, the specific meaning of 'mysticism' needs to be defined by the central features of the total religious complex, not by the elements present of some pure mystical type. The articulate statements of leaders of such mystical traditions seem to me to provide the best evidence; for example, the specific ways in which Śankara links himself to or distinguishes himself from others in the Hindu tradition, or Eckhart's own statements on his relation to the Christian Church. There are certainly difficult problems of interpretation. In Śankara's case hundreds of works are attributed to him, the majority of which are considered by modern scholars to be written by later followers. There is also the question raised earlier as to whether social pressure causes the mystic to conceal radical doctrines in more public utterances. I suspect that such outside pressure is less significant than the internal dialectic of revelation and concealment, sometimes expressed through a systematic view of levels of knowledge, sometimes indicated in positive acknowledgement of the unexpected bestowal of Divine

Illumination. In some cases the social structure of the community, the nature of its rituals, or the motifs in its stories may aid greatly in the interpretation. Whatever the material being scrutinized, it is important to try to determine the most significant whole, at least if it is our aim not only to isolate in our analysis the mystical element but to understand the total religious life of an individual mystic or larger community accepting mystical roles.

For many years the ambiguity of the term mysticism led me to avoid it, especially in studying Indian religious phenomena. The widespread use of the term by modern Hindus, however, is part of the total religious situation that the student of Indian religion and the general historian of religion are seeking to understand. Even more important, the term mystical has been used to point to several important features in the life of many religious communities. It also seems to me that the very ambiguity of the modern term mysticism and the strong evaluations, both positive and negative, accompanying its use may provide a clue to an important problem confronting modern students of religion, who stand in varying degrees of detachment from the religious materials they are examining.

The clearest conclusion of this brief study may appear largely negative: the multiple dialectic in Hindu *bhakti* does not demonstrate its impure or hybrid character as a form of mysticism, since the features of that dialectic are so strikingly reminiscent of western mystical traditions. It might indeed be argued that mysticism is both internally dialectical and culturally hybrid, and that the poles in the dialectic are indirectly connected to an effort to fuse diverse emphases of different religious and cultural traditions.

Those modern South Indians who want to affirm the value of Dravidian culture as well as the Vedic Aryan heritage certainly regard the flowering of Tamil *bhakti* as such a synthesis. The Śrī Vaishṇavas describe their own thought as *Ubhaya Vedānta*: the common truth expressed both in the Sanskrit Veda and in the beloved hymns of their own 'Tamil Veda'.[49]

I have suggested elsewhere that it is the hybrid character of Christian religious language that has made modern western study of religion possible. This language is translated language in which many of the words still point in two directions, both towards some aspect of biblical religion and towards some feature of Greek, Roman, or Hellenistic religion or philosophy.[50] While the term 'mystical' is not a part of the linguistic deposit from the earliest biblical translation, it is also Janus-faced, but in an even more direct way. The pseudonym 'Dionysios the Areopagite' is very deliberately chosen to suggest the fusion of Greek wisdom and Christian faith, since this Dionysios was assumed to be the Greek philosopher converted to Christ by St Paul's preaching on the Areopagus. It is the twin legacy of Athens and Jerusalem, and the repeated efforts to make them one, that constitute the cultural matrix of western mysticism, and the closest analogue to this whole development in Indian religion is *bhakti.*

NOTES

1   Evelyn Underhill, *Mysticism: A Study in the Nature and Development of Man's Spiritual Consciousness* (New York, 1961, paperback edition with a 1930 preface to the 12th edition and the 1st edition); Rufus M. Jones, *Studies in Mystical Religion* (London, 1909); William James, *The Varieties of Religious Experience* (New York; these were the Gifford Lectures 1901–02. Lectures XVI and XVII, pp. 292–328, are printed as a single chapter entitled, 'Mysticism'.); Gershom Scholem, *Major Trends in Jewish Mysticism* (New York, 1941, 1946, 1954); Annemarie Schimmel, *Mystical Dimensions of Islam* (Chapel Hill, 1975). Another scholar who stresses the theistic side of mysticism is R. C. Zaehner. See especially *Mysticism Sacred and Profane: An Inquiry into some Varieties of Praeternatural Experience* (London, 1957) and *Hindu and Muslim Mysticism* (New York, 1960).

There are, of course, many studies of mysticism that give a very secondary place to theistic mysticism. One is W. T. Stace, *Mysticism and Philosophy* (Philadelphia and New York, 1960). The following statements from his conclusion (pp. 341–42) make his position clear:

According to our view, the essence of the introvertive experience is the undifferentiated unity, and 'union with God' is only one possible interpretation of it, which should not therefore be given as its definition. The same experience can be interpreted nontheistically as in Buddhism. . . . The mystic in any culture usually interprets his experience in terms of the religion in which he has been reared. But if he is sufficiently sophisticated, he can throw off that religious creed and still retain his mystical consciousness . . . Buddhism and the higher forms of Hinduism are essentially mystical because the enlightenment experience is their source and centre. But as Professor E. A. Burtt has noted, mysticism, which is a major component in Indian religions, is only a minor strand in Christianity, Islam, and Judaism.'[9]
[Note 9, E. A. Burtt, *The Teachings of the Compassionate Buddha,* New York, 1955, p. 16.]

2 S. N. Dasgupta, *Hindu Mysticism* (New York, 1927). (This was originally a group of six lectures delivered at American universities in 1927).

3 A. Govindāchārya, *A Metaphysique of Mysticism* (*Vedically Viewed*) (Mysore, 1923), pp. 7–9. P. N. Srinivasachari, *Mystics and Mysticism* (Madras, 1951), ch. 1, 'Pseudo and False Mysticism', pp. 1–43.

4 Rudolf Otto, *Mysticism East and West: A Comparative Analysis of the Nature of Mysticism* (New York, 1932), p. 141. This is a translation by Bertha L. Bracey and Richenda C. Payne of *West-Östliche Mystik: Vergleich und Unterscheidung zur Wesensdeutung* (Gotha, 1926) pp. 194–95. I have omitted two sentences in the English translation that are not found in the German text, and have given the German phrases at two points where the translation seems excessively free.

5 Ibid., p. 142.

6 Ibid., p. 143.

7 Ibid., p. 153.

8 Ibid., p. 154.

9 Ibid., pp. 158–60.

10 Ibid., pp. 160–61. 'Mysticism of poise' is a translation of *balanzierende Mystik* (German text, p. 226). To convey Otto's thought in English, I should prefer 'balance' to 'poise', or more freely, would translate 'mysticism of balanced polarity' or 'bi-valent mysticism'.

11 Ibid., pp. 161–62.

12 Ibid., p. v.

13 Ibid., p. 73.

14 Ibid., p. 40.

15 Ibid., p. 42.

16 Ibid., p. 43.

17 Ibid., p. 49.

18 Ibid., p. 50.

19 Ibid., p. 52 (German text, p. 69).

20 Ibid., p. 101.

21 Ibid., p. 165.

22 Ibid., p. 168.

23 Dasgupta, op. cit., pp. viii–ix.

24 Ibid., p. 38.

25 Ibid., 121–22.

26 Ibid., pp. 125–26.

27 It is an intriguing question how Śankara's Advaita, which is one of many varieties of Indian thought and only one of several schools of Vedānta, came in modern times to think of itself and successfully represent itself to the West as the crown of Hindu spirituality and the only philosophi-

cally significant interpretation of Vedānta, the orthodox Hindu systematization of the teachings of the Upanishads. Major contributors in this process were Swami Vivekananda and his colleagues in the Ramakrishna Math and Mission, Mrs Annie Besant and others in the Indian branch of the Theosophical Society, and Paul Deussen, the German orientalist who made Śankara's philosophy accessible to western intellectuals. More recently the entire work of Sarvepalli Radhakrishnan has both reflected and contributed to this point of view. See especially his *Eastern Religions and Western Thought* (New York, 1959). Ch. 2 is entitled, 'Mysticism and Ethics in Hindu Thought' (pp. 58–114).

> Religion generally refers to something external, a system of sanctions and consolations, while spirituality points to the need for knowing and living in the highest self and raising life in all its parts. Spirituality is the core of religion and its inward essence, and mysticism emphasizes this side of religion. (p. 61)
> Mysticism . . . is the admission of mystery in the universe [Note 1. Etymologically considered, the mystic is one who closes his eyes to all external things and keeps silent about the divine mysteries into which he has been initiated.] (pp. 61–62)

The statements just quoted suggest a broad view of spirituality that would fit the theistic schools of Vedānta as well as Śankara's Advaita. That, indeed, is Radhakrishnan's intention, but he makes it clear at many points in his writings that Śankara's position is the profoundest one. In this chapter, which is largely concerned with refuting Albert Schweitzer's characterization of Hindu thought as 'world and life negating', he advances Śankara's explanation of the universe's relation to the Absolute and his interpretation of the Upanishads as containing two doctrines, 'one representing the esoteric truth that Brahman is the impersonal, unknowable Absolute without attributes, the other exoteric, that Brahman is the God who manifests Himself in the universe.' (p. 92)

28 Rudolf Otto, *India's Religion of Grace and Christianity Compared and Contrasted* (London, 1930), p. 25. This is a translation by Frank Hugh Foster of *Die Gnadenreligion Indiens und das Christentum: Vergleich und Unterscheidung* (München, 1930). *Kampf* might be translated 'battle' rather than 'struggle' (p. 13).

29 See discussion above of Otto's views in his *Mysticism East and West*.

30 A. Govindāchārya, op. cit., p. 1.

31 Ibid., p. 3.

32 Ibid., p. 7.

33 P. N. Srinivasachari, op. cit., p. 44.

34 Ibid., pp. 47–48.

35   Ibid., pp. 50–51.

36   Ibid., pp. 194–96.

37   See Norvin Hein, *The Miracle Plays of Mathurā* (New Haven and London, 1972).

A work on the contemporary religious drama is now being prepared by Srivatsa Goswami and John Stratton Hawley. Cf. also Dr Hawley's unpublished Ph.D. dissertation at Harvard, 'The Butter Thief' (November 1977) and the unpublished Harvard Ph.D. dissertation of Donna Marie Wulff, 'Drama as a Mode of Religious Realization: The Vidagdhamādhava of Rūpa Gosvāmin' (December 1977).

38   Recent literature on these topics includes the dissertations mentioned in n. 37 as well as James N. Redington, *The Meaning Of Kṛṣṇa's Dance of Love according to Vallabhācārya* (Madison, Wisconsin, 1975).

39   K. C. Varadachari, *Ālvārs of South India* (Bombay, 1970), pp. 178–79.

A. K. Ramanujan is currently preparing a verse translation of some selections from Nammālvār's hymns, which is to be published by Princeton University Press under the title, *Hymns for the Drowning* (Ālvār means literally, one who is immersed or drowned.).

40   See the comprehensive and well-informed introduction to the post-Rāmānuja's literature of this tradition in Sanskritized Tamil by K. K. A. Venkatachari, *Śrīvaiṣṇava Manipravāḷa* (Bombay, 1978. This was his doctoral dissertation for the University of Utrecht, defended 24 October 1975).

Directly relevant to this topic is the unpublished Ph.D. dissertation for the University of Bombay by Vasudha Rajagopalan Narayanan entitled, '*The Śrī-Vaiṣṇava understanding of bhakti and prapatti*: (From the ālvārs to Vedānta Deśika)', March 1978.

One succinct treatment of the subject is given in Sabapathy Kulandran, *Grace: A Comparative Study of the Doctrine in Christianity and Hinduism* (London, 1964), pp. 170–77.

Cf. also ch. 17, 'Rāmānuja's Relation to His Successors: The Problem of the Gadyas' in John Braisted Carman, *The Theology of Rāmānuja: An Essay in Interreligious Understanding* (New Haven and London, 1974).

41   Carman, op. cit., pp. 65–81, 257–58.

42   Ibid., pp. 124–33.

43   M. R. Sampatkumaran tr., *The Gītābhāshya of Rāmānuja* (Madras, 1969), pp. 210–11, 270. Cf. Carman, op. cit., pp. 190–98.

44   A critical edition, scholarly introduction, and exciting verse translation has recently been done by Barbara Stoler Miller in *Love Song of the Dark Lord: Jayadeva's Gītagovinda* (New York, 1977).

45   The title of a play by Oliver Goldsmith (1728–74). Cf. also the verse of Alexander Pope (1688–1744):

> she who ne'er answers till a husband cools,
> Or, if she rules him, never shows she rules;
> Charms by accepting, by submitting sways,
> Yet has her humour most, when she obeys.

(*Moral Essays*, Epistle ii, To Mrs M. Blount 1, 261)

46   Carman, op. cit., pp. 39–41, drawing on the earliest prose hagiography of Rāmānuja and his predecessors by Pinbaḷahiya Perumāḷ Jīyar, *Arayirappaḍi Guruparamparāprabhāvam* (Trichi, 1968), pp. 176–77.

47   Venkatachari, op. cit., ch. 3, 'Maṇipravāḷa Rahasyagranthas and Independent Works', pp. 95–166.

48   Wilfred Cantwell Smith, *The Meaning and End of Religion: A New Approach to the Religious Traditions of Mankind* (New York, 1962, 1963), pp. 95–166.

49   Carman, op. cit., pp. 44–46, 227–28. Venkatachari, op. cit. ch. 3, 'Maṇipravāḷa Rahasyagranthas and Independent Works', pp. 95–166, Walter G. Neevel, Jr, *Yāmuna's Vedānta and Pāñcarātra: Integrating the Classical and the Popular* (Missoula, Montana, 1977), Cf. Carman, op. cit., pp. 44–46, 227–28.

50   John B. Carman, 'Religion as a Problem for Christian Theology', in Donald G. Dawe and John B. Carman (eds.), *Christian Faith in a Religiously Plural World* (Maryknoll, 1978), pp. 93–98.

JOHN B. CARMAN, Ph.D (Yale), is Professor of Comparative Religion at Harvard Divinity School. He studied at Haverford College, Yale University, and the University of Leiden and has also been a Research Fellow of the Christian Institute for the Study of Religion and Society in Bangalore. Since 1963 he has taught at Harvard, connected with the Center for the Study of World Religions and since 1973 has served as its director. He is the author of *The Theology of Rāmānuja* (1974); co-author, with the Rev. P. Y. Luke, of *Village Christians and Hindu Culture* (1968), and translator of W. Brede Kristensen's lectures in phenomenology of religion, published under the title, *The Meaning of Religion* (1960).

The Mirror Symbol Revisited: Confucian and Taoist Mysticism

JULIA CHING

The psycho-analyst Jacques Lacan[1] speaks of the child's discovery of himself in the mirror, his fascination with his own image, as leading to 'primal narcissism'. His account mirrors, naturally, the Greek myth of *the* primal Narcissus, who discovered and fell in love with his own image in the water. On reading Lacan and hearing him speak at Yale (1977), I was struck by certain similarities as well as differences between Eastern and Western uses of the mirror symbol. These extend beyond the realms of myth and psycho-analysis into those of religious experience, including mystical experience. Here, the image in the mirror no longer represents merely the *external* form of the person as seen by others, but a more interior principle. In both Eastern and Western religions, it frequently represents the soul – or its equivalent. But the functions it serves and the lessons it allegedly teaches are often different. *How* different these are will be part of the burden of this study, as I attempt to unpack the hidden meanings in the mirror symbol used especially in Confucian and Taoist mystical writings.

As a psycho-analyst, Jacques Lacan seeks consciously to de-mystify all experience, by seeking out underlying psychological conditions of human personality. I do not intend in this study, further to *mystify* human or religious experience. My starting point is nevertheless different from Lacan's. I acknowledge and recognize a realm of experience, religious and mystical, which I consider to be not totally comprehensible to psycho-analysis. My use of the mirror symbol will be in accordance with its uses by the mystical writers themselves. I hope that a discussion of this many-faceted symbol will lead to a better understanding of two particular forms of mysticism: Confucian and Taoist.

Let me here state my position on mysticism: I have no desire to appropriate all religious experience as mystical. As I understand it, etymologically the word referred to the mysterious and esoteric, with special reference to ritual mystery. It entered Christian theological usage[2] with a treatise on mystical theology written by Pseudo-Dionysius in the fifth century, and in that usage has come to signify a kind of special communion with God in unusual experiences involving the entire psyche, the whole person. Scholars have discussed the question of *varieties* in mystical experience, such as philosophical and religious, natural and supernatural, Christian and non-Christian. Such discussions are useful, but seldom conclusive. On the one hand, mystical experience is, by its very nature, an elusive phenomenon. Its duration is usually brief, and its rapturous effects suffer diminution as soon as the person reflects over them. Besides, interpretation of such experience is always conditioned by the person's prior beliefs and understanding, both philosophical and religious. Given the intensely subjective character of mystical experience, it would be difficult to reach a consensus on the essential nature of such an experience, even if the interpreters themselves were all mystics.

As a form of psychic consciousness, mystical experience can presumably be subjected to psycho-analysis. A Freudian interpretation seems likely on account of the rapturous joy which accompanies the experience – thus involving a 'pleasure principle' – and because many mystics, like Teresa of Avila and Marie of the Incarnation Guyard (1599–1672), chose to describe their experiences in nuptial terms. When we turn to the examination of the Confucian and Taoist varieties of mystical experience, however, we find a different language. Instead of raptures, we read of peace and serenity; instead of nuptial unions between the soul and God, we learn of the losing of self in nature. Why these differences?

I shall attempt to answer this question in part, whithout prolonged discussion as to whether the differences are basic to the experiences themselves, or whether they merely belong to the level of interpretation. My study will be limited to interpretations, or rather, to interpreting the interpretations.

In the study of comparative mysticism, I have found helpful Friedrich Heiler's monumental work *Prayer*. Heiler develops the archetypes introduced by the Swedish scholar Nathan Söderblom, contrasting mysticism with prophetic piety. He classifies Christianity, Judaism, and Islam as prophetic religions, for which mystical experience has never been essential as they are grounded in divine revelation. On the other hand, Hinduism, Buddhism, and Taoism are 'mysticisms'; their very natures are defined and conditioned by their mystical traditions. Heiler speaks of prophetic prayer as always a dialogue between unequal partners, man and God. According to him, prophetic piety affirms life with joy and resoluteness, because of its faith in God as giver of life, while mysticism tends to flee from ordinary life in order to discover a higher consciousness, preferring asceticism to morality. Prophetic religion emphasizes community and moral action, whereas mysticism tends to be individualistic. Prophetic religion safeguards and maintains a distinction between man and God, so that even the Jewish, Christian, or Muslim mystic engages in a silent dialogue with God in the midst of his ecstasy, without being absorbed into the Godhead. The mysticism of Hinduism or Buddhism, however, consists in the unification and simplification of all psychic activity, achieved by isolation from the world and suppression of the emotions, until all barriers between God and man disappear in ecstatic experience. 'Mysticism is that form of intercourse with God in which the world and self are absolutely denied, in which human personality is dissolved, disappears and is absorbed in the infinite unity of the Godhead.'[3]

Heiler writes about mystical experiences with insight and understanding, although his clear preference is for prophetic prayer – the turning of man to another being to whom he inwardly opens his heart, the speech of an 'I' to a 'Thou'. According to Heiler, the will to live asserts itself in prophetic experience, whereas the mystic 'aims at the extinction of the emotional and volitional life, for the delight of ecstasy can be purchased only at the price of killing the will to live.' His study focuses on prayer – and, if only by extension, on mysticism – in the prophetic religions, especially Christianity. Discussing the Christians and Sufis, in whom the prophetic mode of prayer continues to predominate, he speaks with approval of the 'prophetic passion' which breathes 'warmth and strength' into the mystic's heart. He is more ambivalent about mysticism in itself, whose 'denial of the impulse of life' is born 'of weariness of life'. It is in this vein that he briefly talks about Buddhist mysticism – as a counter-illustration to prophetic prayer. For the most part he refers to Hinduism, Buddhism, and Taoism as 'mysticisms', rather than 'religions'. And he says nothing of Confucianism. His attitudes show the influence of an earlier age in *Religionswissenschaft*, when

Christian theological norms were invariably applied to the comparative study of religions. But he was also ahead of his age in that he examined, not only mysticism itself, but also non-Christian mysticism. His study remains valuable for its presentation of the archetypes, supported as it is by Heiler's vast erudition. There is much that the reader today may learn from the book, even if he does not agree with all the author's presuppositions.

Eastern and Western Mysticisms

'Eastern' and 'Western' are misleading labels, since their connotations depend upon what is considered to be geographically 'central'. Because Western civilization owes so much to the *Mediterranean* area, the East has usually referred to the land east of Europe, and the West to Europe itself. By extension, we have become used to the terms, Eastern and Western religions, referring by 'Western' usually to Judaism and Christianity, and sometimes – logically – also to Islam. According to this norm, Hinduism, Buddhism, and Chinese religions are Eastern. Interestingly, this corresponds to Heiler's archetypes of prophetic and mystical religion. To the extent and for the reason that even the 'prophetical' religions also have developed mystical traditions, it seems useful to consider a few more general differences between Eastern and Western mysticisms, before proceeding to examine the two forms of Confucian and Taoist mysticisms, both of which belong to the Chinese tradition.

It has been pointed out that the great prophets, the founders of the 'prophetic' traditions, were themselves mystics who encountered God in unusual experiences. It has also been pointed out, however, that their prophetic mission was defined less by the experience itself than by the Word of God which they received, and with which they were entrusted for the benefit of *other* men, to whom they must preach it. Here the religious founders, like Moses, Jesus, or Muhammad, could hardly be likened to those followers of their religions who had private mystical experiences which did not add to the content of the original revelation. The revealed Word holds a unique place in these prophetic traditions, both above and unlike the veneration accorded the Vedic Scriptures or the Chinese classics. Indeed, whereas Jewish and Christian mystics prepared their souls for divine union by reverential reading of the Scriptures, the Buddhist or Taoist mystic used *their* classics or sutras only as reference books. They aimed at losing their own selves, at transcending their ordinary sense experience and discursive reasoning.

If a contrast is to be drawn between Eastern and Western mysticisms, the Taoist and Confucian *mystiques* serve as interesting and instructive cases. Classical Taoism is mystical in its inspiration and orientation, although its concerns are, strictly speaking, more philosophical than religious, centred upon man's union with the Tao through contemplation of nature. Taoist popular religion, which claims to be classical Taoism's heir, bears little resemblance to the parent on close examination. It has an enormous pantheon of personal deities, situated in the universe as well as within the human person, a tradition of prayer and ritual, and an esoteric *mystique* of sorts which will be discussed later. It will resist classification either as 'prophetic' or 'mystical' religion.

With Confucianism, obviously the basic inspiration is 'Eastern', though its orientation shows similarities to known characteristics of Western religion in the form of an overriding concern for ethics. Confucianism is intellectual and culture-oriented whereas Taoism prides itself on its anti-intellectualism, both as a philosophy and as a popular religion. Confucians place great importance on the knowledge of the moral self, of one's strengths and weaknesses, for the sake of achieving self-improvement. Confucian meditation stands somewhere between the intellectual concentration of discursive thought, as exemplified by scriptural or classical reading, and the moral concentration of assuring that there is no thought, as practised in Taoism and also Buddhism. The Confucian *mystique* celebrates man's relationship to the universe, both human and natural, reaching for the transcendent through the immanent, the 'divine' through the human. For these reasons, the Confucian term for universal virtue, *Jen* (humanity, love), has acquired a richness of meaning connoting life and creativity, even the Absolute.

However, let us consider Confucianism and Taoism more closely and systematically, one in the light of the other, to see the reflections of each on the other's mirror, and thus avoid misjudging either.

Confucianism and Taoism

What is Confucianism,[4] and what is Taoism? Are they philosophies or religions? Do they have mysticisms? To answer these questions,

I point to a common Chinese distinction, between the terms *chia* (schools of thought, philosophy) and *chiao* (teaching, religion). The former refers merely to the great thinkers and their teachings, the so-called 'great traditions'. The latter refers to the religious and cultic practices associated with the respective systems, and, by extension, to the unique ways in which the great traditions have been appropriated by the people at the grassroots level. A distinction between the great intellectual traditions and the cultic and devotional has been made in all the Chinese traditions: Confucianism, Taoism, and Buddhism.

The Latinized term, Confucianism, is a Western invention which has come down from the seventeenth-century Jesuit missionaries. Their involvement in China gave rise to the so-called Rites controversy surrounding the question of whether to allow converts to continue to take part in such Confucian rites as ancestral veneration. Already, the immense literature which fed the controversy referred to the explicitly religious dimensions of Confucianism: the belief in a supreme deity called Lord-on-high or Heaven, the cult offered by the emperor in his honour, and so on. Important European thinkers took part in the controversial discussions; the most prominent of these were Leibniz, Wolff, and Voltaire.

The Chinese term for Confucianism, *Ju* (scholars, literati), points to its broader character as intellectual culture. It is usually regarded more as *chia* (school of thought) than as *chiao* (teaching, religion), although such terms as *Ju-chiao*, *K'ung-chiao* (K'ung being Confucius' family name), or *Li-chiao* (Li referring to Confucian rituals) are also used. Confucianism is best known for its moral philosophy, as represented by Confucius and Mencius. It is clearly grounded in religion – the inherited religion of the Lord-on-high or Heaven. Confucianism is less known for its mysticism, although the Book of Mencius as well as other works cannot be fully understood except in the light of mysticism.

The *Analects* of Confucius[5] have left behind a description of the Master in a contemplative mood, when he said:

> 'I would prefer to be wordless.'
> Tzu-kung (his disciple), said, 'If you, Master, do not speak, what shall we, your disciples, have to record?'
> The Master said: 'Does Heaven speak? The four seasons pursue their courses and all things are continually being produced. But does Heaven say anything?' (17:19)

The authenticity of this passage is open to doubt. It recalls to mind that Confucius who is created by the Taoist text, *Chuang-tzu*, and who is clearly a Taoist mouthpiece, offering a mystical teaching. One famous passage there expounds the Taoist practice of meditation, of 'sitting and forgetting' (*tso-wang*). It emerges out of an imagined conversation between Confucius and his favourite disciple, Yen Hui:

> Yen Hui said, 'I'm improving.'
> Confucius said, 'What do you mean by that?'
> 'I've forgotten benevolence and righteousness.'
> 'That's good. But you still haven't got it.'
> Another day, the two met again and Yen Hui said, 'I'm improving.'
> 'What do you mean by that?'
> 'I've forgotten rites and music.'
> 'That's good. But you still haven't got it.'
> Another day, the two met again and Yen Hui said, 'I'm improving.'
> 'What do you mean by that?'
> 'I can sit down and forget everything.'
> Confucius looked very startled and said, 'What do you mean, sit down and forget everything?'
> Yen Hui said, 'I smash up my limbs and body, drive out perception and intellect, cast off form, do away with understanding, and make myself identical with the Great Thoroughfare. This is what I mean by sitting down and forgetting everything.'
> Confucius said, '. . . With your permission, I'd like to become your follower.'[6]

Confucianism gives primary emphasis to the ethical meaning of human relationships, finding and grounding the moral in the divine and transcendent. Taoism prefers to turn away from society to the contemplation of nature, seeking fulfilment in the spontaneous and 'trans-ethical'. At the same time it has been suggested that the Tao,[7] a metaphysical Absolute in *Lao-tzu*, represents a philosophical transformation of the earlier personal God of ancient Chinese religion. Certainly, the way it teaches leads to union with itself – a way of passive acceptance and mystical contemplation. Such was the teaching of the great Taoist thinkers, of Lao-tzu and even of Chuang-tzu – although there is now doubt whether either ever actually existed. For men who allegedly chose a life of obscurity and taught a way of silence this fate is, perhaps, not inappropriate.

Whereas Confucius stands as a prophet, offering an ethical teaching grounded in the religious consciousness, Mencius (372–289

B.C.?) projects the image of a teacher of mysticism, proclaiming an interior doctrine, alluding to the presence within the heart of that which is greater than itself. 'All things are present in me. When I reflect upon myself in sincerity, my joy is boundless.' (7A:4) He taught:[8]

> For a man to give full realization to his heart is for him to understand his own nature, and a man who knows his own nature will know Heaven. By retaining his heart and nurturing nature he is serving Heaven. (7A:1)

For Mencius, as for the Christian mystic Gregory of Nyssa (337–400), the heart is the ground of innate principles or virtues, which require only careful cultivation in order to blossom and bear fruit. Both share a belief in human perfectibility, a belief which springs from a shared mystical awareness of a 'divine presence' within.[9] To quote Gregory of Nyssa:[10]

> The Creator who made man in his image deposited the seeds of all the virtues in the nature of the prototype, so that no good might enter from without . . . And there is no other means of attaining what we desire but by doing good to ourselves.

Gregory of Nyssa speaks also of purifying the soul from the movement of passions in order to allow it to contemplate God, its archetype. The Confucian texts prefer to discuss the work of spiritual cultivation in terms of emotional harmony and psychic equilibrium – a harmony of due proportions rather than the absence of passions. The Doctrine of the Mean, one of the 'Four Books', distinguishes between the two states of soul, the 'pre-stirred' state, before the rise of emotions, and the 'post-stirred' state. The *Mean* lies in the harmony of emotions which have arisen, but resembles the equilibrium of the 'pre-stirred' state. The book claims that such harmony puts a person in touch with the cosmic processes of life and creativity:[11]

> While there are no stirrings of pleasure, anger, sorrow or joy, the mind may be said to be in a state of equilibrium. When these emotions have been stirred, and set in their due degree, there ensues what may be called the state of harmony. This equilibrium is the great root of all under Heaven, and this harmony is the universal path of all under Heaven. Let the states of equilibrium and harmony exist in perfection, and a happy order will prevail throughout Heaven and Earth, and all things will flourish.

In this text, the meaning of the word Heaven is ambiguous, shifting from the early reference to a supreme deity (*Analects*), to a vacillation between that and a moral force (Mencius), to the universe itself. Confucian mysticism leans more and more in the direction of pantheism, as attested by the later philosopher, Chang Tsai (1022–77):

> Heaven is my father and Earth is my mother, and even such a small creature as I find an intimate place in their midst. Therefore that which fills the universe I regard as my body and that which directs the universe I consider as my nature. All people are my brothers and sisters, and all things are my companions.[12]

And it is in this direction that Confucian in – or *neo*-Confucian – mysticism shows the imprint of Taoist as well as Buddhist influences, at a time and in a development which represented a conscious *response* of the 'ethical' mind to the more 'religio-mystical'. Neo-Confucianism appropriated Taoist and Buddhist weapons in its struggle against Taoist and Buddhist predominance, returning to the sources of Confucian inspiration to rediscover their hidden mystical strands and reinterpret them in the light of known Taoist and Buddhist categories, while continuing to emphasize man's moral responsibilities to family and society. In an earlier period, the Taoist philosopher Chuang-tzu had said:

> He who has a clear understanding of the virtue of Heaven and Earth may be called the Great Source, the Great Ancestor. He harmonizes with Heaven; and by doing so he brings equitable accord to the world and harmonizes with men as well.[13]

And then, in an ecstatic outburst, apparently addressed to the universe:

> O my Master, O my Master! He passes judgement on the ten thousand things but does not think himself severe; his beauty extends to ten thousand generations but he does not think himself benevolent. He is older than the highest antiquity but he does not think himself long lived; he covers Heaven, bears up Earth, carves and fashions countless forms, but does not think himself skilled.[14]

Harmony with the natural universe brings with it serenity in questions of life and death. Indeed had not Mencius already suggested that it makes no difference to the man who serves Heaven, whether he is going to die young or to live to a ripe old age. Chuang-tzu likewise relates many anecdotes of death, which demonstrate his acceptance of the course of nature. For example, he records[15] a conversation which took place in a dream, in which a skull told him of the happiness of the deceased state, comparing it to that of a king on the throne.

But Taoism is not just passive contemplation. The texts of *Lao-tzu* and *Chuang-tzu* also served a later generation of religious zealots who were anxious to transcend the limited conditions of human existence. Their ambition was to 'steal the secret of Heaven and Earth', to wrench from it the mystery of life itself, in order to fulfil their desire for immortality. They revived belief in personal deities, practising rituals of prayer and propitiation. They fostered the art of alchemy – both the external alchemy, which concentrated upon finding the elixir of life, and internal alchemy, which 'internalized' the Golden Pill, and sought after it through yoga and meditation. They had recourse also to sexual hygiene as another means of prolonging human life. Theirs has been called Taoist *religion* to distinguish it from the classical philosophy of Lao-tzu and Chuang-tzu and its acceptance of both life and death. To quote from their text, *Pao-p'u-tzu*, by Ko Hung (253–333 A.D.?):

> The immortals nourish their bodies with drugs and prolong their lives with the application of occult science, so that internal illness shall not arise and external ailment shall not enter. Although they enjoy everlasting existence and do not die, their old bodies do not change. If one knows the way to immortality, it is not to be considered as so difficult.[16]

This popular Taoist religion developed its own mystical traditions, embellished with stories of wondrous drugs and wonder-working immortals, of levitations, and bodily ascensions to Heaven. It even evolved a kind of 'nuptial' mysticism, manifested in bridal piety, and in the fruit of marital union – the spiritual conception and birth of a child, the 'new self', within the person's spiritual consciousness. This new life is expected to take over the entire personality, as the 'old self' diminishes and disappears. It is in this light that one can attempt to understand the following prayer, addressed to the lunar deity in the middle of the night:

Thou Ruler of the Moon, Mistress of the
Primordial *yin* (female)
Be harmonious with me,
That together we may give birth to a little child
in my cinnabar field.[17]

The Mirror Symbol in Chinese Mysticism

The late Paul Demiéville, sinologist and authority on Buddhism and
Taoism, has left a remarkable article, 'Le miroir spirituel',[18] which
unfolds for us the multiple symbolisms of the mirror as an 'image' of
the soul or spirit. Demiéville's Eastern base is Chinese Buddhism and
Taoism, and his Western base, the Platonic and Pauline traditions as
manifested by the Greek Fathers – with some mention of
seventeenth-century French mysticism as exemplified in the unusual
Marie de l'Incarnation, business woman, widow, mother, and later,
missionary in Quebec, and in the 'quietist' bishop, Fénelon.
Demiéville's article is impressive in its erudition and breadth of scope
and provides a 'counterpoint' to Lacan's use of the same mirror
symbol. I should now like to follow in his footsteps, using the mirror
symbol as a focus for this study of Confucian and Taoist mysticism. I
hope that this will shed light on the subject, against a background of
the wider use of the same symbol in Buddhist and Christian religious
writings, and even, to some extent, in contemporary structuralist
psycho-analysis.

For the Christian, the understanding of the soul as a divine image
stems primarily from the story in Genesis regarding man's creation in
the image and likeness of God. There is, besides, the reference in
St Paul (1 Cor. 13.12) to our knowledge of God in this life and in
Heaven: 'For now, we see in a mirror dimly, but then face to face.
Now I understand in part; then I shall understand fully, even as I have
been fully understood.'

The Fathers of the Church went further. Demiéville refers
particularly to Gregory of Nyssa,[19] who speaks of the soul as a
mirror receiving the image and form of God, so that God becomes
present within it, although remaining there mostly unknown and
hidden, while awaiting the moment of conversion, which is also that
of interior revelation. It is the religious rendition of a Platonic and
Neoplatonic intuition expressed in the dialogue *Alcibiades* through

the elaboration of the Delphic oracle, 'Know thyself'. It reflects an optimistic appraisal of human nature, looking forward to the full blossoming of the seeds of virtue planted in the divine image.

As Demiéville points out, the mirror symbol is found in both early Confucian and Taoist literature. Hsün-tzu (fl. 298 B.C.), a Confucian and reputed rationalist, regards human nature as originally evil, although perfectible by education. He had a remarkable psychological insight albeit he did not analyse consciousness it terms of id, ego, and superego, of libido or of repression. Instead, he distinguishes between the two levels of the psyche, the 'muddy' and the clear, comparing the human mind to a basin of clear water:[20]

> If you place the basin on a level . . . then the heavy sediment will settle to the bottom and the clear water will collect on top, so that you can . . . examine the lines of the face. . . . If you guide [the mind] with reason, nourish it with clarity . . . it will be capable of determining right and wrong and of resolving doubts.

Hsün-tzu sees the mind as possessing contradictory attributes:

> The mind is constantly storing up things, and yet it is said to be empty. The mind is constantly marked by diversity, and yet it is said to be unified. The mind is constantly moving, and yet it is said to be still.[21]

He singles out three qualities of the mind for description: emptiness, unity, and stillness. These appear to be passive qualities yet they are responsible for a fundamental dynamism. These belong to the symbol of clear water, or of a mirror. These make possible that wisdom which is a penetrating insight into all things.

> Emptiness, unity, and stillness – these are the qualities of great and pure enlightenment. . . . He who has such enlightenment . . . has a penetrating insight into all beings . . . and masters the great principle and all that is in the universe.[22]

A naturalist and an atheist, Hsün-tzu might not have been a mystic but he appears to understand the conditions of mystical insight and enlightenment.

The Taoist Chuang-tzu, on the other hand, usually has been considered a mystic. In his writings he has used both symbols – that of the mirror and that of clear water – to represent the mind of the sage. He too sings the praises of emptiness:

Do not be an embodier of fame; do not be a storehouse of
schemes. . . . Hold on to all that you have received from Heaven but do
not think you have gotten anything. Be empty, that is all. The perfect man
uses his mind like a mirror – going after nothing, welcoming nothing,
responding but not storing.[23]

and elsewhere:

Water that is still gives back a clear image of beard and eyebrows. And if
water . . . possesses such clarity, how much more must pure spirit. The
sage's mind in stillness is the mirror of Heaven and Earth, the glass of ten
thousand things.[24]

While such stillness is possible to the mind, it does not come without
effort. It is the sage's lot because of his wisdom and contentment: 'The
ten thousand things are insufficient to distract his mind.'[25] Indeed,
the mind itself must be kept free of dust: 'If a mirror is bright, no dust
settles on it; if dust settles, it isn't really bright.'[26]

The same symbol, the same themes, are taken up by *Huai-nan-
tzu*,[27] the eclectic text of Taoist inspiration from the second century
B.C.

The mirror and water need no intelligence or intention to reflect things. Yet
the circle and the square, the crooked and the straight, nothing can escape
it. (1. 3–4)

This power of reflection is again attributed to stillness:

Man is still at birth; this is the nature received from Heaven. In responding
to things, movement begins. This is a deterioration of nature. (1. 4)

The sage, the man deserving also to rule, is described in cosmic
terms as one standing between Heaven and earth, capable of
reflecting the brightness of one on the other:

He who can cap the great Heaven can tread the great Earth; he who can
mirror the supreme clarity can see the great brightness; he who can stand
erect in the plain can dwell in the great palace. (2. 22)

The value of the mirror lies not only in giving reflections, but
especially in giving accurate reflections; it tells the truth:

He who relies for support on a barrier to look into the bottom of the well
will not see his own pupil even with the best vision. He who borrows the
brightness of a mirror will see in it every inch and every tenth of an inch.
(9. 142)

and:

> When a man mentions your faults, you complain of him. When a mirror shows your ugliness, you praise the mirror. (14: 240)

The best known instance of the mirror symbol in Chinese mysticism comes from the history of Ch'an (Japanese: Zen) Buddhism, and became the occasion for the split between the northern school of 'gradual enlightenment' and the southern school of 'sudden enlightenment'. The story tells of a rivalry between two monks, each desiring to succeed to the patriarchate. The elder and more learned of the two, Shen-hsiu, expressed his insights in these words:

> The body is a bodhi-tree;
> The mind is the mirror bright
> Always and carefully wipe it clean,
> Lest dust fall upon it.[28]

It was a plea for gradual, painstaking cultivation as preparation for enlightenment (*bodhi*). It drew the following response from Hui-neng, a younger man from the south, alleged by some to be illiterate:

> Originally there was no bodhi-tree;
> Nor was there any mirror.
> Since originally there was nothing!
> Whereupon can dust fall?[29]

It came like a thunderbolt. The metaphorical rebuttal was complete, and the poem has been interpreted as a counter-plea for *sudden* enlightenment – the assertion that this goal could be achieved at any time, in any situation. But it also denies the separation of body and mind, the opposition of subject and object. The mirror symbol is invoked only to be superseded. Hui-neng thus manifested his superior wisdom, and eventually succeeded to the patriarchate.

The symbols of clear water and bright mirror reappear in the writings of the neo-Confucian philosophers – these heirs of Mencius drawing also from the heritage of Hsün-tzu, of Chuang-tzu, and of Hui-neng. According to both Chou Tun-yi (1017–73) and Chu Hsi (1130–1200), the sage or perfect man is completely sincere. His mind and heart are like a mirror, quiet and passive, upright when active or moved by emotions.[30] Wang Yang-ming (1472–1529) shows a similar fondness for this metaphor, referring several times to the *gatha* of Hui-neng. He argues that while the emotions of the sage are in accord with all things, yet of himself he has no emotions, just as a bright mirror reflects all things as they come, without itself engaging in either activity or passivity:

> For while the mind and heart of the sage cannot tolerate the least particle of dust, and has naturally no need of polishing, the mind and heart of the average man . . . resembles a spotted and dirty mirror, which needs thorough polishing, to have all its dust and dirt removed. Then will the tiniest streak of dust become visible, and only a light stroke will wipe it away, without anyone having to spend much energy.[31]

In this way he seeks to accommodate the insights of both Shen-hsiu and Hui-neng.

Wang Yang-ming had moved from Confucian studies to the investigation of Taoist and Buddhist beliefs and practices, even abandoning the world for some time. Allegedly, he acquired certain parapsychic powers through his practice of Taoist methods of meditation. But he was troubled by the Taoist and Buddhist withdrawal from action and social involvement. 'I was torn between believing them and doubting them', he said. Not satisfied with his mystical consolations, he was several times near the verge of declaring that sagehood was not universally accessible, since he himself could not get within sight of the goal. For him, the acquisition of wisdom, of the Tao, must be accompanied by the development of a perfect moral character. On this point he remained an unwavering Confucian, never accepting mystical experience as an end in itself, while appreciating it as a strong impetus in one's quest for life's ultimate goals. He decided eventually to return to life's troubles and challenges, as a minor official in the government bureaucracy. His sense of justice led him to a stance of protest and criticism against the injustices of a corrupt administration, and so to adversity in exile. Light came in the middle of the darkest night. In another mystical experience, he discovered that wisdom and perfection are acquired, paradoxically, in the *quest* itself, since, for the man determined to find these goals, every act merges with the whole effort of self-realization, bringing him eventually into the consciousness of the very oneness of his being with all things. He will then find Heaven and earth and all things within his own deeper self. In other words, through moral action allied to knowledge, man comes into vital contact with things – whether persons or events – and transforms them all into his own life, making of all a unity identified with himself. In this light, the Confucian-Taoist adage, '*being* one body with all things' (*yü wan-wu yi-t'i*) could be interpreted as 'making all things (*wu*) one'. In this light, the boundaries between Taoism, Buddhism, and Confucianism are themselves transcended. And yet, in the mystic Wang Yang-ming, a man who learned contemplation in action, including military action – he went on to become a statesman and a general – a man who rose above the divisions between the diverging schools of thought in order to find wisdom, we see more clearly the differing emphases of Confucianism and Taoism and their respective mystical heritages. For *both*, the spiritual mirror represents *both* the self and the world; neither accepts any fundamental ontological dualism. For Taoism, however, the *world* refers more to nature, and for Confucianism it refers more to society and the interlocking world of human relationships, regarded by the world-withdrawing, life-denying ascetic as polluting and ensnaring. As the wise man he became, Wang Yang-ming was able to discover the transcendent in the immanent, the vertical in the horizontal, the Absolute in the relative. By polishing the mirror, he found more than the mirror. He also found what the mirror itself represented.

> [Their hearts are] like mirrors in the mud,
> Enclosing the light within the darkness.
> Dust and dirt once removed,
> The mirror will reflect the beautiful and the ugly.[29]

Conclusion

It is clear that the mirror symbol has stood for a variety of themes in East and West, in Confucianism and Taoism. We have focused on it as a symbol of the mind, heart, or soul. We can therein perceive a distinction between the mirror's dynamic power of reflection, particularly in reflecting, for the Christian, a divine image, and its passive reflection of the natural universe, as in Taoism. In the former case, there is always a certain distance between the subject and the object, the image and its archetype. In the latter case, this is much less true; indeed, in Hui-neng's poem, the metaphor itself is superseded in an illustration of the absence of any duality: body/mind, subject/object, illusion/enlightenment. This is also indicative of the basic difference between prophetic and mystical religions; for the Jewish, Christian, or Muslim mystic a distance between man and God must be preserved, whereas such distance is not as important for the Buddhist or Taoist, who does not acknowledge a personal deity.

The admission of dualism in Western religion has accentuated a relationship of *attachment* between the image and its original, the soul and God – even to the point of describing it in nuptial imagery. When occurring between the self and its own image, as Lacan described, this kind of attachment is narcissism. In Eastern religions, however, both Confucianism and Taoism, it is the mirror's *detachment* from the object reflected which receives attention; things come and go without leaving their traces on the mirror. Thus the mirror itself figures not as a medium for vanity, but as a symbol of transparency and sincerity. Looking into the mirror stands for looking into one's own depths, finding one's real self. In the case of the Confucian, the truth is both beautiful and ugly, so that one might choose to promote the desirable and correct the faulty. In the case of the Taoist, the 'real self' is the universe. To speak of detachment here is thus actually to speak of the continuum of subject and object, of conscious self and unconscious 'nucleus', of man and nature. This is not necessarily ontological monism. It represents a transformed consciousness, achieved by cultivation and purification – as a mirror is cleaned and dusted. Thus the Taoists emphasize the importance of purifying the passions, and the Confucians talk about the due harmony of the emotions. In both cases, the implication is that cultivation is a process of recovery: the recovery of the original purity of the mirror.

There are nuances in Confucian and Taoist mysticism which may be seen in the varying uses of the mirror symbol. For Hsün-tzu, as for the later neo-Confucian philosophers, especially Wang Yang-ming – following in the wake of Buddhist influence – the ascetic accent is stronger. The soul looks into itself to find its true state, to correct its mistakes, to cleanse away its impurities. Meditation is thus oriented toward moral action. Even Chang Tsai's nature mysticism opens him to works of compassion and justice: to respect for the aged, affection for the weak and the orphans, care of the sick and infirm. On the other hand, he sublimates the Confucian virtue of filial piety, carrying it to a higher level of application:

To rejoice in Heaven and have no anxiety is filial piety at its
purest. . . .
He who knows the principles of transformation will carry out well the
work of [Heaven and Earth]; he who penetrates spirit to the highest degree
will carry out their will. Do nothing shameful in the recesses of your own
house and thus bring dishonour to them [Heaven and Earth]. . . . In life I
follow and serve them. In death I will be at peace.[33]

The mind of such a sage is quite different from that of the Taoist
Chuang-tzu, content with reflecting the myriad things of the universe,
accepting change and yet remaining above it. Possibly it reflects a
persistent anthropomorphism; the ancient personal godhead, now
known as Heaven and earth, assumes transpersonal, even impersonal
characteristics. For neo-Confucianism comprises the merging of an
ancient, 'prophetic-like' religion, involving belief in a transmundane
Lord-on-high who wills the good of human kind, with 'pantheistic'
influences[34] from the mystical religions of Buddhism and Taoism.

And what of the mysticism of Taoist religion – the religion of
immortality? Here is a different scenario. Instead of harmony with
nature, we find the desire to manipulate its secrets. Instead of a
continuum of man and nature, an acceptance of both life and death,
we find the persistent quest for the most elusive of life's possible goals:
that of staying for ever alive. The Taoist mystical tradition is
supported by prayer as well as drugs; its fruits are seen in pre-
ternatural feats. Its exuberant celebration of life and self seems to
contrast oddly with the sublime serenity of those very philosophers it
venerates as patriarchs and prophets. On the one hand, it gives
manifestation to man's deepest religious instinct, the desire to
become God-like: *Eritus sicut Deus*. On the other, at least in some
cases, it acts out some of the infantile fantasies exposed by Freudian
psychology. Perhaps, one should say, our infantile fantasies *hide* our
deeper, and deepest, religious instincts – they are really two sides of
the same mirror.

True, certain forms of popular Taoist practices resemble a
combination of religion and eroticism, of asceticism and magic. As
such, they are perhaps a manifestation of the narcissism that
sometimes accompanies mystical consciousness, demanding eternal
raptures. The religious giants of the various traditions, Taoist,
Buddhist, and Christian, distinguish between God, or the ultimate
reality, and the 'spiritual consolations' or rapturous joy that

accompany mystical experiences, in order to assign each its proper priority. But there are mystics in every tradition who confuse the gift with the giver, the joy with the mystery of being. According to the norms of prophetic religions, Christianity, Judaism, or, in our case, Confucianism, mystical experience is not an end in itself. It is a means to the ultimate end – love of God through love of man, or, in Confucian language, the perfect fulfilment of the virtue of humanity, *jen*. Mystical consciousness and knowledge may be a tremendous help in one's efforts to love God, and to develop one's innate human-heartedness, but they are not necessarily signs of perfect love already achieved, or perfect humanity already fulfilled. When a mystic becomes attached to his raptures, or when a would-be mystic becomes enamoured of the joys of mystical experience, and desires them for their own sake, it is a re-enactment of the primal Narcissus falling in love with the beauty of his own image and likeness. Mysticism emerges as a relative phenomenon, best viewed in the light of the particular context.

NOTES

1 Jacques Lacan, 'Le stade du miroir comme fermateur de la fonction de Je, telle qu'elle nous est révélée dans l'expérience psychanalytique', *Écrits* (Paris, 1966), pp. 93–100. See also Jan Miel, 'Jacques Lacan and the structure of the unconscious', in *Structuralism*, ed. J. Ehrmann (New York, 1970), pp. 94–100.

2 Cuthbert Butler, *Western Mysticism* (New York, 1966), Prologue and pp. 181–86.

3 Friedrich Heiler, *Das Gebet* (Munich, 1921). English translation by Samuel McComb (London, 1932). I refer especially to chs. 4 and 5.

4 For a more extensive study of Confucianism, see Julia Ching, *Confucianism and Christianity* (Tokyo, 1977), especially ch. 5, which discusses Confucian mysticism in the light of the Christian.

5 James Legge, tr., *The Chinese Classics* (Oxford, 1930), vol. i, p. 326.

6 Burton Watson, tr., *The Complete Works of Chuang Tzu* (New York, 1968), p. 90.

7 *Tao* refers to the ineffable, the source of all things, the primal 'Mother', the 'void'. Some scholars have suggested that it refers to the deity, others to the first principle in the universe, comparable to the Brahma or Atman of Hindu religion. I would like to suggest here that in fact it represents the philosophical transformation of the deity in ancient

Chinese religion, and I find the fact that it became a deity in popular religious Taoism an interesting corroborative factor. See on this point Tu Erh-wei, *Chung-kuo ku-tai tsung-chiao yen-chiu* ('Studies about the Religions of Ancient China') (Taipei, 1959), Part 4, ch. 2.

8   English translation adapted from D. C. Lau, *Mencius* (Baltimore, Md, 1970), p. 182.

9   If this comparison of Gregory and Mencius seems strange on account of the dogmatic chasm of 'original sin' which should separate the two, let it be called to mind that the Greek Fathers had not given particular emphasis to this doctrine in their struggle against the pessimism and determinism of Gnosticism and Manichaeism, preferring rather to focus upon an 'incarnational theory of redemption'. For Gregory, man's *real* nature remains that defined by the *eros* which continually draws him to divine beauty, and that in spite of the *pathe* which retains and isolates him in a hardened world. For more on this point, see Louis Bouyer, *La Spiritualité du Nouveau Testament et des Pères* (Paris, 1966), p. 426. See also Karl Rahner, 'Original Sin', in *Sacramentum Mundi, An Encyclopaedia of Theology* (Montreal, 1969), vol. iv, p. 329.

10 Paul Demiéville, 'Le miroir spirituel', *Sinologica*, vol. i (1948), p. 133. Demiéville cites from the French version in Hans von Balthasar, *Présence et pensée, essai sur la philosophie religieuse de Gregoire de Nysse* (Paris, 1942), p. 92.

11 English translation adapted from James Legge, *The Chinese Classics*, vol. i, pp. 384–85.

12 English translation adapted from W. T. Chan, *A Source Book in Chinese Philosophy* (Princeton, 1963), p. 497.

13 Watson, op. cit., p. 143.

14 English translation adapted from ibid., p. 90.

15 Ibid., pp. 193–94.

16 English translation in W. T. deBary, ed., *Sources of Chinese Tradition* (New York, 1960), vol. i, p. 260.

17 See Liu Ts'un-yan, 'Taoist Self-cultivation in Ming Thought', in W. T. deBary, ed., *Self and Society in Ming Thought* (New York, 1970), p. 294.

18 For Demiéville's article, see above, n. 10.

19 Demiéville, op. cit., pp. 128–33.

20 English translation adapted from Burton Watson, *Hsün-tzu: Basic Writings* (New York, 1963), p. 131.

21 Ibid., pp. 127–28.

22 Ibid., pp. 128–29.

23 Watson, *The Complete Works of Chuang Tzu*, p. 97.

24 Ibid., p. 142.

25 Ibid., p. 290.

26   Ibid., p. 70.
27   As there is no good English translation for this text, the renditions are my own. For the Chinese original, I used the World Book Shop edition (Taipei, 1969).
28   English translation adapted from Philip Yampolsky, *The Platform Sutra of the Sixth Patriarch* (New York, 1967), p. 130.
29   See ibid., p. 132.
30   Chan, *Source Book*, p. 601.
31   English translation in Julia Ching, *To Acquire Wisdom; The Way of Wang Yang-ming* (New York, 1976), p. 63.
32   Ibid.
33   English translation adapted from W. T. Chan, op. cit., p. 497.

JULIA CHING, Ph.D. (Australian National University). Professor Ching has taught at the Australian National University, as well as at Columbia and Yale and is now an Associate Professor at the University of Toronto. She is the author of several books, including *To Acquire Wisdom: The Way of Wang Yang-ming* (1976); and *Confucianism and Christianity* (1977).

William James's Account
of Mysticism; A Critical Appraisal

JOHN E. SMITH

It is impossible to exaggerate the influence which James's *The Varieties of Religious Experience* has had on philosophical and psychological treatments of religion in this century. The book has not only been widely read and translated into many languages, but it has provided an almost inexhaustible storehouse of recorded experience to be analysed and interpreted even along lines which differ from those marked out by James himself. The significance of the work lies to a large extent in the selective bias which it represents and of which James was thoroughly aware. Unlike many other treatments of the subject, James's emphasis falls neither on religion as doctrine or precisely articulated belief, nor again on religion as cult or liturgical community, but rather on religion as a peculiar force in the *living experience* of individuals. In James's view, religion can be properly understood only by seeing it in its own habitat – which means in the vicissitudes of personal life. As a consequence, James was inclined to regard so-called 'organized religion' as religion at 'second hand' and to set the social expression of religion in opposition to individual experience. This primary emphasis on the personal also led James to subordinate the philosophical and theological dimensions of religion. 'I do believe', wrote James, 'that philosophic and theological formulas are secondary products, like translations of a text into another tongue.'[1] I agree with Royce in objecting to James's view on both heads, but it is not necessary to join the issue at this point because it is generally admitted that mysticism is an essentially individual and personal form of spirituality which must be studied in and through the expressions of individual experience. I shall have occasion, in appraising James's treatment of mysticism, to question whether his subordination of the conceptual order obscured his vision and prevented him from understanding the special form of mysticism to be found in thinkers like Bonaventure, Nicholas of

Cusa, and Spinoza, which is thoroughly dependent on rational dialectic as the means of preparation.

James's attempt to proceed on the basis of the facts of religious experience brings us to a consideration which, though largely methodological, is nonetheless of the greatest importance. In the nature of the case, James derived the experiences on which his study is based from a variety of autobiographical documents – letters, diaries, confessions, meditations – which themselves represent the efforts of their authors to *express* their experiences and what they believe happened to them. It seems to me quite idle to argue, as numerous critics have done, that these expressions are actually *interpretations* reflecting the past experiences, the ideas, and the language of the individual and his social milieu, as if there actually existed, by contrast, uninterpreted experience. The fact is that experience and its expression are as inextricably connected as convex and concave; there is no apprehension of what we have encountered or undergone which is not at the same time mediated in some form of expression, and the *only* forms of expression available are those which determine the individual's historical situation. Current discussions of the nature of scientific knowledge centre on the *interpenetration* of fact and theory; if this is so in fields where the greatest precision of thought is possible, how much more must it hold in the sphere of religion, and especially in mysticism, where there occurs a struggle to express what many believe cannot be said at all! We must rid ourselves of the illusion that there is 'raw' experience and recognize the unavailability of any experience which is not in some way expressed and interpreted.[2]

In approaching his topic, James made use of the specific expression 'religious experience' as a collective name to denote those phenomena in human life which, in his own language, represent the 'cash value' of a whole spectrum of concepts – God, conversion, grace, sin, faith – current in many different religious traditions.[3] Among the several forms of religion James discussed was mysticism and, although it is clear from the organization of his lectures that he regarded this type of experience as one among others, the belief has arisen that 'religious experience' and 'mysticism' were synonymous in James's mind. James was not without responsibility for this identification since there are places both in the *Varieties* and in his letters where mystical states are said to be the 'root and centre' of 'personal religious experience'.[4] On the other hand he recognized forms of spirituality other than the mystical and one certainly cannot construe his title to read 'The Varieties of Mysticism'. James, moreover, not only distinguished between religious and non-religious mysticism, but maintained that there exists a wide range of mystical experience starting with a rudimentary (and not necessarily religious) sense of grasping for the first time the significance of a familiar maxim, and extending to what he called 'professional mystics' deeply immersed in elaborately organized experiences where 'the religious pretensions are extreme'. James, moreover, used his regular method of comparison in serial order; the phenomenon is seen first in its germ and then in its over-ripe form and both are compared with exaggerated and degenerate types.[5] The latter, described by James as the non-religious half of mysticism, are represented by pathological states which he sometimes described as *diabolical* mysticism.

Thus one can see that to identify religious experience with mysticism can lead only to confusion. The mystical consciousness is not the only form of religion, a fact which is underscored by the difference between religious traditions, like Judaism and Christianity, which are *not* essentially mystical, but which have developed mystical forms,[6] and traditions like those of classical Hinduism and Islamic Sufism which are essentially mystical in their fundamentals. We shall have occasion to return to this difference later on; for the present, it is sufficient to notice that religions like Judaism and Christianity in their insistence on the distinction between Creator and creature and on the mediating role of the divine *Word* cannot be understood as mystical through and through, even if both traditions have developed strong mystical strains. By comparison, it is impossible to conceive of the religion of the ancient Vedanta or what Al-Ghazzali called 'the science of the Sufis' as anything other than mystical.

With these preliminary considerations in mind we can proceed, first, to James's own analysis of the distinguishing features of mysticism and its types, and second, to a statement of his understanding of its claims and his view of their validity. The entire discussion will provide a background for a critical appraisal. As will be clear, however, no one can neatly separate exposition and criticism; much is implied by way of appraisal in the manner of exposition and some critical points are best made when an idea or distinction is first introduced. I shall postpone explicit criticism until I have attempted to give as accurate an account of James's position as possible.

James opens his discussion on what some have regarded as a surprising note with the confession that, as regards mystical states, 'I can speak of them only at second hand.'[7] Despite this admission, no one can deny that James had the greatest sympathy for mysticism and that for an 'outsider' he has given a most accurate portrayal of the mystical spirit. In the end there is no doubt that James was 'for' mysticism and opposed to its most unsympathetic critics, and yet he retained a critical attitude in that he regarded the authority of mysticism as limited. His positive attitude is revealed at the outset when he complains about those who use the terms 'mysticism' and 'mystical' as terms of reproach against any view thought to be 'vague, vast and sentimental'. Nothing, unfortunately, has changed in this regard over the past seventy-five years; one still finds this irresponsible and uninformed abuse of these terms by those who want to cast suspicion on any doctrine of which they disapprove. As a safeguard, James set forth four marks for distinguishing the mystical from other types of experience.

Of the four distinguishing features – *ineffability*, *noetic quality*, *transiency*, and *passivity* – the first two are said to be not only essential but sufficient for defining a mystical state, whereas the latter two are, he says, 'less sharply marked', but are usually present. The difference here seems to be based less on universality than on variety and ambiguity. Transiency will be a function of whether the mysticism in question is, in James's language, sporadic or methodical; passivity gave him some pause because of the paradox stemming from the fact that strenuous voluntary forms of discipline and preparation are often accompanied by the firm belief that being prepared to receive an insight is necessary but does not guarantee its coming. In a favourite mystical image, unless the kettle is burnished, it will not reflect the light, but the fact of its being so burnished does not command the light.

By *ineffability*, James meant the impossibility of expressing a state of mind by means of words and concepts. The ineffable must be directly experienced. In this respect, he says, 'mystical states are more like states of feeling than like states of intellect';[8] neither their quality nor their worth can be communicated to a person totally without such experiences. In terms reminiscent of his distinction between *acquaintance* and *knowledge about*, James cites listening to music and being in love as typical examples. In both cases the undergoing, the living through, the acquaintance are essential and without a surrogate.

In citing the *noetic quality* claimed for mystical experience, James calls attention to three distinct points. Although such experience is akin to feeling, those who have it claim to know something as a result. Second, what they claim to know is generally described as insight which eludes the discursive intellect and is felt to be an illumination of great worth. Third, those for whom this illumination is real accord to it 'a peculiar sense of authority'. James took this feature seriously and he sometimes contrasted the scepticism expressed by psychologists and others investigating mystical experience with the unshakeable confidence manifested by their subjects.

The mark of *transiency* refers to the fact that specific mystical states do not last very long – James estimated two hours as an upper limit, and thought less than an hour most common – then fade so that ordinary consciousness and experience once again take command of the person. From a survey of many cases, James concluded that, when past, the quality of such experience can be remembered only partially but it can be recognized on subsequent occasions and further developed.

Passivity has, as indicated, a paradoxical character. Different types of mysticism are associated with different forms of preparation and these involve voluntary operations and self-discipline, often of a strenuous kind. Despite the effort, the mystical consciousness includes a vivid sense of suspension of the will, and of being grasped by a power beyond itself, as if one had been replaced by a superior reality. James connected this feature with the phenomena of secondary or alternate personalities and the power to utter prophetic speech or engage in automatic writing, as if under the command of another. It is important to notice, however, that he excluded these phenomena from the properly mystical when the persons exhibiting them neither recollected them later nor regarded them as having any special significance for their own life and destiny. 'Mystical states, strictly so-called,' he writes, 'are never merely interruptive',[9] but are part of an ongoing life and have a marked effect on that life in the intervals between these heightened experiences.

Turning from these general characterizations, James proceeds to the analysis of typical examples. As indicated above, these examples represent a spectrum; at one end are phenomena without particular religious import and at the other specifically religious mysticism of the sort represented by the Vedanta, St Teresa and St John of the Cross. Rudimentary mysticism points to the well-known experience of being overcome by the feeling that one grasps the meaning and importance of some idea or truth which one has in some sense known all along but never really understood. Luther's experience struck James as typical. Luther had often recited the creed – 'I believe in the forgiveness of sins' – but on one occasion when a fellow monk recited it, Luther reports that for the first time he saw the entire scripture in a new light. Although this illustration comes from the religious context, the experience it represents may occur in connectin with any sort of meaning when there is the grasp of an insight, or the perception of a 'depth', which has been previously obscured by ordinary experience touching only the familiar surface of things.

The next rung on the mystical ladder is a phenomenon which occurs frequently enough to be called by its French name *déjà vu*, an expression which we have adopted into English.[10] James described it as the feeling of having 'been here before', or the invasion of the present by a powerful reminiscent consciousness. He objected to the connection of this experience with insanity which was in his time a familiar way of interpreting it. James viewed it instead as a case of enlargement of perception which is not important enough to be given an exclusively pathological explanation. He would have been amused, and perhaps even annoyed, by the current official definition of *déjà vu* as the 'illusion' of having been some place before on the occasion of being there for the first time. This is surely a definition that embraces an evaluation.

James, as previously stated, arranged the experiences cited in a serial order representing ever 'deeper plunges' into the mystical consciousness. Since it is difficult to speak in quantitative terms about such experience, we may take it that James was referring to the degree of pervasiveness of these phenomena; rudimentary mysticism being the most widespread, *déjà vu* less frequent and so on. Among more singular experiences he places the feelings expressed by Charles Kingsley:

> When I walk the fields, I am oppressed now and then with an innate feeling that everything I see has a meaning, if I could but understand it. And this feeling of being surrounded with truths which I cannot grasp amounts to an indescribable awe. . . .[11]

This description and the one which follows, from the English critic John Addington Symonds, set before us a feature of mysticism which I regard as central and which I doubt James accorded sufficient weight. Describing a trance-like mood which came over him at times of relaxation, Symonds writes:

> It consisted in a gradual but swiftly progressive obliteration of space, time, sensation, and the multitudinous factors of experience which seem to qualify what we are pleased to call our self. In proportion as these conditions of ordinary consciousness were subtracted, the sense of an underlying or essential consciousness acquired intensity. At last nothing remained but a pure, absolute, abstract Self.[12]

With the passing of the mood and the return of ordinary consciousness, Symonds found himself left with a question not unlike the celebrated paradox of the Chinese sage, Chuang Tze, when he asked whether he is a man dreaming that he is a butterfly or a butterfly dreaming that he is a man. Symonds writes:

> Which is the unreality – the trance of fiery, vacant, apprehensive, sceptical Self from which I issue, or these surrounding phenomena and habits which veil that inner Self and build a Self of flesh and blood conventionality?[13]

There are, to be sure, several questions raised by Symonds's experience, but the point I want to underscore for future reference is the idea, *and it expresses one of the truly universal features of all mysticism*, that day-to-day consciousness, shaped by ordinary needs, accompanied by habitual and familiar ways of responding to the world, has in some way to be suspended if some special insight into the nature of things, the true self, the purpose of life is to be gained. In short, there is the belief that the mystical truth is always there, but that ordinary experience stands in the way and must be put aside just as one removes a veil to reveal a treasure which existed all along. One key to unlocking the secrets of the many different forms of mysticism is an understanding of the various modes of preparation or discipline whereby the 'eye of the soul' – to use a favourite mystical image – is cleansed and attains the proper vantage point from which to see.

What are these modes of preparation and how do they relate to the insights that transcend them? The first question is far easier to answer than the second, since the basic facts about many mystical traditions are well known; the relation between the mystical goal and the path leading to it is a matter of interpretation which touches the central issue raised by all mysticism, namely, the status and validity of sheer immediacy. Four principal modes of preparation are to be found in the land of the mystics; all are well illustrated in James's discussion. These modes, though distinguishable, are not necessarily exclusive, and several may be combined in any one tradition. There is, first, preparation through *rational dialectic* intended to lead the mind by a series of rational steps to a grasp of what is beyond all discursive thought; secondly, there is *moral* preparation based on the belief that only the pure in heart shall see God; thirdly, there is *discipline of the body* which ranges from severe asceticism to exercises leading to total relaxation, equilibrium of body and equanimity of mind; lastly, there is the use of *drugs* and *intoxicants* which suspend or limit the restraints imposed upon the self by mundane existence. In all cases, the function of preparation is the same, to remove the veil which prevents the self from seeing the truth.

James begins with the last of these modes – drugs and intoxicants – a way of approach which, as is evident enough, has developed since his time far beyond what he could easily have imagined. 'The sway of alcohol over mankind', says James, 'is unquestionably due to its power to stimulate the mystical faculties of human nature.'[14] Where the sober mood of serious and often strenuous life says, No, intoxication expands, unites, and radiates. 'It is', says James, 'the great exciter of the *Yes* function in man',[15] and must be regarded as 'one bit of the mystic consciousness'. Intoxication, however, loses this status in stupefaction and becomes nothing more than the poisoning of body and mind. Because of his own experimentation with the effects of nitrous oxide, James came to two conclusions which are fundamental for his view of mysticism and his conception of human consciousness. The first is that, although the one who inhales cannot, upon returning to ordinary consciousness, express coherently the depths of truth disclosed, 'the sense', he says, 'of a profound meaning having been there persists.'[16] Second, and more important, James concluded that normal waking or rational consciousness is 'but one special type of consciousness' surrounded by potential forms of consciousness entirely different. This belief is intimately bound up with his idea of 'fringes of consciousness', his doctrine of the subliminal self which is influenced by the Unseen Order, and his rejection of the Cartesian clear 'spotlight' consciousness as a paradigm for all consciousness. I submit that James was not entirely correct in describing himself as one who was acquainted with mystical states only at second hand. The fact is that his belief about multiple consciousness was a direct result of his own experience and he declared that his impression of its truth remained unshaken.

How important this experience was for James can be seen in the metaphysical interpretation he placed upon it which, curiously enough, reminded him of Hegel's thought. All students of James know that he was highly critical of Hegel's rationalism, but here he sees in his own experience of a reconciliation of all the opposites which conflict and lead to human difficulties, the very substance of Hegel's insight. And he claims that his own insight had the precise form of Hegelian reconciliation. Concerning the opposites, James writes: 'Not only do they, as contrasted species, belong to one and the same genus, but *one of the species*, the nobler and better one, *is itself the genus, and so soaks up and abosrbs its opposite into itself.*'[17] In a footnote to this passage, James suggests that Hegel's philosophy must have had its roots in his mystical moods. Whether James was aware of the fact or whether this insight stemmed from his intuitive genius, Hegel had this to say about his own thought in the *Encyclopedia*:

> Speculative truth . . . means very much the same as what, in special connection with religious experience and doctrines, uses to be called mysticism . . . the reason-world may be . . . styled mystical.[18]

The keynote, for James, is a belief in the ultimate melting of conflicting elements into unity; the triumph of the nobler and better genus. This belief was behind his contention that mysticism is fundamentally optimistic in its monism.

The specifically religious dimension of mysticism, according to James, makes its appearance when the experience is taken to mean being in the presence of the Unseen Order or in the immediate presence of God. The sense of such presence may be evoked by the wonders of nature, by an appreciation of the harmony of the cosmos, or by meditation on the self and the feeling of its unity with a cosmic consciousness which at once exalts and swallows the pettiness of all finite egos. 'Even the least mystical of you',[19] he told his audience, must be convinced, first, of the *existence* of mystical moods as states of consciousness having a quite specific character, and, second, of the deep impression which they make on those who experience them. James repeatedly emphasized the importance of the impression made by an experience, its force or effect, and it is not difficult to see why. His pragmatic interpretation of religion is essentially a theory of experience at *work* and therefore it was of the greatest moment for him to underscore the difference in orientation, behaviour, style of life brought about by any form of religious experience. His firm belief was that whatever has visible consequences in the lives of individuals cannot be a non-entity.

It is in connection with James's extended discussion of the mysticism to be found in Hinduism, Buddhism, Islam, and Christianity – cultivated as opposed to sporadic – that the greatest attention is paid to the role of training and preparation in mystical insight. Yoga he rightly understood as a discipline whereby the individual achieves an experiential union with the divine. Assuming the reality of a three-layered consciousness, with an unconscious beneath and a superconsciousness above the ordinary consciousness marked by the feeling of egoism, the aim of yoga is to reach the superconscious state where the individual knows the truth that he is free, loosed from the finite, and identical with the *Atman*. In contrast to the mystical forms previously surveyed, the goal at which the yogin aims is not something which 'just happens'. 'The Vedandists', says James, 'say that one may stumble into superconsciousness sporadically, without the previous discipline, but it is then impure.'[20] The reason that mystics of this type have always spoken of a mystic path or way is that they experience the insight attained at the end as intimately related to what happens to the self in following a regimen that overcomes all the impurities and distractions that prevent any realization of the truth. Consequently for them it would make no sense to think of this fulfilment as something happening fortuitously to an individual from within ordinary consciousness.

Contemporary discussions of the mystical side of Buddhism tend to concentrate on Zen and the goal of *satori* made so familiar to Western readers by the numerous writings of Suzuki. We must remember, however, that at the turn of the century Zen was largely unknown in the West and our knowledge of Buddhist literature, doctrines, practices was less than it is now. James was dependent on studies going back to the middle of the last century when research into the literature and history of the Oriental religions was just getting under way. With his characteristic sense for what is most relevant, however, he chose the example of Buddhist meditation called, in Sanskrit, 'dhyana' and, in Pali, 'Jhana' as representative of the mystical ascent of consciousness (*Samadhi*) to that peculiar Nothingness of *nirvāna* which is at the same time understood as the fullness of life. James's account is not detailed but it does include the four-stage process of meditation whereby one is led to the transcendence of all ideas and perceptions. According to the description which James followed, the four stages involve a progressive overcoming of the distraction or turmoil that mark the surface consciousness. The emphasis falls first on the concentration or the withdrawal of consciousness from objects after the fashion of the tortoise drawing its limbs into its shell. The first stage is a fixing of attention on one point together with the stilling of desire; judgement remains but sense is overcome. In the next stage, discursive reasoning falls away and the self rests satisfied with its own unity. This satisfaction disappears in the third stage where the characteristic Buddhist indifference takes over, accompanied by memory and self-consciousness. The final stage is described as one in which indifference, memory, and self-consciousness are perfected. James expressed doubt as to what memory and self-consciousness could mean at this level and says, 'they cannot be the faculties familiar to us in the lower life.' More recent interpreters come to our aid here with the suggestion that many Westerners misunderstand the progression of consciousness described because of a tendency to think of the disappearance of human faculties as in *sleep*, whereas what is essentially involved is a rearrangement or transformation of these faculties in a state of *tranquillity*.[21] Whether this suggestion would have overcome James's doubt can, of course, only be conjectured, but his query calls attention to an ancient theological problem that mysticism poses in the most acute form. If one speaks of 'self-consciousness' being perfected or transfigured at the culmination of the meditative process, what such 'self-consciousness' means will be dependent on our grasp of it, as James says, 'in the lower life', but the two cannot be entirely the same. We can speak about *jenseits* only in terms derivative from *diesseits*, and yet one is not the other. What self-consciousness means in transfiguration cannot be said, and yet there is the sense that, if the meditative process has any continuity, the self-consciousness which is transformed is the same, at least numerically, as the one known on the hither side of the experience. This problem has often been thought to dissolve in the still higher stages of meditation mentioned in James's account when the meditator says, first, 'there is absolutely nothing'; then says, 'There are neither ideas nor the absence of ideas'; and finally, 'There is the cessation of both ideas and perception'. The final step, says James, is 'as close an approach to nirvāna as this life affords'.[22]

James now considers the other end of the spectrum of mystical types where the religious element is most pronounced and, paradoxically or not, the conceptual articulation increases. Sufism, as represented in the autobiography of Al-Ghazzali, is cited as a typical example of mysticism within Islam, and Christian mysticism is introduced with quotations from St John of the Cross, St Ignatius Loyola, and St Teresa. Although the entire description and interpretation of mysticism ends with an official summary of its distinguishing features and an appraisal of its claims to validity, it is important to notice that his pages on Islamic and Christian forms contain, *en passant*, some highly significant critical judgements which must not be overlooked in the midst of the descriptive detail.

Al-Ghazzali, James notes, left behind one of the few autobiographies which have come down to us from traditions outside of Christianity.[23] This document is invaluable for the insight it provides into the Sufi sect which, together with the dervish groups, are the keepers of the mystical tradition in Islam. That such a tradition should exist at all is surprising in view of the uncompromising monotheism embodied in the faith delivered by Mohammed. Whatever the historical explanation for its existence, there is no question that Sufism represents a significant form of mystical piety. The deepest concern of the Sufis is to detach or purge the heart of all that is *not* God, and this it is claimed can be done only through ecstasy and transformation of the soul. Citing the important difference between knowing what drunkenness is, and *being* drunk, between knowing the nature of abstinence, and *being* abstinent, Al-Ghazzali writes: 'I had learned what words could teach of Sufism, but what was left could be learned neither by study nor through the ears, but solely by giving one's self up to ecstasy and leading a pious life.'[24] The contemplative process sets out from the purification of the self, passes through prayer and meditation, and ends in total absorption in God. Of singular importance is the interpretation of prophetism that is involved. The Sufis, says Al-Ghazzali, see the angels and souls of the prophets, and they alone know by *experience* what prophetism is; all others know nothing but the name. Just as the understanding can grasp intellectual objects not apprehended by sensation, so the prophet has opened to him an illumination which cannot be reached by the intellect. This illumination, however, Al-Ghazzali contends, occurs only in the transport and it 'is like an immediate perception, as if one touched the objects with one's hand'.[25] Without the transport, however, there can be no comprehension.

It is at this point in the discussion that James makes the pronouncements about mysticism in general to which I alluded previously. First, he says, the incommunicableness of the experience is 'the keynote of all mysticism',[26] a judgement which goes back to one of the defining features used to select the subject matter in the first instance. Second, in so far as the mystical truth exists for the individual who has experienced it and no one else, the insight more closely resembles the knowledge derivative from sensations than that represented by conceptual thought. Like Bergson, with whom he was in definite agreement on this point, James invariably opposed the perceptual and the conceptual, seeing the former as knowledge by *acquaintance*, which can be had, but not communicated discursively, and the latter as knowledge *about*, which though remote and abstract can be expressed in conceptual terms. On the other hand, as James points out, many mystics have insisted that our senses are in abeyance and cannot figure in that highest type of knowledge which marks the mystical goal. I shall suggest at a later point that here James grasped a significant feature of mysticism: that it actually represents a pure 'empiricism' in the attempt of the self to encounter truth and reality, naked, as it were, or in the words of Plotinus, 'with nothing in between'. Whether this attempt to transcend all representation and expression is best interpreted in terms of the contrast between the perceptual and the conceptual remains a question.

James's account of Christian mysticism starts with a disclaimer: to present details of the numerous forms of the Christian mystical life in brief compass would be impossible; it is questionable, moreover, whether there are real distinctions of *experience* underlying the logical divisions and subdivisions of mystical types to be found in handbooks on the topic. The phenomena James excluded are, however, important. He disregarded[27] various feats frequently associated with mysticism – hallucinations, levitation, stigmatiz-ation, faith-healing – on the ground that they have 'no mystical significance' because they occur without that consciousness of illumination which was for him 'the essential mark of "mystical states"'. Here we are clearly at the other end of the mystical spectrum, where explicitly religious claims of a cognitive nature are making themselves felt; James sought to evaluate those claims.

We cannot encompass James's entire account of Christian mysti-cism; a few central points must suffice so that we can pass on to his summary statement and final appraisal. In the passages quoted from the writings of St Teresa, whom he regarded as typical, three features of her experience attracted James's attention. First, there was the emphasis on union with God in which all the soul's natural activities are entirely suspended and God raises the soul to himself; secondly, the soul, being without sight or understanding, cannot know *during* the union that it is with God, but, as St Teresa says, 'she sees it clearly later'.[28] Finally, the realization that the soul has been in God is accompanied by an absolute certainty – 'it is wholly impossible for her to doubt that she has been in God'[29] – and this conviction was so strong that St Teresa used it as a criterion of validity. No one who has experienced the union can fail to possess the certainty, and, conversely, the absence of such certainty was for her evidence that no union had actually taken place.

James was especially interested in the kinds of truth which mystics of this type claim to see. Some of these truths are oriented to this world, such as visions of future events, insight into human hearts, a sudden apprehension of the true meaning of a particular biblical text, but by far the most important disclosures have to do with metaphysi-cal and theological insight – the mystery of the Trinity, the divine wisdom expressed in the plan for creation, the manner in which all things exist in God, etc. The important element in all these experiences for James is not, as he says, their being explained from a medical standpoint, but rather their value as indicated by their fruits in and for the life of the individual who has them. For some mystics the other-worldly emphasis is so powerful that practical life in the world becomes virtually impossible. This feature is brought out by the unknown author of *The Cloud of Unknowing* – a work which James does not cite – who argues that it is the duty of lesser mortals to care for the worldly needs of contemplatives who are rendered incapable of looking after themselves. On the other hand, says James, such figures as Ignatius and John of the Cross displayed indomitable will and energy, fruits of their mystical experience. Ignatius was, to James, 'one of the most powerfully practical human engines that ever lived'[30] and all because of his having been 'touched' by God. Interestingly enough, the sort of mystical experience which as James says, 'render[s] the soul more energetic'[31] was seen by him as raising the question of its truth. For, if activity follows the lines marked out by mystical inspiration, an erroneous or misguided inspiration would mean just so much misbegotten energy. The question then is, 'Do mystical states establish the truth of those theological affections in which the saintly life has its roots?' This question, it should be noted, has not to do with establishing the truth of some theological assertions, but rather with a correlation between what James calls 'the theoretic drift' of mystical states and the psychological make-up of the persons who have them.

Mystical states, according to James, are characterized by their optimism and a tendency to monism as a philosophical doctrine. He was impressed by what he took to be a consensus among mystics in these two respects, although later he qualified his claim. Optimism stems from the ultimate affirmation of God, the Absolute, on the far side of a process of negation intended to set God apart from all that is finite and contingent. James saw this affirmation as the mystic's belief in a reconciliation, a rest, an absorption by the Unlimited of all the imperfections attaching to finitude. The function of negation is preliminary, a dialectical path that clears the way for the higher affirmation of the perfection and love at the heart of all things. This path, says James, has a moral counterpart in the negation of the wants and desires of the finite self so that asceticism becomes the avenue to truth.

The monism so prominent in mysticism, as James rightly notes, follows directly from the aim of removing all barriers between the self and the One. He quotes approvingly a passage from Gulshan-Raz, 'In his divine majesty the *me,* the *we*, the *thou* are not found. . . .'[32] Cosmic monism is first manifested in the original mystical experience of unity between the self and the One. James regarded this experience as a pervasive and universal feature of all mysticism and he called it an eternal unanimity that 'ought to make a critic stop and think'.[33] Whatever the case with the critic, James himself did stop and think and several pages later criticized his own words, expressing doubt about the validity of his generalization ('over-simplification') and his appeal to a consensus as a criterion.

With this background we can approach James's critical appraisal of the mystics and their claims. To begin with, there is some confusion in his presentation. Previously I pointed to James's question, Can mystical states establish the validity of theological affections? but no direct answer is given in the pages that follow. Instead we are told that optimism and monism are characteristic of mysticism and the question of validity is postponed. When he finally arrives at an answer, the wording of the question is altered. An italicized summary states that pantheism, optimism, anti-naturalism, twice-bornness, and other-worldliness are essential features of the mystical consciousness and the critical question is then restated: 'Does it [mysticism] furnish any *warrant for the truth* of the twice-bornness and supernaturality and pantheism which it favours?'[34] Happily, James answers this question unequivocally.

Three specific claims are involved: first, that well-developed mystical states have the right to be authoritative for those who have them; secondly, that no authority emanates from mystical states that would make it a duty for others to accept the insights said to be gained; thirdly, the mysticism limits the absolute authority of rationalistic consciousness by showing it to be but one kind of consciousness among others.

Starting with the psychological fact that mystical states *are* authoritative for those who have them, James declares that, if mystical insight is a force by which men live, no critic has the right to insist that the mystic change his ways. The mystic, says James, is invulnerable because, like the sense-bound empiricist, he stands on the authority of a face-to-face presentation of some immediate existence beyond the reach of dialectic.

On the other hand, James contends, mystics have no right to claim that other people should accept the insights of their experiences, even if there were more of a consensus among mystics than there is. It is here that James corrects what he had previously claimed. Asserting that unanimity of experience is actually an appeal to numbers and has no logical force, James writes, 'In characterizing mystic states as pantheistic, optimistic, etc., I am afraid I over-simplified the truth.'[35] He then cites examples of divergent opinions among mystics; some, for example, have been ascetic and some antinomian; some have been dualists and others monists; some have been pantheists while others have insisted on retaining the category of personality as an ultimate. From these facts James concludes that the authority of mystical experience cannot be invoked to support special beliefs such as the doctrine of absolute idealism or monistic pantheism. To strengthen his case James appeals to what he calls 'diabolical mysticism' which exults not in optimism and consolation, but in dread and desolation. These opposing forms, moreover, are said to stem from the same subliminal or transmarginal consciousness.

Despite these difficulties, James still insists that 'the existence of mystical states absolutely overthrows the pretension of non-mystical states to be the sole and ultimate dictators of what we may believe'.[36] He suggests that mystical states, contrary to popular opinion, do not as a rule involve rejection of the ordinary data of consciousness but rather endow them with a new meaning, a new expressiveness and vivacity especially in relation to our active life. It is worth noting that Aldous Huxley, who has fully described his own experiences with consciousness-altering drugs, says precisely what James is claiming:

> . . . I was seeing what Adam had seen on the morning of his creation . . . flowers shining with their own inner light . . . The legs, for example, of that chair – how miraculous their tubularity, how supernatural their polished smoothness! . . . I was so completely absorbed in looking . . . Garden furniture, laths, sunlight, shadow.[37]

James criticizes the rationalists for refusing to consider the *possibility* that familiar facts and experiences may receive a new meaning when viewed in a perspective other than that required for the practicalities of day-to-day living. The emphasis on possibility is entirely in accord with James's proposal that we view mystical states as presenting *hypotheses* that we may ignore, but cannot demolish. The mystic can always enjoy the security of his fortress while he remains within its walls.

James's discussion of mysticism, like the whole of the *Varieties*, suffers from a superabundance of rich fare that has not been thoroughly digested. James himself was aware of the extent to which presentation and description outstripped evaluation in the treatment of his main themes. This outcome can be attributed in part to an emphasis reflected in the subtitle and almost invariably ignored – 'A

Study in Human Nature'. It is my impression that James regarded much of the material he collected – diaries, meditations, auto-biographies – as standing on its own and capable of enlightening the reader without the need for extended interpretation. This approach fits in perfectly with his avowed empiricism and his insistence on grasping what he called the 'particular go' of things. If you want to understand what mysticism is, he would say, you must get as close as possible to the phenomenon itself. There are, however, limitations to this way of proceeding as can be seen in the development of modern phenomenology; there is no royal road from description to the raising of speculative, philosophical issues. Curiously enough, James had himself criticized a simple copy theory of knowledge on the ground that it merely gives us the phenomenon again, whereas we want to understand, interpret, and set it to work in the stream of experience. I am far from saying that James failed to interpret his material. I want only to call attention to the descriptive bias which led him to concentrate on the force of mystical experience in the life of the individual to the neglect of the metaphysical interpretations of reality that abound in the literature. This bias, I believe, accounts for his neglect of what I have called 'rationalistic mysticism' as represented by Bonaventure, Nicholas of Cusa, Spinoza, and even Hegel. For these thinkers rational dialectic is the main form of preparation whereby the mind is brought into the presence of an Ultimate reality transcending discursive form.

James selected his subject matter in accordance with four dis-tinguishing features. The first, ineffability, is surely an essential feature of all mysticism because it is synonymous with the immediacy of experience undergone and implies the co-presence of the self and the Other, whatever form that may take. James was right in seeing ineffability as a pervasive feature among the varieties of mysticism. Ways of preparation differ and many diverse insights are claimed, but essential is the idea of leading the individual to a point where he can apprehend something for himself. The paradoxes of mysticism, and especially the length at which mystics have written about what cannot be expressed, should lead us to stress the mystical claim that there never can be a surrogate for the goal at which the mystic aims. Obviously, if this experience could be transferred or imparted, there would be no need for the insistence on the need to experience immediately what cannot be said. Mystics have, to be sure, articulated their insights in dialectical fashion; they have attempted, for example, to explain how nothingness is the true fulfilment of Being and why the sacred silence is the only true eloquence. But, for the most part, the function of this writing, when it is not addressed to the initiated, may be taken as evocative and indexical. It may serve to engender sympathy and a receptive frame of mind in the reader, or to point to the path that the meditator is to follow. *The Cloud of Unknowing*, for instance, may be read as an extended recipe for meditation by means of the 'cloud of forgetting'.

I would stress another aspect of ineffability, which remains merely implicit in James's analysis, and that is the mystical aim of transcending media of expression entirely. A new note enters here: the central idea is not that something has been grasped that defies articulation, but rather that one seeks to pass beyond the mode of articulation itself in order to *be* or to *become one* with a reality or state of being. In this regard it is not merely that the mystic is unable to articulate the 'love which passes understanding', but rather that, were the most perfect conceptualization possible, it would still not *be* the love that he seeks. Though it may sound strange to some, mysticism is rooted in a decidedly *realistic* motive.

James's second characteristic, the attribution by mystics of a *noetic* quality to their experiences, has usually been the focus of attention for critics and sceptics. It seems fair to say that, if the majority of mystics had not claimed to *know* something, they and their writings would not have given rise to so much discussion and controversy. Although, as James well knew, there are forms of mysticism in which the claim to knowledge is not primary, it is also clear that a steady undercurrent in much mysticism is the belief that there are truths which elude ordinary consciousness and that these truths can be grasped only when the limitations of discursive thought have been transcended.

In considering the noetic claim, James, quite rightly, I believe, defended the validity and importance of the insights of those persons who had them, and at the same time denied that any claim can be made for their authority over others. To the extent to which actually going through the process of preparation and reaching the goal is essential – and it is – those standing outside the mystical circle can participate only dialectically through logical reflection on what mystics write, especially when it is cast in a metaphysical mode. What

Kingsley, or Symonds or St Teresa saw, heard, felt, etc., is, in a sense, not discussable from outside, although, as James well knew, attempts have been made to *explain* it in psychological and even medical terms. But in the case of such figures as Bonaventure, Nicholas of Cusa, and Meister Eckhart, who provided metaphysical development of their insight, one obviously can consider their ideas from the outside and seek to determine their meaning and coherence. When Bonaventure, for example, tells us that every form of seeing is a *reflection* of light, but that the source of all light itself is perfect darkness, we see at once what he means. If the first premise is correct, then the source of all light could not itself be seen without there being a more ultimate source for it to reflect, which, of course, runs counter to the original supposition. Or, when Nicholas of Cusa says that he grasped the coincidence of the opposites in his vision and saw the identity of finite and infinite, we can follow his thought, strange as it sounds. Each finite thing represents an infinity of perspectives on an infinity of things and thus the finite, though finite, has a point of coincidence with the infinite. What I am suggesting is that the outsider can participate dialectically with the mystical insight when it has been elaborated philosophically, but in that case his judgement of its validity will also have to be dialectical. The authoritativeness of Bonaventure's or Nicholas's insight *for themselves* might ultimately arise from the fact that they 'saw it at once', but for everyone else its validity would have to rest on other grounds. James nevertheless was quite right in proposing that the deliverances of mystics, or at least some of them, be taken as *hypotheses* to be considered on philosophical grounds once they have been properly articulated. In other words, insights could be delivered via the mystical route without their objective validity being dependent on the manner in which they came.

More important for James in his appraisal of the noetic claim was his insistence that the mystic does bring into view other forms of consciousness than the ordinary form accompanied by discursive reason. I am willing to follow him in this contention, but I do not believe he saw clearly enough the differences between two forms in which this other consciousness manifests itself. Roughly stated, the difference is between an other consciousness which supplements ordinary consciousness and sustains some relation to the familiar world, and the sort of consciousness which purports to disclose a world entirely discontinuous with the world in which we normally live. Other consciousness may be viewed as a new awareness of certain features of the familiar world that have been obscured by an ordinary consciousness wholly determined by the utilitarian demands of everyday life in a precarious world.

Let us consider two examples. In so far as we approach the world as theoretical knowers in the pursuit of scientific knowledge, we focus attention on those features of things capable of treatment in scientific categories, and in a technological age that means a type of understanding aimed at control of the environment; all else is omitted as irrelevant. On the practical side, our activities in the world and with other human beings are severely restricted by our needs, desires, and the pressures exerted by time and space as well as the demands made by our occupation and family life. These daily pressures work as so many screens and filters which allow us to take in, to see, to appreciate just so much of the world as is essential for practical purposes. We never totally *see* anything with which we are practically involved. The reason why we cannot say what colour eyes a good friend has is not that we cannot remember, but that we have never really *looked at* them. The occluded dimension is often identified as the aesthetic and this is unobjectionable if the term is understood in a broad way to mean an appreciation for the being and value of things in themselves.

The mystical quest for the other consciousness, by whatever means, is precisely an attempt to get past the screens and filters of ordinary consciousness which, though necessary for survival in the world, stand as obstacles to the appreciation of whatever does not 'count' for the attainment of some practical result. The concept of the *ecstatic*, the 'standing outside of oneself', vividly expresses the idea that the standpoint of ordinary consciousness is set aside, and a new vantage point is attained from which a world hitherto ignored is apprehended. The new consciousness seems, however, to be oriented to hidden and obscured dimensions of *this* world, rather than to a totally other world disconnected from our present life.

Another example of a new consciousness making itself felt when we are no longer under the sway of everyday awareness can be found at vital and extraordinary turning points in the human cycle – birth, death, choice of vocation, marriage. These 'rites of passage' are distinguished from the ordinary events of everyday life because they are fraught with significance for life as a whole. Our ordinary way of looking at the world must be suspended or to a degree arrested so that concern for the ground of our being and our destiny can make itself felt. A wholly secular life is one in which the utilitarian consciousness, completely engrossed with the successful conduct of mundane business, encompasses all that an individual thinks and does. No other consciousness is allowed to break through and the turning points which are grasped by the religiously oriented personality with concern and awe, are reduced by the secularized man to ordinary events. One can see this phenomenon in reverse in some forms of the Puritan consciousness whereby *every* moment of life is viewed under the aspect of eternity and divine judgement, so that the sacred dimension swallows the whole of life and it seems that there is no secular life at all.

In these illustrations the new consciousness has both a definite relation to and a value for life in the everyday world. That is to say, there is some continuity between the several forms of consciousness involved. There are, however, other claims, as James pointed out, which assert that suspension of ordinary consciousness means disclosure of, or contact with, a world that is wholly other and discontinuous with the world we know. I would agree with James that this sort of experience can have meaning only for the one who has it and any noetic claim made for it must likewise be limited.

There are, I believe, three other features of the immediacy of insight to which mystics point, but James mentions only one of them. There is, first, what has been called *synoptic grasp*, or seeing a meaning 'all at once' and without a sense of succession. The words of a grammatically correct and meaningful sentence succeed each other in a unique serial order, and they are spoken or read in that order and no other. Understanding their meaning, however, is not a serial affair because one might be able to attach some meaning to each of the successive terms without grasping the meaning of the whole. In the temporal aspect of the sequence, moreover, the earlier members precede the later and are over or past before their successors come, but the mind grasping the completed thought expressed in the sentence must take all the words at once as if the delivered thought made the succession irrelevant.

A second feature frequently associated with mystical immediacy is the phenomenon of *appropriation* or the insight that some idea, conception, truth applies to or describes *me* and my situation. It is of the nature of thought to express itself in universals of various types, and discursive thought has an innate tendency to veer away from the individual and unique. But even 'the individual' as a category is a universal since it denotes a multitude of items, so that to reach the point of reference to 'John Jones' as this individual and no other requires a further effort. Add to that the demand that the one doing the thinking also be the one to whom the thought applies or is relevant, and we have reached the notion of appropriation. The grasp of the self-reference has to be a first-person immediate affair because the very being of the reference consists in *my* seeing that some truth in question is true about *me*. Some other person's concept that this truth is true about me is something entirely different. The apprehension of the truth and its being a truth about me must occur for me simultaneously. We often say, 'It suddenly dawned on me . . .' or 'In that instant it came home to me . . .' and in these cases we are referring to appropriation. Notice that the apprehension is a singular affair and is by no means the same as the general concept of there being truths which are true about me even when I am the one who entertains this concept.

The third feature to which I wish to call attention *was* noted by James, namely, the apprehension of a new and total perspective on our life or the facts of the world. We sometimes try to express this, not perhaps very clearly, by saying that we now see things in a 'new light'. The experience of Luther, mentioned previously, furnishes an excellent illustration. It is well known that the repetition of a familiar creed in a liturgical context leads to a triumph of the poetical over the theological so that the mind is often directed not to the meaning of the terms but to the cadence and the aesthetic quality of the recital. Luther said that the phrase 'the forgiveness of sins' which he had heard many times and had often recited himself suddenly grasped him on an occasion when another monk uttered the words. He said that he saw the entire gospel message transformed in the light of this phrase as for the first time.

Thus far we have considered James's first two characteristics of mystical states – ineffability and noetic quality. The other two do not require extended treatment. Transiency is an obvious feature when the experiences in question are clearly defined, and we have already referred to the paradox of passivity which includes both the sense that one can prepare oneself with conscious effort and at the same time be passive in the seeing or experiencing of whatever comes. It is wholly uncharacteristic of mysticism for the subject to think of the final state as one that he produces or elicits as the result of preparation.

I believe that James paid insufficient attention to the relationship between the mystical goal and the path by which it is reached. I contend that a large part of the meaning and intelligibility to be attached to the final vision attained in many forms of mysticism derives from attempting to understand what was negated, transcended, or absorbed along the way. The goal cannot be understood all by itself even for the one who follows the meditative or reflective pattern. I do not claim that what I am saying holds for every type of mysticism, but it clearly is valid with reference to those mystics who adopted the path of rational dialectic as the proper means for leading the mind to an insight or into the presence of the One transcending all distinctions.

The best way to approach the problem is to ask what meaning can be attached to the Buddhist 'absolute emptiness', for example, to the 'profound silence' of Meister Eckhart, or to the 'sacred void' of numerous mystics if we try to penetrate these notions in complete detachment from the web of thought and experience of which they are the culmination. In each case, to be sure, the expressions mentioned do represent the heart of the mystical position, but taken by themselves and in 'wholly immediate fashion', they have little or no meaning. The 'absolute emptiness' and the 'void' are – well – just empty, and, as for the silence, it obviously cannot be said! But if one connects these expressions with a dialectical reflection and sees them as attempts to express the goal of mystical experience, they take on a significance they would not otherwise have.

The Buddhists tell us that 'emptiness' is not to be understood on a *relative* plane as absence or extinction, but only on the basis of the pure experience which is the mind reflecting itself and no other content. This is what is called *sūnyatā* and it is reached only through a meditative process which involves a progressive transcending of distinctions. It is precisely in this process that the absolute emptiness comes into view. 'In Buddhist emptiness', Suzuki writes, 'there is no time, no space, no becoming, no-thing-ness; it is what makes all these things possible; it is a zero full of infinite possibilities; it is a void of inexhaustible contents.'[38] We have, then, a most remarkable sort of emptiness and something very different from what the term would ordinarily be taken to mean. But that is just the point; we are not to understand in terms of ordinary meanings that are closest to hand, but rather in terms of the final outcome of a process of negation which at the same time brings the absolute beginning into view. This outcome itself cannot be said and we face the recurrent mystical paradox. 'To say "empty" ', Suzuki says 'is already denying itself. But you cannot remain silent. How to communicate the silence without going out of it is the crux.'[39]

The Zen solution to this problem (it does not hold for all Buddhism) is an attempt to go beneath language in the direction of indices or pointers which are meant to induce an insight which is not said. To bring the mind to a realization that reality is absolute emptiness, the Zen master may fold his hands over his chest, shake the tea plant, or strike a blow with his stick. The most intriguing paradox in all this is that we know, in some difficult to define sense, what it is that cannot be said!

In a similar vein, let us consider the recurrent mystical emphasis on the 'profound silence'. Once again we are not dealing with a beginning, but with an outcome, and its significance will be entirely lost on anyone who does not understand how that outcome was reached. The mystics of the great silence all begin with a dialectic of negation that has two aims: first, to overcome the barriers between the finite self and God or the One; secondly, to negate every form of expression which implies that God is a finite being among other beings. Both aims are concerned with a removal of finitude. The path inevitably leads to silence because every form of speech reveals itself as something determinate or finite – this and not that. The dialectic of speech leads us to see that the final reality must transcend speech and this is the reason why the dialectic of Eckhart, for example, ends in the profound silence which was invariably symbolized by the desert. The loquaciousness for which mystics are famous does not in any way contradict the ultimacy of silence, because the language is largely expressive, an outpouring of joy and of thanksgiving at having attained the mystic goal. In this sense, the writing is not an attempt to say what cannot be said, but rather expressions of praise and jubilation flowing from the heart which has become one with God.

Earlier on I called attention to James's contrast between the perceptual and conceptual orders and his tendency to associate mysticism with the former because of its emphasis on direct experience and acquaintance. I do not mean to deny the element of truth in this judgement, but I now wish to consider my previous suggestion that this identification, together with James's repeated subordination of the conceptual order, had the effect of clouding his vision and causing him to pass over a very significant form of mysticism in which rational dialectic plays a major role. I first became interested in mysticism as a result of perplexity over a seeming paradox: a number of thinkers in the western tradition who may legitimately be labelled as mystics were also great rationalists, great knowers, and, in some cases, mathematicians. Think of Pythagoras, Plotinus, Bonaventure, Nicholas of Cusa, Spinoza, and Hegel. How is it possible that mysticism, so often associated with the irrational, the non-rational, the immediate and even the mysterious, could manifest itself in the thought of these individuals, each of whom regarded concepts as the touchstone of rational thought. Russell, in a well-known essay, set mysticism and logic in opposition to each other. With more historical accuracy and deeper philosophical results, he might have considered the relations between mysticism and mathematics and thus have thrown some light on this peculiar combination.

I do not claim to have a complete explanation for this phenomenon, but there are some considerations which can help us to understand how there can be a marriage of a certain kind of mysticism with the strongest sort of rationalism. In the first place, there is the central fact that the mystical immediacies are in every case results and not starting points. This fact is a commonplace among students of mysticism, but it may well elude those who are thoroughly imbued with the idea that all knowing *starts out* from immediate certainties of some sort. The truth is that all of the rationalists mentioned above insisted upon the essentially discursive or mediated character of thought and hence for no one of them is there immediate knowledge at the beginning of the intellectual venture. However, and this is the crucial consideration, their denial of initial immediacies did not prevent them from believing in the reality of a kind of immediacy *at the end* of a dialectical process. This immediacy is a kind of intellectual apprehension, intimately related to the rational process which brings it about. Mysticism and rationalism can come together because the process whereby the mind is led to the goal can be seen as a thoroughly rational one governed by clear logical transitions; only the goal itself is a final step beyond discursive thought, but it is a step that no one can take who has not passed through the dialectical development. The final seeing is done with the 'eye' of the mind.

I know of no finer illustration than that provided by St Bonaventure's treatise *The Mind's Road to God*. Bonaventure was, of course, writing within the Christian tradition and his thought is cast in an Augustinian mould. The work has a place within the framework of what Augustine called 'faith seeking understanding'. Bonaventure's reflection is therefore not set forth as an argument, but, like Anselm's *Proslogion*, there is in it a crucial logical transition of the utmost importance for the final step of the journey. *The Mind's Road* is a rational, reflective meditation describing, in the author's words, the ascent of the soul to God. In accordance with the ontological tradition in which he stood, Bonaventure aimed at leading the mind to a point which is at the same time the presence of the *uncreated* light, and his venture is thus quite different from that of inferring God's reality on the basis of some present finite fact which needs a cause or reason to be.

Bonaventure's central image of the universe as a *mirror* of the divine, has a dual significance: first, the world of nature *external* to the self provides a reflection of God, and, secondly, the self or mind is an *internal* mirror and each reflects in its own way what is *above* both of them. Bonaventure strikes the characteristic mystical note at the outset, calling attention to preparation; it is necessary, he says, that the 'mirror of the mind be clear and polished' if it is to reflect that light through which all understanding comes.[40] Should that preparation be lacking, the mind will fail completely to grasp the significance of the outer mirror which is nature. In the language subsequently developed, God appears in nature in the form of *traces – vestigia –* whereas he manifests himself in the mind in the form of an *image*. Bonaventure's point is that if the mind does not first know itself as the internal mirror and is not prepared to reflect the light, it will fail to see in the external mirror those traces of the divine that help lead the mind to the end of its journey. With the image of Jacob's ladder in mind, Bonaventure says that we must put 'the whole sensible world before us as a mirror, by which ladder we shall mount up to God'.[41]

I shall not attempt to chart the entire journey of the mind, but rather to point out certain landmarks. As God is contemplated both *through* and *in* the sensible traces furnished by nature, man's intellectual powers are called into play and he discovers the laws and proportions of all things, but most important of all he grasps the significance of *numbers* – 'number is the outstanding exemplar in the mind of the Maker, and in things it is the outstanding trace leading to wisdom.'[42] Thus is established the crucial connection between mysticism and mathematics; the necessity attached to mathematical truths as gained through necessary inference always represents for this type of mysticism an essential paradigm of the presence of the uncreated light.

Passing from the external mirror to ourselves, we are led to reflect on our own capacity to grasp essential truths of reason and in so doing we arrive at a certain perplexity. How is it possible for the mutable human mind to apprehend an unchangeable truth? The answer represents what I referred to earlier as an important logical transition, which pushes this meditative approach to the edge of explicit argument. The mind could not apprehend such truth, says Bonaventure, if there were not a light 'shining without change'[43] and such a light cannot, without contradiction, be identified with the natural light of human reason. There is here a certain tension between the rationalistic element, which would insist that there is such a light and that, since we do apprehend the unchangeable truth, we *must be* in its presence, and the mystical element, which leads to *contemplation* of the light or *being in* its presence. These two elements exist side by side in the reflective understanding of the soul as the image of the divine. The sciences, says Bonaventure, have infallible rules 'like rays of light descending from the eternal law into our minds'[44] so that our minds can lead us through themselves to the contemplation of the eternal light.

We cannot, according to Bonaventure, understand all of this with the force of our own unaided faculties because the image in us has been obscured – which for Bonaventure means being mired in the sensible world – and must be reformed by the gifts of grace. With the aid of illumination, we come to a true understanding of how we are mirrors of God and 'that we are led into the divine by the powers of the rational soul itself.'[45] At this stage attention shifts to Being itself without which the intellect could know nothing at all.

Being as the condition for all beings, and light as the condition for all that is seen, become the final objects of contemplation, and at the end of the process the mind passes beyond itself. Here the mystical element prevails and form is transcended; 'In this passage, if it is perfect,' says Bonaventure, 'all intellectual operations should be abandoned, and the whole height of our affection should be transferred and transformed into God.'[46]

I know of no more appropriate example of the interlacing of rationalism and mysticism than this gem of logical meditation. The approach it represents will inevitably be alien to anyone who, like James, has small sympathy for rationalism and too closely identifies mysticism with feeling and the perceptual order. But such an imposing tradition cannot be passed over, particularly because of the persistent efforts of its proponents to set forth the ultimate limits of reason in an intelligible way.

It may indeed appear that I have forgotten James or that I am judging him in terms of what he did *not* say. It is, however, important to notice that omissions are frequently quite revealing because they call attention to a selective emphasis. Clearly James did not stress the mysticism typical of a Bonaventure, but instead emphasized mystical forms in which other consciousness is prominent, because of his general understanding of religion in terms of the effects wrought by the 'unseen power' in the subliminal consciousness. In this sense mysticism provided support for the conclusions that sum up the *Varieties* and offered something in the way of evidence for what James called his 'piecemeal supernaturalism'.

At this point and against the background of what has gone before, the question of the relation between mystical experience and enduring religious traditions can fruitfully be raised. Two questions, or perhaps two aspects of the same question emerge; one concerns James's own view of this relationship based on his general conception of religion, and the other focuses on his interpretation of the role of the mystic in the 'varieties' of religious traditions. These two questions, though obviously related, are not the same; their answers should contribute something of significance to the underlying theme of this volume.

We have seen the supreme importance James attached to feeling, to direct experience, and above all to the individual in solitude as the main locus of religion. As James's colleague and friendly critic, Royce, pointed out decades ago, James tended to regard institutional religion embodying tradition as a 'second-hand' affair to be described as 'conventional' in comparison with the vivid workings of faith in the depths of individual lives. No sectarian demanding a personal profession of faith (as opposed to the inherited faith of someone born into an established church) could have been more insistent than James on the primacy of individual commitment. It should be pointed out, however, that James overlooked the important distinction between organization and community and thus greatly underestimated the importance of the social dimension in religion. Nevertheless, that was the trend of his thought and must be reckoned with.

While, as has been noted, James did not identify religion as such with mysticism, there can be no doubt that he saw in this form of spirituality a supreme manifestation of religion in the life of the individual self. On the other hand, he understood very well the force exerted by the particular character of a religious tradition on the type of mysticism appearing within it. Within Christianity, for example, the strong emphasis on human individuality makes possible a mysticism like that of Eckhart with its conception of an uncreated *Funklein* of divinity in each person. The mysticism of classical Hinduism, on the other hand, moves in a quite different direction because the central notion of Brahman implies an overcoming of the distinctions that would otherwise prevent the believer from grasping the identity of the *Atman* and *Brahman*. It would therefore be quite correct to say that James did not view mysticism as a unified, transhistorical form of religious experience, but rather as one having several distinctive forms depending on the 'variety' of religious traditions in the background. This judgement is supported by a point brought out earlier on, namely, James's own correction of his previous exaggeration of the unanimity to be found among mystical writers.

Let us now consider the second question: how did James perceive the impact of mystics on the enduring religious traditions from which they sprang? To answer this question requires some interpreting, because James did not address himself to it directly. But I believe a clear answer can be arrived at on the basis of his treatment of the relevant facts. First, there are numerous indications that he regarded the mystics within a particular religion as embodying and manifesting in their own lives the essential faith of that tradition in a pure or exemplary form. This is certainly consistent because, as we have seen, it is in individual life that James finds what is most authentic in religion. The emphasis on the immediate, moreover, implies the priority of actual love, faith, hope in the mystic's life as contrasted with verbal and ritual articulations of these virtues. There is, presumably, no mysticism at 'second-hand', nor could it possibly assume any merely conventional form.

From this manifestation of authenticity there follows a second clue as to the place of mysticism in historical religions. It also helps to explain the tensions engendered by mystical experience and expression within established ecclesiastical frameworks. The life and thought of a mystical figure stand, in effect, as a *touchstone* of authenticity, a critical model of man's relation to the divine. The very being of the mystic passes a form of judgement on the conventional religion of his tradition, and, like all such judgement, it is unsettling and often resisted by ecclesiastical authority. The immediacy at the heart of all mysticism appears as a threat to the many forms of mediation between man and God that form the substance of a liturgical community. The mystic appears, as it were, to circumvent an established order, despite the fact that, as James pointed out, the vast majority of mystics understand their experience as a supreme exemplification of the essential faith of their tradition.[47] What most attracted James to mysticism becomes clear at this point; it brings religion back again to the individual and is a constant reminder to institutional religion that no individual should be subordinated to any system.

NOTES

1   William James, *The Varieties of Religious Experience* (New York, n.d.), p. 422. All subsequent quotations from the *Varieties* are cited from this modern Library edition.

2   For more on this issue, see S. Katz, 'Language, Epistemology, and Mysticism', in his edited collection *Mysticism and Philosophical Analysis* (London and New York, 1978), pp. 22–74.

3   See 'Religious Experience' in *Encyclopedia Britannica*, 15th edn, pp. 647–52. As far as I have been able to discover, James was the first to use 'religious experience' as a technical term, although others before him like Jonathan Edwards and Schleiermacher had directed attention to the same experimental phenomena which formed the subject matter of the *Varieties*.

4   *Varieties*, p. 370.

5   At the outset of the *Varieties*, James justified his citing of exaggerated
     cases on the ground that they more readily and clearly manifest what is
     characteristic of the particular type of experience.

6   The expression 'mystical Christianity' is *not* redundant.

7   *Varieties*, p. 370.

8   Ibid., p. 371.

9   Ibid., p. 372.

10   Freud discussed the phenomenon of 'having already seen this or that'
     under the name of *déjà vu* in *The Psychopathology of Everyday Life*
     which appeared in German in 1904 and was translated by A. Brill into
     English in 1914. There Freud not only refused to call the phenomenon
     an 'illusion' but mentioned his own experience of it. He explained it as
     the recurrence of an unconscious fantasy and was at some pains to make
     sure that it should not be taken as evidence of anything in the way of
     clairvoyance or pre-existence. See *The Basic Writings of Sigmund Freud*,
     ed. Dr A. A. Brill (New York, 1938), pp. 168–70.

11   *Varieties*, p. 375.

12   Ibid., p. 376.

13   Ibid., p. 377.

14   Ibid., p. 377.

15   Ibid., p. 378.

16   Loc. cit.

17   Ibid., p. 379. James was quite right in his interpretation of Hegel; in all of
     Hegel's dialectical resolutions there is a clear asymmetry in that they
     proceed from the more concrete or inclusive term which is to include the
     other and not vice versa.

18   *The Logic of Hegel*, tr. William Wallace from the *Encyclopedia* (2nd edn,
     London, 1892), sec. 82, p. 154.

19   *Varieties*, p. 388.

20   Ibid., p. 392.

21   See Edward Conze, *Buddhist Meditation* (London and New York, 1956;
     reprinted Harper Torchbook, 1969), pp. 17ff.

22   *Varieties*, p. 393. That James's presentation of Buddhist contemplation,
     though brief, is well founded, can be seen by comparing it with the more
     recent account by Conze cited in the previous note.

23   There is here a topic which calls for investigation aimed at answering the
     question whether works like Augustine's *Confessions*, Pascal's *Pensées*,
     Wesley's *Journal*, Edwards's extensive autobiographical writings and
     many, many others are unique to the Christian tradition and are to be
     explained in terms distinctive of it.

24   *Varieties*, p. 394. James reproduced several pages of the autobiography,
     and prefaced them with the words 'M. Schmölders has translated a part
     of Al-Ghazzali's autobiography into French'. What follows, however, is

in English, and there is no indication whether James made the translation or adopted it from someone else.

25 Ibid., p. 396.

26 Loc. cit.

27 Ibid., p. 399, n. 2.

28 Ibid., p. 400.

29 Loc. cit.

30 Ibid., p. 404.

31 Ibid., p. 406.

32 See *Varieties*, p. 411.

33 Ibid., p. 410.

34 Ibid., p. 413.

35 Ibid., p. 416.

36 Ibid., p. 418.

37 Sybille Bedford, *Aldous Huxley, A Biography* (New York, 1974), p. 538. The passage above is from *The Doors of Perception*. Miss Bedford writes, 'Now, what Aldous experienced under the drug was a change in *everyday* reality.' Italics in original.

38 D. T. Suzuki, *Mysticism: Christian and Buddhist* (New York, 1957), p. 28.

39 Ibid., p. 29.

40 St. Bonaventure, *The Mind's Road to God*, tr. George Boas (New York, 1953), p. 5.

41 Ibid., p. 10.

42 Ibid., p. 20.

43 Ibid., p. 24.

44 Ibid., p. 27.

45 Ibid., p. 32.

46 Ibid., p. 44.

47 For more on this aspect of mysticism see Steven T. Katz's essay in this volume and his earlier essay, 'Language, Epistemology, and Mysticism', loc. cit., pp. 22–74.

JOHN E. SMITH, Ph.D. (Columbia University), B.D. (Union Theological Seminary, N.Y.), LL.D. (University of Notre Dame). Among his books are *Royce's Social Infinite* (1950); *Reason and God* (1961); *The Spirit of American Philosophy* (1963); *Experience and God* (1968); *The Analogy of Experience* (1973) and *Purpose and Thought: The Meaning of Pragmatism* (1978). In addition he has published more than one hundred articles in such journals as *The Review of Metaphysics*, *Religious Studies*, *The Journal of Philosophy*, *Thought* and *The International Philosophical Quarterly*. He taught at Vassar College and Barnard College before joining the faculty at Yale in 1952. Professor Smith has served as President of the American Theological Society, the Metaphysical Society of America, the Hegel Society of America and the American Philosophical Association. Presently he is Clark Professor of Philosophy at Yale.